Getting Started in
Security
Analysis

Peter J. Klein

John Wiley & Sons, Inc.

New York • Chichester • Weinheim • Brisbane • Singapore • Toronto

Published by John Wiley & Sons, Inc.

Published simultaneously in Canada.

Library of Congress Cataloging-in-Publication Data:

ISBN 0-471-25487-8

Printed in the United States of America.

10 9 8 7 6 5 4 3 2 1

Getting Started in

Security Analysis

The Getting Started In Series

Getting Started in Stocks by Alvin D. Hall

Getting Started in Security Analysis by Peter J. Klein

Getting Started in Futures by Todd Lofton

Getting Started in Mutual Funds by Alan Lavine

Getting Started in Metals by Jeffrey A. Nichols

Getting Started in Rare Coins by Gregory C. Roy

Getting Started in Bonds by Michael C. Thomsett

Getting Started in Options by Michael C. Thomsett

Getting Started in Real Estate Investing by Michael C. Thomsett and Jean Freestone Thomsett

For
Sidney "Sonny" E. Ackerman,
my grandfather,

and
Irene, Courtney, and Kelly,
my world

Acknowledgments

I want to thank the numerous colleagues and professors who have put up with my incessant questions and pondering at the lectures, seminars, and courses that have made up my academic and professional career. Special thanks to the following: William Avera, CFA; Randall Billingsley, CFA; Vincent Catalano, CFA; Don Chance, CFA; Carl Crego, CFA; Richard De-Mong, CFA; Jack Francis; Robert Johnson, CFA; Charles Jones, CFA; Allan Marcus; Richard McEnally, CFA; Jack Rader, CFA; Carl Schwezer, CFA; Vincent Su; and Andy Temte, CFA. In addition, The Association of Investment Management and Research (AIMR) deserves a round of applause for their efforts to increase the academic awareness in the investment management profession.

In addition to my academic mentors, the following colleagues deserve special thanks for their frequent "raising-of-the-bar"; without this push, it would have been too easy to give up midstream: Barry Buchsbaum; Neil Caren; Robert Clark; Al Coletti; Steve Dannhauser; Lawrence Davidow; Elliot Denrich; Larry Doyle; Joseph Fuschillo; Ted Goldman; Ron Goldstein, CPA; Peter and Maris Gordon; David Gutwirth; Marten Hoekstra; Stewart Kamen; Thomas Lukacovic, CFA; Stuart Lustberg; Francis McGrail; Edward Moy; Alan Ripka; Michael Ryan, CFA; Jonathan Sack; Steven Sack; Thomas Salshutz; Andrew Semjen; Greg Sherwood; Scott Sherwood; Robert Singer, CPA; Steven Stern; John Sullivan, CFP; and Anthony Turco.

For that special ilk of investor known as my client (or more closely defined as *partner*) a very special thank you is offered for providing business insights often missed by Wall Street analysts, understanding with regard to my hectic schedule, constant efforts at keeping me humble and most importantly, their friendship. Most particularly the following receive my kudos: Kelly Chen, Claire Friedlander, Paul Golub, Robert Grajewski, Norm and Sandy Gruber, Murray Kaye and his "boys", Dick Kitts, John Morse, Mitch Nichnowitz, Harry and Lilly Novinson, Joe and Nancy Payne, Peter Perry, Jacob Solome, Brooke Trent, Andy Tunick, Joe Walsh, Paul Watson, Jules Weiss, Carley Zell, and Stacy Sack Zuckerman.

No work of this type could be possible without assistance from a top-notch office. Monique Abel, Rosemary Davitt, Scott DeLucia, Kevin Dowd, John Hennigan, Mary T. Nigro, and Jane Voorhees have all played a special part in bringing this book to completion. In addition, a very special acknowledgment is bestowed on Brian Iammartino of The Wharton School at The University of Pennsylvania; Brian's input and technical prowess have been invaluable in completing this project.

Claudio Campuzano, Mina Samuels, Jacqueline Urinyi, and Mary Daniello at John Wiley & Sons, and the team at Publications Development Company of Texas provided editorial assistance in developing a format for this work that could be understood by the typical investor. Robert Zenowich provided valuable editorial reworking. Without their help, this book would still be an open file on my laptop.

Lastly, a great big thank-you goes out to my family—without their understanding, compassion, and faith, I certainly would not have had the mettle to carry on when things looked their most bleak. Special thanks to Rose Ackerman, Roland and Deb Buzzard, Mrs. Peter Cassia, Michael and Anne DuBois, Rich and Karen Kerr, Mr. and Mrs. Richard Kerr, Christopher J. Klein, Michael and Joanne Klein, Anthony and Christine Petronella, the Schilling Family, Carole Turco, Vinny Turco, Mr. and Mrs. George Walsh, and Tommy Walsh. To my loving wife and wonderful children—"Daddy's home"!

P. J. K.

Contents

Introduction   1

PART ONE: TOOLS OF THE TRADE   11

Chapter 1
Accounting   15

Chapter 2
Economics   35

Chapter 3
Investment Mathematics   71

Chapter 4
Quantitative Analysis   89

PART TWO: FUNDAMENTAL FINANCIAL
SECURITY ANALYSIS   109

Chapter 5
Equity Analysis and Valuation   111

Chapter 6
Credit Analysis   147

PART THREE: PORTFOLIO MANAGEMENT   179

Chapter 7
The Investment Management Process   181

Epilogue   255

Appendix A
Internet Directory   259

Appendix B
Selected Tables   267

Bibliography   279

Index   281

Getting Started in

Security Analysis

Introduction

You are about to begin a journey into the science of investment analysis. Many of you may think that using the word science to describe the activities of Wall Street is a misnomer. Luck, chance, or voodoo are probably closer to your explanation of investment activity. I hope to convince you otherwise. As you make this journey, it should become obvious that investment analysis and its related extensions are rigorous enough to be taken as an actual science.

Like other scientific disciplines, investment analysis requires a working knowledge of its basic concepts. Part One explores these concepts, with considerable emphasis on exercises that hone awareness, expertise, and understanding of this once arcane subject. A century ago, the task of investment counseling belonged to men of prudence who, for fear of being wrong, usually invested funds with guaranteed returns and did not rely on scientific discipline. The fear of not being beyond reproach—otherwise known as "reputation fear"—provided enough guidance for these men. Typically the wealthy and elite, they did not see the utility of investment analysis for the simple reason that they did not have to—they were already rich.

Today, investment analysis plays a meaningful role in planning for a comfortable financial future. This book provides the reader with a firm foothold on this important subject (although the basic concepts may prove helpful in many of life's other exercises). Mastery of investment analysis takes much more than a cursory read through this text; it requires years of study and perhaps decades of practical experience. My hope is to provide today's investor, novice or seasoned, with enough understanding to simulate the workings of Wall Street analysts. An investor, after reading this manual, will have a fundamental store of financial information; will understand the terms, pricing, and research of a financial services provider; and will find the daily financial papers more interesting.

Many investors of the 1990s are well aware of the basics of financial planning through exposure to myriad seminars, books, magazines, and Web sites. They need the next level of information. Just think about how many of your friends understand the risk-return trade-off (more risk, more return), asset allocation (spreading assets around into many classes), and the need for long-term investing habits. But how many wish they understood how a company's shares are valued, or how the workings of regression analysis and the typical economic releases in a given month directly affect the value of their investments? Part One is designed to provide this essential background.

Part Two, "Fundamental Financial Security Analysis," sets forth the notion that the tools described in Part One can be of practical use only if the investor understands how a given company is valued. Thus in this Part, I explain the methodology behind the valuation techniques of a company's equity and debt securities:

> With tomes of data available, how should we quantify the value of this company? Which calculations must be executed to ascertain the true value of this company?

Consequently these valuation techniques build on the lessons of Part One. Without a firm understanding of the tools analysts use, it is impossible to firmly grasp the true valuation process.

Part Three, "Portfolio Management," is a discussion of the investment management process—the symbiosis of the tools and valuation techniques with the financial planning process. It includes an examination of the laws and regulations that govern this highly regulated industry. To fully grasp these legal constraints, today's serious investor must understand and be able to use the investment management process.

Lastly, as a housekeeping item, the reader should be aware of some literary licenses taken in this text. The pronouns "he" and "she" are used interchangeably throughout; this is done for stylistic simplicity and does not reflect the current percentage breakdown in the investment analysis field. The terms VFII (Very Financially Interested Individual—pronounced "vif-fee") and NFII (Not Financially Interested Individual—pronounced "nif-fee") are introduced early on in this text and refer to the current investment-user market. People who have started to read this book should consider themselves either a VFII or a reformed NFII. The terms *analyst, practitioner,* and *investor* (seasoned or novice) are also interchangeable throughout this work, and in each case the word refers to the user of investment analysis. From professional to novice, all analysts should be in the continual learning phase. The professional analyst specializing in real estate may require a briefing on the workings of the equity market, just as a seasoned investor could be brought up to date on the changing dynamics of macroeconomics releases.

While the ultimate purpose of this book is to educate today's proactive investor in the science of investing, by no means can it serve as a proxy for a complete education in this expansive field. It can, however, provide the investor with a solid foundation of knowledge. Any interested investor (VFII) can request an incessant flow of research reports from either his representative at the issuing firm or the company itself (most companies will release the research reports; however, they require the prior permission of the analyst's firm to do so); but understanding jargon-laden reports usually takes more than a cursory background in the subject.

INVESTMENT REPORT CHECKLIST

As a first step toward a better comprehension of the research reports issued by firms, it is a good idea to study what the professional groups look for in a quality report. The Association of Investment Management and Research (AIMR) has published a new (1996) version of its *Standards of Practice Handbook*. It is the source of the following checklist (reprinted with permission). This list is used for illustrative purposes only and is not intended to be all-inclusive. These investor guidelines are helpful for when determining whether the writer of the research report exercised diligence and thoroughness (as required by Standard IV-2) in compiling the report:

   ✔ *Macroeconomic factors.* Analyze the impact of domestic and international fiscal and/or monetary policies, currency exchange rates, and business cycle conditions on the company or its industry.

   ✔ *Industry considerations.* Investigate the industry (or, if a diversified company, the principal industries) of the issuer of the security. Considerations should include historical growth and future potential, the nature of worldwide competition, regulatory environments, capital requirements, methods of distribution, and external and internal factors that might change the structure of the industry.

   ✔ *Company's (or issuer's) position in the industry.* Analyze the company's strengths and weaknesses within the industry environment.

This analysis should not only be based on discussion with the company's management, but should also include information from competitors and such trade sources as distributors.

✔ *Income statement and statement of cash flows.* Review statements for a period covering two business cycles and investigate reasons for annual and seasonal changes in volume growth, price changes, operating margins, effective tax rates (including the availability of tax loss carryforwards), capital requirements, and working capital.

✔ *Balance sheet.* Investigate the reasons for historical and prospective changes in the company's financial condition and capital structure plus the conformance of accounting practices to changes either proposed or implemented by accounting rule-making bodies.

✔ *Dividend record and policy.*

✔ *Accounting policies.* Determine policies and examine the auditor's opinion.

✔ *Management.* Evaluate reputation, experience, and stability. Also evaluate the record and policies toward corporate governance, acquisitions and divestures, personnel (including labor relations), and governmental relations.

✔ *Facilities/programs.* Review plant networks, competitive effectiveness, capacity, future plans, and capital spending.

✔ *Research/new products.*

✔ *Nature of security.*

✔ *Security price record.*

✔ *Future outlook.* Examine principal determinants of company operating and financial performance, key points of leverage in the future (e.g., new markets and geographical expansion, market-share improvement, new products/services, prospects for profit margin improvement, acquisitions), competitive outlook, major risks (e.g., competition, erosion of customer base, abbreviated product life cycles, technological obsolescence, environmental hazards), and financial goals (for the short and long term) and the analyst's level of confidence in achieving them.

The preceding checklist should not be viewed as a complete methodology from which to judge the competency of a research report, but it certainly lends itself to further investigation. The *Handbook* goes on to state, "Members (of AIMR) must take responsible steps to assure themselves of the reliability, accuracy, and appropriateness of the data included in each report." From the investor's standpoint, joining the AIMR as a Charterholder or member has special value when seeking clear and concise information.

A proactive investor never stops honing his skills, permitting his intuition a better shot at being right. Perhaps he will search for the characteristics common to the best companies. Identifying this set of traits could allow the investor to find the next great company and, hopefully, a great (read: inexpensive) stock. Remember to make this differentiation between company and stock. A great company may be so outstanding that the market will bid up its share price to a level that makes the stock an imprudent candidate for any true fundamentalist. Value investors seek to purchase equities whose fundamental value has not yet been discounted by the market. While the value investor's analysis will be sensitive to the equations in this text (Dividend Discount Model, DuPont Method of the Return on Equity Equation, sustainable growth), it will also call on a considerable understanding of qualitative and management analysis.

Borrowing from the tenets of value investors, I have developed a methodology that gives the investor a starting point for fundamental equity analysis. The acronym PATIROC summarizes the characteristics critical to the equity investor:

- ✔ People.
- ✔ Assets.
- ✔ Technology.
- ✔ International Strategy.
- ✔ Return.
- ✔ Operations.
- ✔ Cost-Effective Management.

PEOPLE

People make a company. A company that inspires its employees and creates a strong, cooperative morale will benefit in the long run. When deciding whether to purchase the equity of a company (stock), an investor should make it part of due diligence to try to learn something about the employees (and the culture of the firm). I don't mean just to top management (CEO, CFO, or investor relations director), for they are often well trained to represent the facts in a somewhat optimistic, overly biased tone.

Try to find out about the employees of the company—the middle management and the factory or "line" workers. They represent the true test of the morale of a company:

> How do the frontline employees feel about their company? Do they participate in the company's retirement plans? Go to company functions? Understand the business and, furthermore, are interested in the success of the company?

Several years ago during one of my equity searches, I came across a company that had this positive "People" characteristic. The company was a fast-growing enterprise that rewarded its employees for achievements above stated goals with stock options. Some employees on the factory floor had over $1 million in stock options. These employees were happy, to say the least, and it showed in the way they spoke about their company and its market share, competition, and new ventures. To an investment professional this was like stepping into nirvana, except that when I asked the human resources director about the prospect of doing investment seminars, he responded, "Our employees would be happy to teach your clients about investments, but wouldn't that be kind of strange, since they're your clients?" After I caught my breath, I realized that he was dead serious and that I should seek other potential educational seminar opportunities.

Another element of this characteristic is the function of ownership; that is, who are the shareholders, the equity partners, of the company? We want to enjoy the company of smart investors (those professionals with an outstanding record of performance) and most importantly, of management. Insider ownership is compiled and published on a periodic basis (see Appendix A) and could give the investor valuable insights about the intentions of senior management.

> Is this management long-term in their expectations or are they seeking the quick buck? How much of total compensation is made up of stock options? What is the value of management's share position? Have they purchased more shares during the recent price decline?

While answers to such questions can be informative to the investor, there is a caveat—because of the increasing use of stock options, many of today's senior management may choose to sell (or "exercise" in the parlance of options) their shares merely as a means of diversification rather than as a portent of an imminent price decline.

ASSETS

A strong balance sheet is a wonderful characteristic for a company in search of fame and fortune in the annals of great stocks. Assets take many different forms, the most obvious and arguably the easiest to spend being cash or cash equivalents (short-term money market instruments). But when utilized properly, certain noncurrent assets (typically, assets that cannot be translated into cash within one operating cycle) can be top performers for a given company. Take, for example, the new factory with the very best in high-tech machinery or the 30,000 acres of land in the Pacific Northwest that happens to be within one hour's drive from the MicroSoft World Headquarters. While these assets are not easily converted into cash, they are certainly assets. Furthermore, the land can be carried at cost (not current market value) on the company's balance sheet. The well-trained "asset hound" seeks to break down a company's balance sheet in search of either the underutilized asset or the undiscovered or unrecognized (by accounting tenets) asset. In many situations, as value investors come to realize, the sum of the parts equals more than the whole.

TECHNOLOGY

Effective application of the newest technical advances makes a business more efficient. Inefficient use of or lack of technology, can consequently, doom an enterprise to underperformance. A business in the 1990s cannot operate in the same fashion as it did 15 years ago—when, for example, was the last time you purchased a good that was not scanned in some way? This often pervasive act of electronic accounting has a significant dividend to the merchant—inventory control. These cash registers (a term that probably will soon be as antiquated as buggy whip is today) are often plugged into a database that can analyze each store's sales, margins, discounts, returns and, most importantly, need for reordering. Some economists postulate that this information-driven inventory control mechanism (technology dividend) contributes to the current period of continued low inflation.

Dedication to research and development, within a company's given area of focus, belongs in this category. Often the most savvy investors seek those companies that have consistently posted high R and D expense ratios (as a percentage of revenues). This type of research support differentiates the serious player from those companies (or managements) that are in just for the quick buck. While it may be a non-income-producing expense today, this dedication often pays off. For example, a biotechnology company may have committed millions of dollars over the past four years to a particular new drug discovery technique. This technique, based on genetic research, then yields a major breakthrough that provides the company a significant joint-venture relationship with a major pharmaceutical company.

INTERNATIONAL STRATEGY

Only the company that can successfully implement an international strategy can fully compete in the new global community. The expanded marketplace (read: global community) for a company's goods and services, subjects a company to different currency flows as well as increased competition. Economists have also pointed to this increased market as a contributing factor to the low inflation currently enjoyed by the restructured U.S. corporation. How can a large U.S.-based producer of paper raise its prices aggressively when several internationally based companies stand ready to gobble up market share? The proactive treasurer (and entire financial management team) in a globally sensitive company needs to be aware of the new playing field to maintain effectiveness.

RETURN

This is the lifeblood of a well-run company; without it, sooner or later, the company will die. Equity investors invest their capital in shares of companies that they expect to post a worthwhile return. This return, or its expectation, provides the groundwork for the share value. In some cases, investors will use a price-to-earnings ratio or perhaps, as described in Chapter 5, a Dividend Discount Method to arrive at a fair value for the company's shares. As discussed in Chapter 1, the investor needs to pay careful attention to the manipulations of net income that affect the ultimate value of the shares.

OPERATIONS

This characteristic reveals the inner workings of the company. How does this business operate? What is the industry like? Competitors? In this category, the investor seeks to identify the company as a business, pure and simple. The investor attempts to divorce himself from the emotions of stock investing and focus on the value of the business, per se. Investors should seek companies with a franchise value, that is, a product or service that is duplicated in a multitude of markets. Companies that come to mind in this category are McDonald's, PepsiCo, Coca-Cola, and Wells Fargo Bank. In addition to having a franchise value, the company should also be an adept acquirer:

> What happens if the company's market share peaks? What will drive forward the company's top line and market share expansion?

Acquisitions can be an important part in this equation. The investor should seek companies that have a strong competitive advantage in the acquisition exercise:

> Does management endorse expansion through acquisitions? Are they patient enough to wait for the right price? Do they have the assets (high cash levels, low debt levels) to support such a campaign?

COST-EFFECTIVE MANAGEMENT

Perhaps a more euphemistically sensitive title would be "lean" (but then the acronym wouldn't be as catchy). In any sense, the more frugal a company is with its expenses the more likely it is a tightly run ship. And companies run this way typically have greater staying power in a bad economy or market (for their products). All too often, small companies raise capital through the equity market only to spend millions on a "world headquarters"—a 30,000-square-foot architecturally imposing structure, landscaped on a 10-acre campus sporting flags from every nation, expensively appointed in imported carpets and mahogany furniture. In no way am I suggesting that a growing company should avoid spending money to improve its working environment or competiveness within its market. But there is a limit to what can be classified as an expense—or simply expensive. An expense is an expending of capital with a probability of a return to justify that expense; conducting business in an expensive way is often proof that a company is out of control. If you were the owner of a small hardware store in town and a candidate for a clerk position walked in and demanded $15 per hour, hiring this applicant would be expensive (unless the person possessed some extrasensory abilities to attract a strong increase in hardware buyers in the town). On the other hand, if you decided to hire three clerks at $5 per hour each, to work the floor simultaneously in order to achieve a "full-service" hardware store strategy (to differentiate from the warehouse strategy of the large chains), then this expense can be justified (as an attempt to increase market share through a differentiation strategy).

While these "PATIROC" characteristics are not the only traits that define a good company, they certainly give the investor the right direction. With these screens in place, the investor has the further responsibility to be skeptical of price. Don't overpay for a great company. Should the music ever stop, even for a quarter or two, the price action in the stock would be unforgiving. Look for great companies with specific characteristics, and then apply a good dose of skepticism to the price of the shares. Investing in a great company with an inflated price tag does not make much fundamental sense. As mentioned in Chapter 5, Michele Clayman's research on "excellent companies" demonstrated that they do not stay excellent forever. For this dynamic reason, we, as prudent equity investors, must have a well-defined exit strategy that focuses on changes which can affect the company's ongoing operations or stated value. Such changes includes the departure of senior or founding management, industry fragmentation, new product or company entrants—most pervasive—the increased valuation of the company's share price. While all investors hope for an increase in the share price of the underlying equity, one needs to be acutely aware of the implications toward value:

> Is this increased valuation warranted or is it due to external market forces (too much capital chasing too few good investments)? Has the company's management endorsed, by increasing their own positions, this increased share price? Is this price appreciation industrywide? Does it speak to euphoria or is it firmly footed in sensible valuation?

To achieve success, equity investors must often ask themselves these questions, always second-guessing their research to uncover any flaws. Maybe that is why it can be such a gut-wrenching but rewarding exercise.

Finally, throughout this journey, please remember that investment analysis is not a game but rather a venerable discipline firmly entrenched in many scientific disciplines. As a means of support and proper manners, however, I still offer all readers good luck.

Part One

TOOLS OF THE TRADE

Part One requires the working knowledge of certain important disciplines that are firmly footed in the mathematical and economic sciences. Any financial analyst needs to study these disciplines—work with them time and time again—before being ready to progress farther into the financial analysis maze. As with many other professional pursuits, most of the early work (grunt work, "paying your dues," "coming up the ladder") builds a foundation on which the higher skills depend. They are the building blocks that the investor will use countless times in the construction of a portfolio.

The tools of financial analysis are as critical to investment success as surgical instruments are to a brain surgeon. With a working knowledge of these tools, the financial analyst, whether a beginner or a seasoned investor, will have the skills to recognize a timely investment opportunity.

The four tools of financial analysis are:

1. Accounting for business transactions.
2. Economics.
3. The mathematics of finance.
4. Quantitative analysis using basic statistics and regression analysis.

The focus of Chapter 1 is less the basics of accounting (exhaustive coverage of that topic is beyond the scope of this work) than it is specific items of importance to today's analysts and investors. These include merger/acquisition accounting methodology and the valuation implications of managerial accounting policies (depreciation methods, inventory recognition, etc.). A working knowledge of these areas enables the investor to dissect the company's accounting statements in search of any inconsistencies or red flags. In this case, the investor acts as a detective, searching through data from sources initiated by several types of media, to identify information that permits an analysis and subsequent valuation.

Additionally, careful examination of financial statements can lead to a better understanding of management's policies and style:

> Does management have a conservative or liberal bias with regard to accounting policies? By which method are noncurrent assets depreciated? Are inventories valued using a LIFO (last in-first out) or FIFO (first in-first out) basis?

Answering such questions can lead to a more comprehensive valuation of any company.

Chapter 2, "Economics," focuses on the items, such as government indicators and international parity conditions, that concern today's investors (novice or professional). Studying these areas is essential for attaining a more complete picture of how economic events affect the valuation of financial instruments:

> What does the Purchasing Power Parity equation say about the price of foreign goods (in the United States) given an increasing value of a foreign currency versus the U.S. dollar? When are the 12 leading indicators released and what do they tell us about the economy? Does the economic business cycle permit an advantage in timing of the stock market?

The basic economic premise—the theory and practice of supply and demand models ("Microeconomics")—is not directly covered in this text, for its full examination requires a more extensive review.

Chapter 3, "Investment Mathematics," deals with the underpinnings of the entire study of investment finance—the mathematics behind the future value of money. After a discussion of the different formulas used to calculate this all-important mathematical concept, several problems are presented that permit the practitioner a repetitive learning format. This "problem set" format lends itself to much of this chapter, for *investment mathematics,* simple enough in theory, requires the practical understanding that comes with repetitive problem solving (e.g., What is the future value of $1000 in 6 years at a compounded rate of 6% per year? What is the internal rate of return, or valuation, of a specific real estate project?).

Chapter 4, "Quantitative Analysis," is the final chapter in Part One. The quantitative approach to investment analysis is critical when the investor is making a hypothesis about the relationship between independent variables and a particular firm's earnings. Again, the problem set format is used to further reinforce the practical applications of this theory (in addition, the appendix in Chapter 4 covers regression analysis).

Accounting

This chapter, you will learn the following aspects of accounting:

- ✔ The balance sheet and income statement.
- ✔ The basics of managerial accounting.
- ✔ Purchase and pooling methods of merger/acquisition accounting.

The practice of accounting is the tabulating and bookkeeping of the capital resources (in currency terms) of a particular firm. The actual entries listed on the accounting statements do not tell us anything concrete about the firm's business activities, but reflect how accountants record these activities. That is not to say that accounting statements are without value; they are among the most important pieces in the valuation puzzle, but without careful study, they do not reveal any information of consequence. This inadequacy of accounting data lies within the procedures themselves; in most cases, an investor needs to be proficient in this art to gain any insight into the future prospects of the concern in question.

OVERVIEW

Before embarking on the exercises involving accounting, it is important to discuss briefly the three theories used in accounting for financial assets. Each differs in the way it affects valuation:

1. The classical theory.
2. The market-based research approach.
3. The positive accounting theory.

In the classical theory approach, the value of accounting methods is measured by the accuracy of the information presented on the value of the firm. Essential to this approach is that investors take this information at face value, study it, and act according to its implications. For example, if accounting data illustrate that a particular firm accounts for its inventory by the LIFO (last in-first out) method, then it would be prudent (for the analysis of this firm) that the investor be aware of the effects of inflation on the inventory's valuation. Why? Because inflation will increase the value of the newest inventory (last in) and therefore increase the cost-of-goods-sold expense (first out) on the income statement, which in turn decreases the gross profit.

The market-based research approach gained prominence in the late 1960s when accounting research shifted from the classical theory to the financial theory approach. A critical factor in this shift was the development of the efficient market hypothesis and the modern portfolio theory. These theories suggested further research into the effect of accounting information on the valuation of a firm was an exercise in futility. After several years of empirical research, however, it has been found that the market-based research approach is largely unfounded, and therefore, for all practical purposes, today's investor can ignore it.

The positive accounting theory suggests that accounting theory does not stand alone but interacts with other information provided by the company's operations. Perhaps the decisions made by management affect the accounting data provided to investors. It would seem obvious, in today's environment of stock option incentives, that management would have a vested interest in the reported accounting statements and subsequent effects on the share price. This suggests not that management is fudging the numbers to benefit the share price, but instead is adopting certain (legal and typical) accounting practices to achieve that benefit. It seems likely, given this theory, that management would adopt a liberal accounting methodology. What implication does this hold for financial analysis? Be careful and dig deep for the information you seek.

This chapter looks at only the accounting methods most important to the investor by reviewing the most common accounting statements—balance sheet and income statement.

THE BALANCE SHEET

The balance sheet serves as a snapshot of the current net worth of a particular firm at a given moment in time. It illustrates, in some detail, the asset holdings (fixed and current) as well as the liabilities in such fashion that the offsetting amounts equal the net worth of the company (equity). The following definitions permit a better understanding of this financial statement (see Appendix B, Table B.1).

Assets

The first major section of the balance sheet lists assets, including the following.

Current Assets.   This consolidation entry includes assets that can be converted into cash within one year or normal operating cycle. The following entries are components of current assets:

- ✔ *Cash.* Bank deposit balances, any petty cash funds, and cash equivalents (money markets, U.S. Treasury Bills).
- ✔ *Accounts receivable.* The amount due from customers that has not yet been collected. Customers are typically given 30, 60, or 90 days in which to pay. Some customers fail to pay completely (companies will set up an account known as "reserve for doubtful accounts"), and for this reason the accounts receivable entry represents the amount that is expected to be received ("accounts receivable less allowance for doubtful accounts").
- ✔ *Inventory.* Composed of three parts: (1) raw materials used in products, (2) partially finished goods, and (3) finished goods. The generally accepted method of valuation of inventory is the lower of cost or market (LCM). This provides a conservative estimate for this occasionally volatile item (see Aside: LIFO versus FIFO).
- ✔ *Prepaid expenses.* Payments made by the company, in advance of the benefits that will be received by year's end, such as prepaid fire insurance premiums, advertising charges for the upcoming year, or advanced rent payments.

Fixed Assets (Noncurrent Assets).   Assets that cannot be converted into cash within a normal operating cycle. The following are fixed assets:

✔ *Land, property, plant, and equipment.* Those assets not intended for sale and used time and time again to operate the enterprise. The typical valuation method for fixed assets is cost minus the accumulated depreciation—the amount of depreciation that has been accumulated to this point.

Liabilities

The next major portion of the balance sheet lists liabilities, including the following.

Current Liabilities. This entry includes all debts that fall due within 12 months (or one operating cycle). By matching the current assets with the current liabilities, the investor can get a good idea of how payments will be made on current liabilities:

✔ *Accounts payable.* Represents the amount the company owes to business creditors from whom it has purchased goods or services on account. This is often referred to as "Trade-Related Debt."

✔ *Accrued expenses.* The amounts owed and not yet recorded on the books that are unpaid at the date of the balance sheet.

✔ *Income tax payable.* The debt due to the Internal Revenue Service (IRS) or other taxing authorities but not yet paid. These are, by definition, accrued expenses, but because they are tax related, they carry with them a certain importance to the analysis of the firm.

Long-Term Debt. These are debts due beyond 1 year (or one operating cycle).

Stockholders' Equity

The last major section of the balance sheet is the stockholders' equity section, which includes the following:

Stockholders' Equity. The total equity interest that all shareholders have in the company. Stockholders' equity, like any other equity, is the net worth remaining after subtracting all liabilities from all assets. The true measure of the firm's reputation as an outstanding company resides in its ability to grow this equity amount. The book value of a firm is calculated as the stockholders' equity—the assets minus the liabilities.

Retained Earnings. The amount of earnings, above the dividend payout, accumulated by the firm. Although retaining earnings may be an appropriate strategy at a given point in a firm's life cycle, it can also be an invitation to a corporate raider seeking a cash cow investment opportunity. Furthermore, a company retaining too much of its earnings can open questions about why these cash flows haven't been reinvested in high net present value (NPV) projects so the company can continue to grow. (Is this firm running out of good opportunities?)

THE INCOME STATEMENT

Whereas the balance sheet is the record of net worth for the firm, the income statement illustrates the firm's operating record. In this statement, the firm's income and expenses are reconciled to arrive at a value of net income for the period in question. Very often, the analysis of equities focuses on this net income value (earnings). The information gleaned from one particular year is not as critical to the analysis of a particular firm as the data for several years or, better yet, the projected (future) earnings information.

To put the corporate accounting statements in perspective: The income statement is similar to your personal tax filing for a given year; reconciling income (W-2, capital gain and dividend earnings, etc.) versus expenses (mortgage expense, business expenses, etc.). The balance sheet, on the other hand, is similar to your personal net worth statement that you might organize for an estate plan document or mortgage application.

The following definitions should aid in understanding this financial statement (see Appendix B, Table B.2):

✔ *Revenue.* The amount received by the company for rendering its services or selling its goods. The total revenue is calculated by simply multiplying the number of goods sold by the price per unit (quantity sold × price per unit). Revenue always initiates the income statement because, by definition, it is the starting point of operating activities. Net total revenue takes into account any returned goods and allowances for reduction of prices.

✔ *Cost of goods sold.* The primary cost expense in most manufacturing companies—all the costs incurred in the factory to convert raw materials into finished product. The cost of goods expense also includes direct labor and manufacturing overhead associated with the production of finished goods. The *fixed cost* is the amount that will not typically increase with increases in output of the finished product; it includes expenses in operating an enterprise (e.g., rent, electricity, supplies, maintenance, repairs), often called "burden," "fluff," or "overhead." A *variable cost* can be directly traced to the production process and therefore will typically increase as the number of units produced increases (e.g., raw material costs, sales commissions).

✔ *Gross profit.* The amount of excess of sales over the cost of sales. Gross profit is often represented as a ratio (in percentage form):

$$\frac{\text{Gross profit margin}}{(\text{expressed as a percent})} = \frac{\text{Gross profit amount}}{\text{Revenues}}$$

The following example illustrates the gross profit margin (see Appendix B, Table B.1):

Revenues (or sales)	$6,019,040
COGS	3,912,376
Gross profit	$2,106,664

Therefore the gross profit margin is $2,106,664 divided by $6,019,040 or 35%.

Note. Depreciation is a noncash charge and therefore is not included in this calculation; instead, it is an accounting reconciliation that is more critical in the after-tax profit calculation.

✔ *Operating expenses.* This line item serves as a heading for the consolidation of the nondirect costs incurred in the operations of a business. Selling, general, and administrative expense is the most typical operating expense for a company. As businesses differ, operationally and economically, so will their allocations toward operating expenses. For example, the computer software development company will have a higher commitment toward operating expenses (salaries, bonuses, educational seminars, marketing, etc.) versus a wholesale manufacturing company, whose largest costs are typically the raw materials used in the production process. Sales, general, and administrative expenses (SG&A) are important items in the analysis of a company for they illustrate the management's fiscal restraint or resistance to temptation. When a VFII notices the sales of a company increasing but the SG&A growing at a faster rate, a yellow flag of caution is raised. Components of SG&A include salaries, commissions, advertising, promotion, offices expenses, travel, and entertainment expenses.

✔ *Operating earnings before depreciation (earnings before interest, taxes, depreciation and amortization—EBITDA).* Known as a measure of cash flow for it factors out the noncash charges included in depreciation and amortization expense. Many analysts, especially those specializing in relatively new, very capital-intense industries (telecommunications and cellular communications), rely on this measure as the true earnings of the company.

✔ *Depreciation and amortization expense.* The estimated amount that management expects to use in the future to replace its operating facilities. It can be thought of as an escrow account where the company sets aside a specific (defined by tax policies, equipment's salvage value, and estimated useful life) amount each year to be used in the future to repurchase the operational necessities (plant and equipment) of the enterprise. Amortization is depreciation, but instead of referring to a tangible asset, it refers to an intangible asset (e.g., goodwill, patents).

✔ *Operating earnings.* Earnings attributed to the activities of the company without any impact from the financing of its balance sheet. This earnings figure is used in the calculation of an "enterprise value" or value of the business as if it were a private concern.

✔ *Interest expense.* Amount that equals the company's outstanding debt multiplied by its debt expense (i.e., interest owed to bondholders). Under current corporate tax law, the debt payments made to bond holders are tax deductible: This amount is subtracted from the operating earnings before calculating the taxes.

✔ *Income tax expense.* Tax rate (approximately 36% on the corporate level) multiplied by the pretax earnings.

✔ *Net income.* Earnings, plain and simple—the last entry on the income statement, the bottom line. Ironically, it is the opening entry for much of what is known as fundamental analysis—the analysis of a business utilizing quantitative models to determine the earnings and subsequent valuation.

Having defined the basic components to the accounting statements, we can begin to analyze these components. Managerial accounting simply refers to using and analyzing accounting data to maximize the resources of the company. Decisions about the method chosen to depreciate an asset (straight-line or accelerated) could be crucial to the profitability

LIFO versus FIFO

Last in-first out (LIFO) and *first in-first out* (FIFO) are methods by which inventory is valued on a company's balance sheet. The typical company is continually purchasing new goods and selling existing goods, both of which come from the inventory account. The method used to determine the value of the inventory account is as follows:

Beginning period inventory value +

Value of new purchases −

Inventory used in COGS =

Ending period inventory value

Whether the LIFO or FIFO method is used in inventory valuation determines whether the amount expensed as cost of goods sold (COGS) comes from new purchases (LIFO) or existing inventory (beginning period) as in FIFO.

The following guidelines shed some light on this occasionally confusing area:

LIFO

Undervalues inventory (given increasing prices) on balance sheet because the more expensive items are expensed as COGS rather then being kept on the balance sheet as inventory—hence, last in-first out. This method became more widely used during the inflationary 1970s, when companies attempted to match their current operations with current costs so as not to incur artificially high profits (for with high profits come very real high taxes).

FIFO

Correctly values inventory on the balance sheet (in inflationary environment) due to an expensing (as COGS) of the previously purchased (at lower prices) goods, therefore providing an inequitable match of revenues with COGS, resulting in an overstatement of earnings and subsequent tax expense.

of a company. The decisions surrounding the evaluation of a company's fixed cost structure (the allocation of costs that do not change with the level of output, e.g., rental cost) versus its variable cost structure (expenses that vary with the amount of output generated, e.g., raw materials, selling expenses) could also be crucial to future planning.

The following problem set focuses on the fundamentals of managerial accounting.

<hr>

PROBLEM SET
MANAGERIAL ACCOUNTING

Question 1

The Brittany Company, which manufactures robes, has enough idle capacity available to accept a special order of 10,000 robes at $8 per robe. A predicted income statement for the year without this special order is as follows:

	Per Unit		Total
Sales	$12.50		$1,250,000
Manufacturing costs:			
Variable	$6.25	$625,000	
Fixed	1.75	175,000	
Total manufacturing costs	8.00		800,000
Gross profit	**$ 4.50**		**$ 450,000**
Selling expenses:			
Variable	$1.80	$180,000	
Fixed	1.45	145,000	
Total selling expenses	3.25		325,000
Operating income	**$ 1.25**		**$ 125,000**

Assuming no additional selling expenses, what would be the effect on operating income if the company accepted the special order?

Answer

The important facts in this problem are:

1. The idle capacity situation that currently exists within the company; this relates to a fixed cost structure that is able to take on more capacity without increasing its (fixed) costs.
2. The rather large size of the order that is being considered.
3. The assumption that no further selling (variable) costs would be incurred in this order.

The following computation breaks down the accounting data to better illustrate the problem:

The Brittany Company			
	Contribution Approach	*Effects of Special Order*	*With Special Order*
Sales	$1,250,000	$80,000	$1,330,000
Variable costs	800,000	62,500	885,000
Contribution	$ 450,000	$17,500	$ 444,500
Fixed costs	325,000	0	320,000
Net	$ 125,000	$17,500	$ 142,500

The preceding calculations indicate that it would be advantageous (to the tune of $17,500 additional profits) to accept this special order.

The other (quick and intuitive) method is to examine the per unit costs:

✔ Revenues from special order are $8 per unit.

✔ Variable costs per unit are $6.25; assume that due to idle capacity there are no additional fixed costs.

✔ Net profit is therefore $1.75 per unit, or $17,500 for 10,000 units.

Question 2

From a particular joint process, The UTA Company produces three products X, Y, and Z. Each product may be sold at the point of split-off or processed further. Additional processing requires no special facilities, and production costs of further processing are entirely variable and traceable to the products involved. In 199x, all three products were processed beyond split-off. Joint production costs for the year were $60,000. Sales values and costs needed to evaluate UTA's 199x production policy follow:

Product	Units Produced	Sales at Split-Off	If Processed Further Sales	If Processed Further Additional Costs
X	6,000	$25,000	$42,000	$9,000
Y	4,000	41,000	45,000	7,000
Z	2,000	24,000	32,000	8,000

Joint costs are allocated to the products in proportion to the relative physical volume of output.

A. Determine the relative unit production cost for X, Y, and Z.

B. To maximize profits, UTA should subject which products to additional processing?

Answer

A. First, calculate the additional cost per unit by simply dividing the additional costs by the number of units produced.

Relative unit production costs for additional processed product for X, Y, and Z:

X $9,000/6,000 = $1.5 per unit

Y $7,000/4,000 = $1.75 per unit

Z $8,000/2,000 = $4.00 per unit

B. Next, calculate the incremental increase in revenues that the further production would bring, as well as the subsequent net income.

X: $42,000 (end revs) − $25,000 (split-off revs) = $17,000 (incremental increase)

$17,000 (add'l revs) − $9,000 (add'l costs) = $8,000; therefore accept additional output.

Y: $45,000 − $41,000 = $4,000

$4,000 − $7,000 = ($3,000); this is a negative value (loss) therefore reject additional output.

Z: $32,000 − $24,000 = $8,000

$8,000 − $8,000 = $0; although not a loss, this represents a break-even amount and is therefore also rejected for additional output.

Question 3

The following information is given for the Lone Hill Company:

Initial cost of proposed new equipment	$130,000
Predicted useful life	10 years
Predicted salvage value (end of life)	$10,000
Predicted savings per year in operating expenses	$24,000

Ignoring income tax effects, answer the following:

1. What is the depreciation expense per year by straight-line method? What are two other methods? What makes them different? How do they affect the reported net income of company?
2. What is the predicted increase in future annual net income?

Answer

This example involves evaluating the straight-line depreciation method, one of the most common methods in accounting. In the straight-line method, the calculation is as follows:

$$\text{Depreciation expense per year} = \frac{(\text{Initial cost} - \text{Salvage value})}{(\text{Useful life})}$$

Apply this method to the data in the problem:

$$\text{Depreciation expense per year} = \frac{(\text{Initial cost} - \text{Salvage value})}{(\text{Useful life})}$$

$$\frac{(\$130,000 - 10,000)}{(10 \text{ years})} = \$12,000 \text{ per year depreciation expense}$$

The accelerated depreciation method (ACRS) and the sum-of-the-years digits (SOYD) both permit higher depreciation expenses and consequently lower pretax earnings (and lower taxable expense) and ultimately lower reported net earnings.

Now evaluate the effects on future annual income from this choice of depreciation method.

The expected increase in future annual net income (ignoring income tax effects):

$$\begin{array}{ccc}
\text{Predicted annual savings in} & \text{Depreciation} & \text{Increase in} \\
\text{operating expense} & - \quad \text{expense} & = \quad \text{net income}
\end{array}$$

$$\$24{,}000 \quad - \quad 12{,}000 \quad = \quad \$12{,}000$$

MERGER ACCOUNTING METHODS

As investors have confronted the now-common (practically daily) occurrence of merger/acquisition activity in their portfolios, they have sought methods to efficiently evaluate the new entity. The dialogue from press releases will almost invariably discuss the potential *synergies between both companies* and the now *global reach* of this new entity, and add many enthusiastic comments about the *future impact of this marriage*. The front page of every business daily will have photographs of the two CEOs glowing and toasting the new company (they probably have the most to gain); perhaps even a new logo and advertising campaign will be introduced. Once the postannouncement hype dies down, however, the question of valuation and impact on the share price is still up in the air. Valuation of this new entity in part depends on the accounting methodology used to combine both companies.

How do we get a handle on this arcane science of merger and acquisition accounting? How are the assets combined on the balance sheet of the new company? Are there any implications that would affect the income statement (and reported earnings) of the combined entity? For trend analysis, will this new entity and its financial statements be easy to decipher?

Two methods are used in the accounting for mergers and acquisitions: the purchase and pooling-of-interest methods. Each method has its nuances toward valuation and rules that permit its use. In the material that follows, an attempt is made to summarize these nuances.

The Purchase Method

The acquiring company assumes all the assets and liabilities of the target company by purchasing all its outstanding equity at a given price (as designated in the acquisition agreement). The assets and liabilities of the target company are marked to market (fair market value). The purchase price of the company (the number of shares outstanding multiplied by the per share purchase price) is compared with the "fair market value of net assets" (FMVNA) and any resulting value which is above this FMVNA is known as goodwill.

Goodwill is an intangible asset (brand names, market share, brand recognition, etc.) that is purchased and then amortized each year over a period defined by the Internal Revenue Service (APB 17 allows for amortization of goodwill from 10 to 40 years, but it is not deductible for tax purposes). A significant amount of goodwill can go a long way to reduce net income (as reported to investors but not to the IRS) but, in the same token, significantly increase the balance sheet values.

Financial statements that are combined from the effective date of the merger create a difficulty for trend analysis. If Company X acquires Company Z on September 30 (assume a calendar fiscal year) the combined (new) company's income statement will falsely indicate a big increase (due to the combined income) for the fourth quarter. A NFII who didn't take the time to understand the implications of this acquisition might conclude that the company is undergoing "phenomenal growth" when, in reality, it has purchased this growth. Meanwhile, the VFII will consider important questions:

> Did Company X overpay for Company Y? Does definable synergy exist between their businesses? Can the combined company reduce significant overhead?

The Pooling-of-Interests Method

This method unites the ownership interests of two companies into one new entity; it refers to merger, and not acquisition for the simple reason that no acquiring is taking place but rather a pooling of interests.

Use of the pooling method is limited to mergers that meet the following conditions:

✔ The two companies must be independent.
✔ Voting common shares can be the only issuance.

✔ Stock repurchases are prohibited.

✔ Equal benefits (of the transaction) are enjoyed by all shareholders.

✔ Disposals of significant businesses are prohibited.

The combined companies are accounted for using historical cost values; there is no markup (or down) to fair value. This can impact the future income statement (of the combined company) by recognizing a future sale (of an asset that has been carried at cost) as a large gain in the period of the sale. The sale can also be used to offset any losses on other asset sales or simply to report higher earnings.

Financial results for prior periods (for up to the prior 10 years) are restated to recognize the merger. This "fictitious history" suggests that the companies have been one entity for a longer period than they actually have been. This can have a detrimental effect on the understanding of the valuation of the company.

The following example should help in solidifying this topic.

PROBLEM SET
MERGER/ACQUISITION ACCOUNTING

Question 1

Assume the following balance sheet data for Company A and Company B:

	Company A	Company B
Inventory	$100	$400
Accounts receivable	50	100
Property	200	350
Total	$350	$850
Accounts payable	$ 30	$100
Long-term debt	70	200
Common stock	200	400
Retained earnings	50	150
Total	$350	$850

Now make the following assumptions:

1. The fair market value for Company A's inventory is $200 and property is $300.
2. The transaction is assumed to have occurred within the year in question.

Case 1: Company B acquires Company A for $800 using the purchase method. Illustrate the new company's balance sheet.

Case 2: Companies A and B decide to merge their businesses (in a "share-for-share exchange") accounted for using the pooling method. Illustrate the resulting balance sheet.

Answer

	Case 1	Case 2
Inventory	$200 + 400	$100 + 400
Accounts receivable	50 + 100	50 + 100
Property	300 + 350	200 + 350
Goodwill	350	0
Total	$1,750	$1,200
Accounts payable	$30 + 100	$30 + 100
Long-term debt	70 + 200	70 + 200
Common stock	800* + 400	200 + 400
Retained earnings	150*	50 + 150
Total	$1,750	$1,200

*When B acquired A, it purchased all its equity (common stock and retained earnings) for $800 and thereby the former amounts for these items (for Company A) no longer exist in the combined entity.

Notes:

1. Goodwill is recognized in Case 1 because the purchase method is used. It is calculated in the following manner:

   FMVNA of Company A:

Inventory	$200
Accounts receivable	50

Property	300
Accounts payable	(30)
Long-term debt	(70)
FMVNA of Company A	$450

The purchase price is $800, therefore the resulting Goodwill value is $350 ($800 minus $450).

2. As the assumption stated, the transaction occurred within the given year. If the problem called for more than one year of data, the following adjustments would be required—

   a. Case 1 data would have been affected for the period that the transaction took place (prorated if in the middle of the year) and not for previous years.

   b. Case 2 data would have been restated for all periods (up to 10 years) to affect the impact of the merger.

The Income Statement measures the effect this acquisition/merger would have on the operating results of the combined entity.

Income Statement

An assumption, for illustration purposes, is made that Companies A and B had reported the same figures for the past three years (1991–1993). In addition, it is assumed that the tax rate for both companies is 40%.

Assume the following Income Statements for Companies A and B (before any consolidation activity):

	Company A 1991–1993	Company B 1991–1993
Sales	$400	$1,000
Cost of goods sold	100	500
Gross margin	300	500
Other expenses	50	150
Depreciation	50	100
Pretax earnings	200	250
Tax expense	80	100
Net income	$120	$ 150

Note. Depreciation in both cases is based on a salvage value of $50 and a depreciation period of 3 years. The depreciation expense, using the straight-line method, is calculated as follows:

Case 1: Property asset value (balance sheet value is cost because we know that the market value is $300 and that the asset is being recognized using the lower-of-cost-or-market [LCM] method and that there is no accumulated depreciation) of $200 minus salvage value of $50 is a depreciation base of $150 which is then divided by 3 years to calculate the $50 depreciation expense.

Case 2: As indicated: $350 − $50 = $300 which is then divided by 3 years to calculate the depreciation expense of $100.

Question 2

Construct the combined entity's revised income statement for the following cases:

Case 1: Company B acquires Company A using the purchase accounting method and amortizes the goodwill cost over 10 years. The effective date of the acquisition is June 30, 1992. Both companies report on a calendar (December 31) fiscal year.

Case 2: Company A and B merge as of June 30, 1992.

Answer

	Case 1			Case 2		
	1991	*1992*	*1993*	*1991*	*1992*	*1993*
Sales	$1,000	$1,200	$1,400	$1,400	$1,400	$1,400
Cost of goods sold	500	550	600	600	600	600
Gross margin	500	650	800	800	800	800
Other expenses	150	175	200	200	200	200
Depreciation	100	125	150	150	150	150
Amortization	0	17	35	0	0	0
Pretax earnings	250	333	415	450	450	450
Tax expense	100	133	166	180	180	180
Net income	$ 150	$ 200	$ 249	$ 270	$ 270	$ 270

Notes:

1. Using the purchase method, the income statement is restated for only the period that the transaction takes place. Therefore, in Case 1 (above), 1991 is illustrated with no effect of Company A's data (entirely Company B's data), 50% impact for 1992 and 100% for 1993. Here we are given a false record of this company's growth rate; it is important to realize that this growth was not internally generated but purchased. Now the analysis focuses on what price was paid for this growth and does the acquisition make sense (on a business level—are there synergies or cost savings?).

2. The amortization expense in Case 1 is calculated as follows:

   1991:   No effect

   1992–2002: Due to the acquisition on June 30, 1992 the combined entity's income statement is impacted beginning in this year. We know from the combined company's balance sheet data (see Question 1) that the goodwill amount is $350 and that, as per the given, it will be amortized over 10 years—therefore the amortization schedule would be as follows:

   1992: $17 ($35/year for half year)

   1993–2001: $35

   2002: $17 ($35/year for half year)

3. Using the pooling method, each year is restated for the merger and each entry is added together to calculate the data for the consolidated income statement. As it is plain to see, this creates a fictitious history for this company—Has the company actually earned $270 annually for the last 10 years?

As shown in the previous problem set, the balance sheet and income statement become quite different statements when compared between the two methods. These methods have important effects on credit (ratio) analysis as well as valuation analysis.

In the purchase accounting method, assets are marked to a true or fair value as of the time of the transaction. This causes a "correct" depreciation expense to be tendered against the income statement resulting in an understatement of reported earnings. In addition, the initiation of goodwill and its resulting amortization further leads to an understatement of net income (for book purposes, not for tax purposes). However, the most entangling by-product of this method seems to be the discontinuity and subsequent futility of trend analysis caused by the non-restatement of financial statements as well as the origination (on the financial statements) of the acquisition on the effective date.

In the pooling method, there is an understatement of assets due to the use of historical values; this leads to an understatement of depreciation expense (less asset values leads to less depreciation on those assets), an overstatement of earnings before taxes, tax expense, and consequently net income. Furthermore, in the pooling method, a fictitious history of the company is created, which may cause inconsistencies for those sad few who are not in tune with these implications. Most would agree that the fictitious history created by the pooling method is far better than the trend analysis fiasco caused by the purchase method.

Now that we have covered the basics of accounting, with the definitions of the typical financial statements and discussed merger/acquisition accounting (an area of accounting that has received much attention of late), we can turn our attention to the next tool—economics. While the previous information on accounting is not sufficient to perform an audit on a corporation, the lessons should provide the VFII with solid footing in this often confusing and forgotten building block of analysis.

Chapter

Economics

In this chapter, you will learn:

1. The international parity theorems that serve as the underpinnings for financial currency and international trade valuations.
2. The U.S. government's monthly economic releases.
3. The business cycle and the implications to investment timing.

Economics can be a paradoxical science; whatever you would normally think to be a correct and logical relationship turns out to be the complete opposite. The majority of nonfinancially interested individuals (NFIIs) would regard a strong growth economy as the best possible scenario for an increasing valuation of financial assets. However, this scenario could actually portend greater inflation (the nemesis of financial assets) and higher interest rates (to combat these higher rates, see "Purchasing Power Parity" later in this chapter) and lower valuations for financial assets because the cash flows generated within will be discounted at higher rates, resulting in lower present values (see Chapter 3).

Another NFII may associate a strong U.S. dollar with increasing interest rates because "higher interest rates generate a greater demand for the domestic currency." But one theoretical application of international parity conditions states that as domestic interest rates increase (vis-à-vis foreign interest rates), the value of the domestic currency (vis-à-vis the foreign currency) actually should weaken to allow parity (at which no arbitrage or "free-profit" opportunities exist) between both nations.

Opportunities also exist whereby a well-positioned (within the Wall Street community) VFII can profit through rare mispricing or inefficiencies that exist, albeit for only a brief moment, between foreign currencies and interest rates. This type of arbitrage, defined as the ability to purchase a certain asset on one market and then sell the very same asset on another market at a higher price without any risk, is known as interest rate arbitrage. However, like any inefficiency in the market, the opportunity quickly disappears as the buying action of profit-hungry investors force the inefficiency back into parity.

DETERMINING THE HEALTH OF THE ECONOMY

At this point, we face one of the more daunting tasks of any investor—surveying the health of the current economy. This text covers macroeconomics only on a cursory basis because the myriad of economists, investment strategists, and others of this guru sect force efficiency (or information flow) in the marketplace. The volumes of research orchestrated by these men and women drive the investing public's info flow into a state of efficiency. With all this information at their fingertips, how could investors of sound mind and reasonable resources make mistakes?

In the ivory towers of Wall Street, the sources of this economic research have a difficult time determining the health of the economy. A report by Stephen McNees (see Bibliography) states that there is a wide disparity between the forecasts of these professionals and the actual outcomes. Although these forecast errors are often adjusted through the revision process, there is no guarantee of continued improvement. Furthermore, for certain financial variables (e.g., interest rates, stock prices), naive models (simple statistical models) are typically no better than the professional forecasts. Some releases of macroeconomics variables (e.g., gross national product, consumer price index) are consistently bested by the professional's forecast, but the margin for superiority is small. So what is an investor to do? If trained economists can't judge the health of the economy with consistent accuracy, what is the likelihood that today's typical investor can?

Well, candidly, he cannot. But what the investor can do is understand the underlying tenets of macroeconomic relationships and therefore learn to judge the value of financial assets under certain scenarios. For example, the investor who notices a trend of increasing new home sales can surmise that the revenues (and possible, as a consequence, the share price) of companies in the building products and mortgage industries should increase. To further fine-tune his hypothesis, this VFII could employ some simple regression analysis (see the appendix in Chapter 4) to calculate the correlation (if any actually exists) between an increase in this macroeconomic variable and the earnings of the companies that fuel this business. However, the flag of caution is raised, for it may not be as simple as just described. Perhaps there is a lag between the increase in new home sales and the effects on the suppliers to that industry. Or this macroeconomic trend may be an aberration. How "good" is the release? Is it two months old? Is this indicator subject to revision, and if so, what has been the trend in this regard?

This chapter summarizes the major economic releases. Like the information throughout this book, this summary can serve as a factsheet or guideline. An investor today need not understand all the intricacies involved with economic indicators but rather must grasp the effect on financial assets when these releases are made public.

Consider this example. An investor has decided to position $100,000 into zero-coupon treasuries maturing in 25 years (February 15, 2022) for his pension account. The cost of each bond is approximately (as of 1/15/97) $174.24 ($1,000 face value at maturity) and therefore has a stated yield to maturity of 7.090% (ignoring any fees, commissions, or markups).

Price	Yield to Maturity
$174.24	7.09%

The following chain of events occurs:

1. Friday at 8:30 A.M. (EST), the Department of Labor reports a significant and unexpected (and this is the key—for if it was expected, then the bond market would have already adjusted) decrease in the number of unemployed (or increase in the non-farm payrolls). This is a negative for the bond market because stronger growth (the more people employed the more they can spend) usually leads to higher inflation. Inflation is the nemesis of the fixed income market, for it depreciates the buying power of a fixed rate of return.

Unemployment Rate	Inflation
Decreases	Increases

2. Futures on interest rates begin to decline in price immediately (increase in yield).

Inflation	*Interest Rate (Futures) Price*	*Interest Rate (Futures) Yield*
Increases	Decreases	Increases

3. Treasury bond prices also decrease sharply, and therefore yields on treasuries are now 7.22%.

Treasury Bond Prices	*Treasury Bond Yields*
Decreases	Increases

4. The price of the zero-coupon bond is now $168.98 (offered price or buy price) per bond, with a yield to maturity of 7.22%.

Price	*Yield to Maturity*
$168.98	7.22%

The trade would now cost only $16,898 versus $17,424, for a savings of $526, or 3% of the investment. Not much of a difference, especially in the long run, but multiplied by several other similar occasions or a more significant investment (if the pensioner was to purchase $500,000 face amount—$84,490 versus $87,120—the savings would have been $2,630) and it is evident why a VFII may consistently outperform his uninterested counterpart.

I am not advocating timing of the bond market (or any other market for that matter); but careful attention to such a glaring potential loss (or gain, for economic data in the other direction) can add a percentage point or two to an investor's total return. Today's investor should be fully aware of the risks (and rewards) of a particular investment opportunity: Don't just take your financial services provider's (FSP) advice, no matter how professional his judgment may be, but rather question it, be proactive, and debate the issue at hand. Ultimately, this FSP's advice should be more than adequate. However, his support of the idea really determines his worth. Does he have a true conviction—and here is the crucial part—based on some definable and accurate analysis, or is he just selling you something? Is this FSP truly committed to the science of his profession, or is he simply towing the firm's line and reciting the "morning research call"? Fortunately, I have the pleasure and good graces to work in an environment that promotes the professional development of colleagues who value the science of the investment management process.

This attention to detail permits the VFII to consistently outperform even the luckiest NFII year after year. The underlying premise of this book is to help the average investor become a more astute investor who understands the relationships between financial assets and the economy, an investor who is able to read and understand the *Wall Street Journal,* the *Economist,* and a brokerage firm's research report with ease and enjoyment. An investor who develops a "think tank like" relationship with his FSP—in which ideas are shared on a more evenly aligned playing field. I am sure that many FSPs will admit that many of their best investment ideas have come from discussions with clients. Occasionally, a client would recognize certain trends in his own industry that may have implications for a particular company or another industry. Or perhaps a client would become a big fan of a particular new product (or service) and then, with the help of the professional, investigate the company's investment merits. This, in my estimation, is the foundation of the "New Age" of investment management—the sharing and free exchange of information and ideas between investors and professionals for the achievement of a common goal—profits. Clearly, the implications of this "joint-venture" can be extraordinary.

INTERNATIONAL INVESTING

International investing has grown in importance over the past two decades, due in part to the outperformance of the MS EAFE (Morgan Stanley Europe Asia Far East) index (18% average annual return) versus the U.S. stockmarket (9.9% average annual total return of S&P index) between 1970 and 1989. But many constraints exist to international investments besides the obvious political risks (the concern of a riot or some other political turmoil would disturb the financial markets) and currency risks (said to be the greatest "driver" of return and, consequently, the greatest risk, for an international investor). These include technical or accounting differences between nations, which make analysis particularly challenging, and the cultural knowledge required to make intuitive suppositions about future trends. Other concerns for the investor who seeks returns outside his home country include psychological barriers (i.e., cultural differences), legal restrictions (i.e., insider trading laws), transaction costs, and discriminatory taxation (i.e., limitations on repatriation of profits).

The massive scope of international investing is quite beyond the lessons in this manual; it is possible, however, to shed some light on this new and chaotic area of investments. The currency market can provide a focus for the discussion of the differences between investments in different nations.

Let's start at a very simple quote of $1(American) to 1£ (British). The quote (indirect quote format) of the number of foreign currency units per 1 U.S. dollar is the format used in the case that follows. The inverse of this quote would provide the number of U.S. dollars per unit of foreign currency.

As the dollar increases in value:

1. The exchange rate between the dollar and the pound will increase (e.g., the number of pounds it takes to "buy" one dollar will increase). Starting from our base case scenario (1£ = 1US), the exchange rate would go to 1.2£ = $1 for a 20% increase in the dollar. The reciprocal exchange rate 1£ = $.8333 (1/1.2) is another way (direct quote format) to write the same exchange rate. If an American were traveling in London during this base case scenario (1£ = $1), he would have to cough up $1 to ride the subway (assuming that the subway costs 1£); upon returning to London during our "dollar appreciation" case scenario, the American would only need $.83 to take the same ride. This demonstrates the benefit of having a strong currency (while visiting a nation whose currency is weakening).

2. The economic incentives increase for domestic importers, because the currency they use to purchase foreign goods increases in value. Meanwhile, the fortunes of domestic-based exporters would be under pressure, as their goods become more expensive for foreigners to purchase. Now here is where it gets interesting— because of the strong domestic currency, a major foreign exporter (whose currency is weak) to the strong-currency nation has the ability to lower prices (in domestic terms) because on conversion (from domestic currency to foreign currency) this exporter will receive more domestic currency for each of the stronger currency paid for the product. Remember, the foreign exporter does not care if his currency has depreciated versus another nation, because he will use his currency in his nation and therefore doesn't need to convert it into another currency.

In summary:

Value of Dollar	Exchange Rate (U.S./Foreign Currency)	Foreign Goods Purchased with U.S. $	U.S. Goods Purchased with Foreign Currency
Increases	Increases ($ buys more of foreign currency)	Less expensive	More expensive

Another example can clarify this important notion:

1. A Japanese car manufacturer exports cars to the United States, and expects to receive 10,000 Yen (¥) for each car sold.

2. The base case scenario is an exchange rate of $1= 100¥, so the Japanese company expects to price the cars at $100, therefore permitting their 10,000 Yen inflow on conversion.

3. But the exchange rate changes ($ appreciates versus the Yen) and is now 150¥ = $1. Now, the Japanese company can lower their U.S. price (and possibly increase their market share) to $66.66 per car to maintain their 10,000 Yen inflow ($66.66 × 150¥ to the $ = 10,000 ¥).

The flip side of this equation is the impact on domestic inflation; because the foreign exporter lowers his price (because of changes in the currency), the domestic manufacturer (of the same good) must also lower his price to stay competitive.

In these situations, the corporate finance department of multinational corporations will employ hedging strategies to permit risk management with currency fluctuations. By utilizing derivative products such as options, swaps, forward contracts, and futures, a multinational corporation (MNC) can lock in currency exposure today for some future time period.

Now, look at what happens when the dollar decreases in value:

1. The exchange rate—the number of units of foreign currency per $1—also decreases and therefore, the amount of foreign currency needed to purchase $1 decreases (to $1 = .90£).

2. The economic incentives for domestic importers decrease (their currency, used to purchase foreign goods, is decreased in value), while the fortunes of domestic-based exporters increase (their goods are less expensive for foreigners to purchase).

In summary:

Value of Dollar	Exchange Rate (U.S./Foreign Currency)	Foreign Goods Purchased with U.S. $	U.S. Goods Purchased with Foreign Currency
Decreases	Decreases ($ buys less of foreign currency)	More expensive	Less expensive

There may be several different cause-and-effect reasons for a particular currency to appreciate or depreciate vis-à-vis another currency. Methods to forecast exchange rates are firmly embedded in theoretical and restrictive assumptions about how perfect and efficient trading (of goods, services, and capital) between nations is assumed to be. In the real world, however, these assumptions are lifted to reveal many uncertainties about the future growth and impact of inflation, and the effects on the currency markets. An evaluation of these restrictive assumptions yields some intriguing facts:

✔ Goods cannot be transferred between nations instantly.

✔ Shipping costs are prohibitively high.

✔ Import restrictions (tariffs and quotas) affect international trade.

✔ Cultural differences make consumption standardization between nations very difficult, and usually drastically flawed.

International parity conditions are explored in greater detail in the appendix to this chapter including the discussion of interest rate arbitrage as well as problem sets to sharpen skills in this area.

GOVERNMENT RELEASES AND INDICATORS

The economic information released by the government periodically, collectively known as indicators, supposedly indicates the health of the economy. My skepticism is a by-product of the very nature of these releases (usually representative of a lag of 1 to 2 months) and the empirical evidence that supports the notion that even with all this information at their computer-tapping fingertips, economists have a pretty difficult time being consistently accurate with their macroeconomic views.

Although the current process of economic releases is better than in most developed countries, small inconsistencies remain, including the revision procedure and the measurement protocol for many of the more

What Is Inflation?

You probably can think of a description or even a definition of inflation—it is what you feel when you go to the checkout counter at the supermarket. When I find myself enduring this experience (in my household, thankfully, about once every three months), the numbers just fly by in some type of exponential gaze. I usually ask the checkout operator, armed with the newest in bar technology, to slow down (and I am often in a rush) because I think there is a problem with the machine. How could these prices be so high if the CPI just came out last week and registered a decline in the core rate of inflation? The price on that cereal box *must* be a mistake! How much per pound for those mangoes?

Empirically, the inflation effects on interest rates, known as the "real" rate, is simply the product of the nominal interest rate and the inflation rate, seen as:

Nominal interest rate = Real interest rate × Inflation rate

This equation is embedded in the theory known as the International Fisher Parity Condition.

If the rate of inflation is 4% and the nominal rate was 6%, what is the real interest rate?

We could use some algebra to get:

6% = 4% X which equals 1.5%

Or we could apply the approximated linear relation:

Nominal rate = Real rate + Inflation

We get a lower number when actually calculating the multiplication instead of the arithmetic because multiplication affects numbers faster and more significantly than arithmetic. The simple reason for this is that elusive tenet of finance known as compounding.

Two economic views differ significantly on the subject of real interest rates:

✔ Fluctuations of interest rates are caused by revisions in inflationary expectations, since real rates are very stable over time. As explained by Alan Shapiro (1992), "If the required real return is 3% and expected inflation is 10%, then the nominal interest rate

(continued)

What Is Inflation? (Continued)

would be 13.3%. The logic behind this result is that $1 next year will have the purchasing power of $.90 in terms of today's dollars. Thus, the borrower must pay the lender $0.103 to compensate for the erosion in the purchasing power of the $1.03 in the principal and interest payments, in addition to the $.03 necessary to provide a 3% real return" (*Multinational Financial Management*, 4th ed.).

✔ Keynesians' provide a different view: Monetary shocks leave short-term inflation unaffected because of "sticky" goods prices (prices take time to adjust to inflationary pressures), whereas real rates react immediately to liquidity conditions. For example, if a sudden contraction in money supply growth leads to an immediate increase of nominal interest rates, then the real interest rate will increase because money becomes rare while short-term inflation expectations are unchanged.

important releases. However, there is a continual effort for improvement in this critically important area; most recently, the Boskin Commission has embarked on the monumental task of rethinking the measurement of the critically important inflation measure known as the Consumer Price Index (CPI). Although the details of the commission's findings will not be final for some time, the economic data release process is as reliable and accurate in the United States as any other developed nation. Can it be improved? Of course, what government-related activity can't benefit from some improvement? In the United States, the market (and its participants) demand the most accurate information possible from the suppliers of this data.

How should the investor use the multitude of economic data that is reported each day? Which reports are important and which are not? What effect does an economic report have on a given portfolio? The effect depends on the type of portfolio (equity or debt) and the magnitude and direction of the economic release. The simple rule of thumb is this: As the economy expands, pressure exists on the Federal Reserve to increase short-term interest rates to mitigate any potential inflationary effects. As interest rates increase, the present value of future earnings decreases and thereby the value of financial assets, which are based on the present value of future cash flows, also decreases. So, in a nutshell, as the economic reports "hit the tape" the investor must decipher whether the report is above or below consensus estimates (an average of the Wall Street community's economists forecasts) and furthermore whether this portends an expanding or contracting economy.

One way to think of this mechanism is by relating the economy to a car engine—the more gas the driver gives (by stepping on the accelerator), the more the engine will rev, and if the engine revs up too fast for too long, it will overheat. With the economy, liquidity (or capital) is the fuel, interest rates act as an accelerator to the economy (lower rates accelerate economic activity, higher rates slow activity) and inflation is the symptom of an overheating economy. So the question for the investor monitoring the economy should be whether the economic release signals increased or decreased economic activity and whether a trend up or down can be determined over several releases.

The investor should also pay attention to the specific industry being studied to determine its current economic picture. The economy does not move in lockstep but is segmented, and consequently certain sectors will grow at different rates and times than others. For example, the housing market could be in a growth pattern, evidenced by the upward trend of new home sales and housing starts/building permits, but the manufacturing sector could be registering a slowdown, evidenced by a downward trending National Association of Purchasing Managers (NAPM) report. While the investor holding shares in home-building companies would be expected to receive a positive outlook for the earnings of these companies, the effect of this growth could affect an increase in interest rates and thereby reduce the demand for new homes (due to increased mortgage rates). This two-tiered guessing game keeps Wall Street's cadre of economists, analysts, and strategists busy each weekend. In its basic form, stock prices move up or down depending on two factors—earnings and interest rates; as explained in Chapter 5, the current value of an equity is the present value (using a discount rate) of future cash flows (earnings).

In evaluating the economy as a whole, how does an investor know which indicator should be analyzed to base his decision of interest rate forecasts? Which indicators are more sensitive to the inflationary threats in the economy? Enter the Federal Reserve; a group of top economists, practitioners, and academics who attempt to determine the temperature of the economic engine.

> Perhaps an increase in housing data is due to some seasonal affect, or perhaps it is just consequence of an enduring period of low interest rates and high personal savings. Maybe, at this current juncture, the increase in housing data is being met with

How the Federal Reserve Works

If the Fed wants to stimulate the economy:

✔ *Decrease in federal funds rate.* This is the rate set by the Fed for overnight loans between member banks, so they can meet their reserve requirements. These loans are typically made to smaller, regional banks by larger, commercial banks.

✔ *Decrease in discount rate.* This mechanism is rarely used and that is perhaps why it receives such fanfare when it is used. The discount rate is the rate charged to member banks for loans directly from the Fed.

✔ *Federal Open Market Committee (FOMC) activities:* If the Fed requires its member banks to hold more capital in reserve, that action provides more capital for the bank to lend out to customers thereby stimulating the economy and lowering the cost of capital (interest rates). The mechanism used in this procedure is the Fed's buying of U.S. Treasury securities from the member banks, thereby increasing the member bank's reserves.

If the Fed wants to restrict economic activity:

✔ *Increase in the federal funds rate.* As with anything, if you desire to decrease demand of any good, in this case capital, you need only to increase its price, in this case, interest rates. An increase in the federal funds rate would make banks more prudent with their reserves so that they would not have to borrow at the higher rates. A bank would be less likely to make a borderline credit quality loan, because if the bank fell short on reserves and had to borrow, the costs of this borrowing would have a negative impact on its profits.

✔ *Increase in the discount rate.* Like the preceding, an increase in the discount rate would also have a contractory effect on the banks' profit margins and therefore would be expected to slow down lending activity. Once again, if businesses are unable to obtain capital inexpensively, they may choose to postpone their plans for expansion, new equipment, or new employees. This type of action has its impact throughout the economy.

✔ *FOMC activities:* Here, the Fed sells U.S. Treasury securities to the member banks (which are required to buy a predetermined amount) thereby reducing the capital that the banks have on deposit and consequently available to lend.

sufficient supply and therefore, price pressures are not much of a concern.

The preceding musings are, I expect, the type of discourse that is often analyzed by Federal Reserve governors and their staffs. An investor should be aware of the Fed's current concern and the indicators that relate to this concern. Recently, the Fed has been most concerned about the 30-year low in the unemployment rate, which typically, in the past, has been a portend of higher economic activity (the more people making money, the more they can spend) thereby increasing the threat of inflation. The Fed's current infatuation with inflation has made the markets quite sensitive to swings on the mornings that employment data are released (especially the "employment cost indicator"). Several years ago, the "release-of-concern" was the deficit data and prior to that the trade-gap data. The point here is important—the Fed is as fickle as the economy and therefore an investor needs to be aware of the current "indicator-du-jour" to understand how the impact of a certain release will affect the market. It is important to differentiate the investor's concern with economic releases with regard to the effect on the market and on an investment portfolio. A word of caution to the investor who is under the impression that an understanding of economic indicators is the key to the temple of investment outperformance: Economic releases are volatile and fickle. An investor cannot fully rely on one dataset to make a decision, but must assemble a bevy of releases (over time) to make an effective analysis of expected future conditions. That is not to say that the market itself will be so tempered in its reaction to the latest economic release—the traders, who make their living on volatility and volume, will ensure that any reaction is anything but boring.

In addition to the fickleness of the market and uncertainty about the importance of economic releases, the media romanticize each tiny movement as an earth-shattering development. This is not to say that the increased awareness of financial information, due to the different media sources (cable television, Internet sites, and dedicated financial radio stations) is a negative. Just the contrary, it probably accounts for more of the increase in individual investor participation than any other single source. However, my concerns lay with the media's overemphasis on the economic report of the day, challenging the investor to make decisions based on this volatile information flow. While this information is pertinent to traders and speculators of this fast-money ilk, it may not be material to the investor who has a farther investment horizon. However, the investor should not ignore this data, for when analyzed over some period, it can provide insights to the economy on a whole as well as specific industry sectors.

Keeping with the function of this book, we have provided details of only the most important economic releases. For simplicity and ease of use, 42 different economic indicators typically monitored by Wall Street investment firms are organized into 13 different categories:*

1. *Employment and Unemployment*
   Change in payroll employment (thousands).
   Unemployment rate, civilian (annual %).

2. *Income and Production*
   Gross domestic product, 1987 dollars (annual%).
   Personal income, current dollars (monthly %).
   Index of industrial production (monthly %).
   Rate of capacity utilization, all industry.

3. *Consumption*
   Retail sales, current dollars (monthly %).
   Retail chain store sales index, 1977 = 100 (annual %).
   Personal consumption expenditures (monthly %).

4. *Housing*
   Housing starts (annual 000's).
   Building permits (annual 000's).
   Existing home sales (annual 000's).
   New homes sold and for sale.

5. *Autos*
   Retail unit sales of new passenger cars (annual mils).

6. *Credit*
   Consumer installment credit, net extensions ($Bil).

7. *Deficit*
   Federal budget ($Bil).

8. *Trade*
   International trade balance ($Bil).

9. *Confidence Measures*
   Conference Board Business executives expectations.
   Conference Board consumer confidence index (1985 = 100).

---

* *Source.* PaineWebber Economics Group, 1997.

10. *Composites*
   Leading indicator composite (monthly %).
   NAPM composite diffusion index.

11. *Financial Indicators*
   Dallas Fed exchange rate indexes (1985 = 100).
   Federal Reserve Board trade-weighted exchange rate (1973 = 100).
   M1 (simple annual %).
   M2 (simple annual %).
   3-month Treasury bill rate.
   30-year constant maturity Treasury bond yield.
   S&P 500 stock price index, (1941–1943 = 100).

12. *Prices, Costs, and Productivity*
   Consumer price index, all urban (monthly %).
   CPI ex food and energy (monthly %).
   Producer price index, finished goods (monthly %).
   PPI ex food and energy (monthly %).
   Agricultural price index (1990–1992 = 100).
   West Texas Intermediate crude oil, spot price ($/barrel).
   Productivity, nonfarm business (annual %).
   Unit labor cost, nonfarm business (annual %).
   GDP deflator, 1987 (annual %).

13. *Business Sector*
   Advance report on durable goods (monthly %).
   Manufacturing (monthly %).
   Manufacturing and trade (monthly %).
   Corporate profits in current $ ($Bil).

Table 2.1, at the end of this chapter, illustrates a typical month's most important economic releases in calendar format. The following are the most important (to the financial markets) indicators.

Automobile Sales

U.S. automobile manufacturers release data on car and light truck sales three times a month: the first 10 days, the middle 10 days, and the final 10 days (although this last release can range between 8 or 9 days in February to 11 days in the 31-day months). This release is measured as an annual rate representing the retail unit sales (millions) of new passenger cars. Domestic and foreign are each stated separately.

Manufacturer's Shipments, Inventories, and New Orders for Consumer Goods

This is the volume of new orders, in addition to the amount in inventories and shipments received by manufacturers of consumer goods. This indicator is representative of the business sector of the economy. It is measured as a monthly rate in percentage terms and serves the 30-day period ending two months earlier (i.e., first week in July report is for May period). The lag of this indicator is its major weakness; furthermore, it is released about two weeks after that month's *Index of Industrial Production.*

National Association of Purchasing Managers (NAPM) Report on Business

NAPM has more than 40,000 members in the United States and Puerto Rico. This report has been issued by NAPM since 1931 (except during World War II). NAPM is our first complete assessment of manufacturing, a sector that is strongly correlated to the total economy. Over 300 industrial purchasing executives serving 21 industries in 50 states are represented on the Membership of the Business Survey Committee. The Committee is diversified by Standard Industrial Classification (SIC) category, based on each industry's contribution to gross domestic product (GDP). These executives must respond to the following areas:

- ✔ Inventories.
- ✔ Vendor performance/supplier deliveries.
- ✔ Employment.
- ✔ New orders, backlog of orders, new export orders.
- ✔ Imports.
- ✔ Production.
- ✔ Prices paid index.

NAPM is measured through a questionnaire that purchasing executives respond to by indicating either *Up, Down,* or *Unchanged* for each area in the preceding list. The report is calibrated in percentage terms: Above 44.5% indicates an expanding manufacturing sector and below 44.5% a contracting sector. The resulting single index number is then seasonally adjusted to allow for the effects of repetitive intrayear variations resulting primarily from normal differences in weather conditions, institutional arrangements, and differences attributable to holidays. All seasonal adjustment factors are supplied by the U.S. Department of Commerce and are subject annually to relatively minor changes when conditions warrant them.

The Employment Situation

This economic release covers the change in nonfarm payroll employment. In addition, the *unemployment rate* is stated (annual percentage rate of civilians who have filed for unemployment compensation) as well as the *Employment Cost Index* (average hourly earnings). This crucial report is broken down into two separate surveys: an establishment survey and a household survey. The establishment (industry) survey looks at the payroll employment (hours, wages, and overtime) of the following industries: goods producing, manufacturing, construction, mining, service producing, transportation, public utilities, wholesale trade, finance, insurance, and real estate.

The household survey, on the other hand, dutifully queries 59,500 households (although I know no one who has ever received such a call) on the status of employment. The first question—"Do you have a job?"—is used as an estimate of the labor force figure (or in other words, the base against which the unemployment rate is measured). The status of job seeking is determined by asking, "Are you looking for a job?" The answer to this question is used to establish the unemployment rate.

The *employment situation indicator* is measured in thousands of newly employed; the total amount and the manufacturing-only amount are both stated. It is released by the Labor Department at 8:30 A.M., EST on the first Friday of each month and covers the previous month.

On each Thursday at 8:30 A.M. (EST), the Department of Labor reports the number of new unemployment claims for the previous week. The "rolling nature" of this report allows the unemployment situation for the month to be estimated very accurately, and any aberrations to this widely expected reading on employment may disturb the markets. As stated earlier, it is not the release that can be disturbing, but rather the amount of change compared with the consensus forecast. And forecasts for employment situation releases are anticipated to be more accurate than other releases.

The Index of Leading Economic Indicators

In the first week of each month (actually the last business day of the previous month) the Conference Board (a not-for-profit economic research concern with more than 2700 corporate and other members in 60 nations) releases the Index of Leading Economic Indicators (LEI). Up until early 1996, the U.S. Department of Commerce had taken the responsibility for reporting this important composite indicator. The underlying premise of this release is its strong correlation with the future direction of the economy. The design of the LEI allows it to serve as a barometer of the future direction of the economy. The LEI is actually a composite of 11 separate indicators, each of which is separately reported throughout the month. In this way, government economists hope to create one indicator that forecasts the future direction of the economy with a good amount of accuracy.

Has it worked? The jury is still out, but this index has been reliable in predicting down-turns in the economy 8 to 18 months in advance; however, it has also rung a false alarm about once each cycle. In the Fall 1984 period, the LEI suggested a weaker than expected rate of growth in 1985, despite professional forecasts of a strong economic expansion. As it turned out, the LEI beat the forecasters for 1985—a year of subpar growth.

Most of the components that make up the LEI are what you would expect from a release that tries to forecast the future:

✔ *Contracts and orders for plant and equipment.* As orders for new equipment increase, the future would appear bright. A typical owner of a manufacturing plant is certainly not going to buy new equipment unless he expects a strong level of growth well into the future. This same premise can be extrapolated, in a more basic sense, to your own situation. Would you feel comfortable putting an extension onto your home when your business is not growing? Or when there have been layoffs in your division at the office?

✔ *Permits issued for new housing, formation of new businesses, and manufacturer's new orders.* When the number of permits issued for new housing is on the decline for several consecutive months, an investor could make the supposition that either we are approaching a recession or, more likely, are already in one. The housing sector has a great impact on the total economy, from interest rates to related industries (furniture, landscaping, remodeling, etc.), due to its relative high correlation with the consumer, whose purchasing habits typically account for more than 66% of GDP. The formation of new businesses acts like a proxy measure of the level of optimism about the future and the willingness of investors and businesses to invest and spend. As more businesses come into the economy, not only does the level of the economy grow but the comfort level of many investors also grows. This will snowball into greater consumption and investment.

The basic principle of the LEI is that changes in the business cycle can be a guide to the future direction of the economy, and its forward-looking nature guarantees close attention from Wall Street. The LEI is measured on a monthly rate in percentage terms for the time period of the previous month (i.e., in late July the report comes out for June); this remains one of its major criticisms.

The LEI is a composite of 11 different indicators:

1. *Average workweek of production workers in manufacturing.* Due to the uncertainty associated with timing of the business cycle (the economic outlook in the early stages of a recovery or in the early stages of a recession), employers are more likely to adjust the hours of existing workers before hiring new workers during a recovery or laying off workers during a recession. Therefore, this average workweek is an important look into the head of the production manager in charge of hiring and firing.

2. *Average initial weekly claims for state unemployment insurance.* Like the preceding indicator, this indicator, which shows the increases and decreases in unemployment (released on Thursday mornings), reflects the business expectations of the demand for labor.

3. *Manufacturer's new orders for consumer goods and materials, adjusted for inflation.* Business commitments for new resources and materials are an indication of future economic activity as well as demand for the labor needed to produce the final goods.

4. *Vendor performance (companies receiving slower deliveries from suppliers).* This is an interesting approach to determining the strength (on a forward basis) of the economy—the speed by which vendors deliver orders is an inverse relationship with the strength of the economy (i.e., the economy is strong when delivery time is slow). The reasoning may not be clear at first—slower delivery times indicate a large amount of back orders, representing a stronger economy.

5. *Contracts and orders for plants and equipment, adjusted for inflation.* As mentioned, the increased amount of contracts or orders reflects a stronger economy.

6. *Building permits for new private housing units.* Also as mentioned, the increased level of permits for new construction has a direct, positive relationship to a stronger economy.

7. *Change in manufacturers' unfilled orders, durable good industries.* The rate of accumulation of inventories indicates the expectation of future sales.

8. *Change in sensitive materials prices.* Sensitive materials refer to those with a longer production lead time (e.g., farm products, mineral, and scrap products), therefore making their price more sensitive to sharp changes in demand.

9. *Stock prices, 500 common stocks.* Stock prices, in the words of Federal Reserve Chairman Alan Greenspan (December 1996) could indicate a level of "irrational exuberance" among avarice-minded investors. However, the fact that stock price levels reflect investor expectations of economic growth is firmly grounded in research and empirical evidence. High stock prices make it easier for businesses to raise funds for plant and equipment by selling new stock on the public market. Conversely, low stock prices increase the likelihood that firms will expand by using debt rather than equity financing. In addition, the typical household generally feels more wealthy as its equity investments are rising rather than falling. The dramatic increase in the percentage of equity investments in the typical household's total net worth calculation is becoming more of an acute concern.

10. *Money supply (M2), adjusted for inflation.* This indicator speaks to the amount of liquidity in the economy. As the amount of financial liquid assets increases, the purchasing power available to business and household transactions (materials, capital goods, labor resources, "big-ticket" consumer items) increases. Money supply could either mean savings and checking account balances (M1), or M1 plus money market balances, otherwise known as M2—a more complete measure of total liquidity.

11. *Index of consumer expectations.* Two organizations report a measure of consumer confidence—University of Michigan's Survey Research Center (index of consumer confidence) and the Conference Board ("consumer confidence index"). As expected, these indicators report on the turning points of the business cycle before they are recognized in the economy. As with many leading indicators, one is cautioned to their basic nature; that is, these indicators are more sensitive to the future trends in an economy than to specific forecasts.

As of August 1996, the Conference Board is considering a proposal of eliminating two indicators (change in unfilled orders, durable goods industry and change in sensitive material prices) from the leading indicator index due to their poor forecasting power in the past decade. Furthermore, there seems to be a movement at the Conference Board toward adding to the LEI an indicator representing a yield-curve component (a spread-based indicator quantifying the difference between the 10-year Treasury note rate with either the 3-month or 1-year bill rate). A recently published report by two economists at the Federal Reserve Bank of New York credits the yield curve with strong predictive powers of upcoming economic downturns (about four quarters before a recession's onset). For example, if the 10-year rate is 121 basis points (1.21%) higher than the 3-month rate, the chances of a recession are only 5%. Conversely, if the short-term rate is 240 basis points higher than the 10-year rate, the chance of *not* having a recession is only 5%. This Federal Reserve study is firmly entrenched in the expectations hypothesis of interest rates, which states a correlation between long-term rates and current investor expectations for inflation: A normal-shaped yield curve (higher long-term rates than short-term rates) illustrates that investors expect inflation in the future and thereby fixed-income investors require a higher rate to go out longer on the curve, whereas an inverted yield curve (short-term rates higher than long-term rates) illustrates little fear of future inflation and therefore a recession is looming.

It is important to examine the basic tenets surrounding the formation of the leading economic indicators, as well as the related coincident and lagging indicators. Although the LEI is most commonly used in investment finance (for its forward-looking design), the coincident and lagging indicators can also provide important levels of study for industry analysis. The leading, coincident, and lagging indices of economic activity are based on the concept that each phase of the business cycle (see Figure 2.1) contains the seeds of the following phase. This system, adapted from the early twentieth-century business cycle concepts of Wesley Mitchell, assesses the strengths and weaknesses in the economy for clues toward the future growth rates as well as cyclical turning points (shift from recession to expansion).

The three classifications—leading, coincident, and lagging (LCL)—refer to the turning points in the business cycle:

1. The *leading index* attempts to pinpoint the time when the economy begins to shift from a contracting phase (recession) to an upward bias or recovery.

2. The *coincident index* mimics the cyclicality of the overall economy and tends to coincide with recessions and expansions.

3. The *lagging index* turns down after the beginning of the recession and turns up after the beginning of the expansion.

The underlying tenet of LCL format is the notion that the entire economy revolves around the future expectations of profits in corporate America. That is to say, as business executives believe the sales and profits of their company are on the rise they will begin to institute a more aggressive production campaign, coupling that with a stronger purchasing and investment commitment. This increased activity will eventually lead to a peak in the economic cycle to be followed by a slower, more contracting phase of the economy (see box, "Business Cycle and Investments"). The LCL provides a method to pinpoint these turning points and allows management to plan important investment strategy policies.

Business Cycle and Investments

The *trough* pinpoints the part of the business cycle where corporate sales and investment reach depressed levels with considerable excess in plant capacity. As sales increase, profit expectations begin to creep higher and business managers begin to plan for increased production, increasing working hours, and gradually rehiring previously laid-off labor.

At the *middle recession* phase of the cycle, businesses become uneasy (perhaps due to the higher costs of capital) and begin to pull back on their reins by reducing orders for equipment, cutting back on inventories, and laying off workers. Incomes begin to be reduced (due to the layoffs) and consequently consumers become wary (decrease in spending).

At the *peak,* workers, machines, and materials are beginning to be utilized at capacity and this strong demand exerts increased price and wage pressures (*Can you smell a hint of inflation?*). Businesses begin to increase their debt loads to finance the expanding levels of inventory and fixed asset commitment. This increased demand for borrowing leads to higher interest rates, which indicates the peak of the economic cycle.

At the *middle recovery* point in the cycle, employee incomes begin to rise, which stimulates personal consumption expenditures (consumer confidence increasing), thereby leading managers to initiate expansion (modernization) of production facilities. These corporate expenditures on capital goods require added jobs and subsequently higher income and consumption levels.

At the end of the recession (beginning of the recovery), credit terms begin to ease and housing construction tends to increase. This leads to increased consumer confidence (in addition to spending), as most determine that the worst (of the economic cycle) is coming to an end.

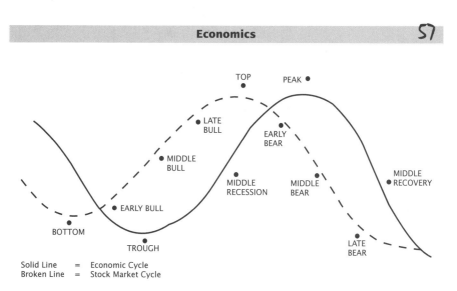

FIGURE 2.1 Business cycle and relative stock performance.

Personal Income and Expenditures

Personal consumer expenditures are stated in this report, as is the calculation of real disposable income and the personal savings rate. The personal consumption expenditures category is the largest segment of the gross domestic product (GDP) accounting for nearly 66%. For this reason, a strong level of consumer spending is often viewed as favorable for the economy as a whole. In addition, the consumer spending statistic is divided into two segments—durable and nondurable goods. Durable goods are those that last longer, are larger and often more expensive, and are more sensitive to changes in the business cycle. The typical consumer would think longer before purchasing a durable good (automobile, furniture, appliances, etc.) than a nondurable good (easily replaceable items, such as food, clothing, sundries).

The personal consumption expenditure is measured as a monthly rate (change from previous report) and is reported in percentage terms. This indicator covers the time period for the prior month and is released at 10 A.M. Eastern time.

U.S. International Trade in Goods and Services— Merchandise Trade Balance

This represents the dollar value difference between U.S. exports and imports on a seasonally adjusted basis. Trend analysis plays an important function in this indicator, for it points to either an expansion or contraction of the trade deficit. Implications are more pronounced in the currency markets: The dollar will be bolstered with a declining deficit because it reflects a more economically sound government trade policy and therefore the currency becomes more attractive to foreigners. The merchandise trade balance is measured in billions of U.S. dollars on a seasonally adjusted basis. Reflecting the time period of two months prior to its release, this indicator is often viewed as somewhat lagging.

The Producer Price Index

The producer price index (PPI) measures prices at the wholesale level only (formerly called the wholesale price index). The PPI is a leading indicator of inflationary trends in the economy, for it measures the price changes that have not yet moved through the economy. Price increases on the wholesale level take time, often as much as several quarters, to move to the consumer level.

This makes intuitive sense, as the following scenario shows:

1. You are a manufacturer producing widgets in a highly competitive industry.
2. You begin to notice price increases in your raw materials.
3. Deciding to lock in these prices before they rise any further, you purchase more of the raw material than normal.
4. The new widgets are more expensive than those previously in inventory, lowering your profit margins. If it wasn't for the highly competitive nature of the widget industry you would raise your prices, but you fear retaliation by competitors who may have seen the price increases coming before you did and stocked up at lower prices. If you raised your widget price you could leave yourself open to a severe decline in market share. You must wait until the industry, on a whole, increases price (see discussion of consumer price index).

The Labor Department reports the PPI approximately two days before the consumer price index and indicates the average percentage change from the previous period (month prior).

Consumer Price Index

The consumer price index (CPI) is a measure of inflation that is often most directly attributable to the individual investor—the percentage change in the rate of inflation that directly affects your pocket over time. To obtain a more definitive explanation of the inflationary trends within the economy, the Department of Labor compiles a sample basket of goods representing the typical consumer's purchasing habits. The consumer price index measures the monthly changes associated with this basket. This report is published in the month following the measurement (in June the CPI for May is reported). It is presented as the percentage change over the prior month. However, the percentage change from the same month the year earlier is much more sensitive, for it factors out the monthly statistical deviations ("noise").

Often we are told that the CPI (also reported in PPI) may have increased by 0.02% for the month, but the core rate of inflation, which factors out the volatile food and energy sectors, was down 0.01%. This testifies not only to the volatility within those sectors (for the government would not have had—or the markets would not have demanded—to break them out separately if they weren't so volatile), but also to the sensitivity of the U.S. markets to their old nemesis (recall the Misery Index). It is interesting to witness how the economic system becomes sensitized by the market and the demands of the investors (suppliers of the capital).

A formidable effort has been placed on the redefining of the CPI; specifically a recent assessment that suggests the CPI overstates inflation by as much as 1.1%. As in most scientific disciplines, however, an argument suggests the opposite—that the CPI actually understates the true rate of inflation. This view is based on the notion that housing (the largest component of the CPI, accounting for approximately 40% of the basket of goods and services) is vastly understated. Mr. Stephen Roach, chief economist of Morgan Stanley Group and an advocate of the understates theory, postulates that the difference in housing measurement could add as much as 0.6% to the CPI.

Gross National Product

Gross national product (GNP)—a measure of spending and income on a domestic and international basis—is the most extensive measure of macroeconomic activity in the U.S. economy. The GNP summarizes the total economic output of the nation with two different methods; the demand method and the income method. The demand concept (also known as the product side) refers to end-use markets for goods and services produced, whereas the supply method (income side) attempts to reconcile the costs involved in producing these goods and services. The following example illustrates the components of these two methods (% data are estimates from July 1986, Survey of Current Business, Bureau of Economic Analysis, U.S. Department of Commerce).

Demand Method

Personal consumption expenditures		65%
Durable goods	9.0	
Nondurable goods	22.6	
Services	33.4	
Gross private domestic investment		16.6
Business plant and equipment	11.5	
New housing construction	4.8	
Inventory change	0.3	
Net exports		(2.0)
Exports	9.2	
Imports	(11.2)	
Government purchases		20.4
Federal	8.9	
State and local	11.5	
Total		100%

Supply Method

Compensation of employees		65.6%
Wages and salaries	42.8	
Supplements	10.1	
Unincorporated business profits	6.4	
Farm	0.7	
Nonfarm	5.6	
Rental income		0.2
Corporate profits		7.0
Net interest		7.8
Sales and property taxes		8.3
Depreciation allowances		10.9
Business transfers, government subsidies, government enterprises		0.3
Statistical discrepancy		(0.1)
Total		100%

The GNP is reported on a quarterly basis (as an annualized rate) by the Bureau of Economic Analysis (division of the U.S. Department of Commerce) and is subject to revisions throughout the following months and even into the next couple of years. As a matter of fact, a Wall Street adage suggests that if you want to know what the actual GNP was (grew at) this year, talk to me in about three years when the revision process finally posts the amount to the record books.

TABLE 2.1   Economic Releases Calendar

Week 1

Leading economic indicators for months prior (released last business day of previous month).

National Association of Purchasing Managers Report for previous month.

Construction expenditures for two months prior.

Personal income and expenditures for two months prior.

Domestic and imported car sales for previous month.

The employment situation for previous month.

Week 2

Producer price index for prior month.

Retail sales for prior month.

Consumer price index for prior month.

Capacity utilization for prior month.

Industrial production for prior month.

Week 3

Manufacturing and trade inventories and sales for two months ago.

U.S. international trade in goods and services for two months prior.

Housing starts and building permits for prior month.

Week 4

National Association of Realtors existing home sales for prior month.

Advance report on durable goods for prior month.

APPENDIX—INTERNATIONAL PARITY CONDITIONS

Two methods are typically relied on to forecast exchange rates:

1. *Balance of payments method.* As in many economic scenarios, supply and demand describe the price of the good being exchanged; in the case of currency, the exchange of financial "goods" between nations determines the price (exchange rate) charged in the market.

2. *Asset market approach.* In this approach, we rely on two parity conditions to provide some guidance to the future exchanges rates between nations. The concepts surrounding purchasing power parity (PPP) and interest rate parity (IRP) are critical to understanding currency exchange rate forecasting.

Interest rate differentials and inflation rate differentials remain the most common and practical drivers to currency exchange rate movement, although these parity conditions do not affect the short run for several reasons. Before exploring the parity conditions and their individual nuances, it is necessary to define certain terms:

Spot rate. Rate of exchange between two currencies; refers to immediate delivery.

Forward rate. Rate of exchange between two currencies; the rate is set today but not recognized until a date in the future. The Foreign Exchange Expectations Theory suggests that the forward exchange rate should be the unbiased predictor of the future spot rate.

Interest rate. Rate charged for money; usually quoted as an annual rate.

Inflation rate. Rate of consumer price increase over a specified period.

PURCHASING POWER PARITY

States that spot exchange rates will adjust perfectly to inflation differentials. If prices of goods rise greater in nation one relative to nation two, then nation one's currency must *depreciate* to maintain a similar real price for the goods in both countries.

If it holds (a matter of debate, at least on the practical level), the purchasing power parity (PPP) implies that the real (inflation-adjusted) "cost" of any good is identical for investors in any country. In lay terms, purchasing power parity presumes the cost for a McDonald's burger is equal, no matter in which nation it is being purchased and with which currency.

As any traveler to the Far East would attest, PPP does not hold, at least not in the short run (research by Adler & Dumas suggests that inflation differentials contribute less than 5% of the short-term volatility in exchange rates). Although the empirical evidence suggests that PPP is useful in forecasting exchange rate movements over a longer term period, according to Bruno Solnik (1991), "Usually it has taken more than several years for the deviation from PPP to be corrected in the foreign exchange market."

Why doesn't this parity condition hold in the short run? Consider the following factors:

✔ *Cultural differences.* Different cultures consume differently; for example, people in the Far East are much more prolific savers than people in the West, who are predominately spenders. The standard of living is a good deal higher in the West, but this alone does not fully account for the huge differences in cultures.

✔ *Measurement difficulties with consumer basket differences.* Inflation is typically measured via a basket of goods currency weighted to a level value. But other nations may value their basket differently due to the resources available to that nation. Furthermore, inflation among nations is not uniformly measured in this basket format, which only increases the difficulty in measuring this intangible value.

✔ *Transfer costs, import taxes, and restrictions.* These restrictive measures on trade subject a cost structure into the parity condition that was never anticipated (or more likely just neglected) by the economic theorists who first postulated these theories. With costs like taxes and shipping impeded against trade, how could one expect to have a parity condition (which reflects the effect of one variable on another) hold in the short run? Time is needed to work through these additional costs.

Considering the preceding information, one may question the benefits of using the PPP in exchange rate forecasts. In the short run, PPP is not much help, partly because of the restrictions previously mentioned and the fact that exchange rates move very frequently while inflation adjusts slowly over time. But how about in the long run? Long-run exchange rate forecasting is important for two reasons:

1. Multinational businesses use these forecasts to calculate their exchange rate exposure (and the respective risk management techniques) during a given period.

2. Government policymakers utilize these forecasts when determining an effective monetary and fiscal policy plan.

As it turns out, PPP is quite intuitive in forecasting exchange rates over the long run. Empirical evidence (Hakkio, 1992) illustrates that the exchange rate will revert toward the PPP-expected rate within one to six years. Statistical tests established that exchange rates will have differing probabilities (for convergence toward PPP) for different currencies but will average about 59%. That is, if two currencies are currently not in parity, then one could postulate that, on average, there is a 59% chance that these currencies will converge within a one- to six-year time horizon. Furthermore, the number of years it takes to converge and the probability of convergence will differ between nations (currencies). For example, the U.S. Dollar/British Pound exchange rate has the highest probability of convergence (79%), as well as the shortest time horizon to converge (typically within 3 years).

How is all this helpful to today's investor? Assume a U.S.-based investor is evaluating a U.K.-based investment, and during his due-diligence correctly determines (a VFII, no doubt) that the currency effect will be a major contributing factor to the expected return of this investment. He further learns that the British pound and U.S. dollar are trading far from where their relative inflation measures would postulate (the pound is trading too cheap vs. the PPP condition). If this investor's time horizon is greater than, say, four years, then he can be relatively comfortable with the supposition that the pound will appreciate (vs. the dollar) over this horizon. If this investor enters ("puts on") this trade while the pound is trading below its parity value and then sells this investment when the pound has appreciated, he has added value to the transaction beyond that of the fundamental analysis of the security.

Mathematical Notation

$$PPP = \frac{1 + \text{Inf (foreign)}}{1 + \text{Inf (domestic)}} \times \frac{\text{Forward exchange rate (fc/\$)}}{\text{Spot rate (fc/\$)}}$$

Example: Inflation rate is 7% in France and 4% in the United States; if the spot rate ($f/\$$) is $75f/\$1$, then the PPP suggests that the exchange rate on the forward market should be selling for $77.16f/\$1$.

Intuitively, this makes sense—prices are higher in France compared with those of the U.S., and therefore the Franc is depreciating vis-à-vis the dollar. Alternatively, it could be illustrated that the American purchasing a good in France, which has increased in price, would need the offsetting gain in currency power to permit parity.

Quick Math Method

Inflation differential between two nations is 3% (7% − 4% = 3%). Therefore, the Franc would need to devalue (because French inflation is higher than U.S. inflation) versus the dollar by approximately 3%.

$$\frac{75f}{\$1} \times 1.03 \ (3\% \ \text{devaluation}) = \frac{77.25f}{\$1} \ (\text{Parity level})$$

INTEREST RATE PARITY

Interest rate parity (IRP) states that the interest rate differential must equal the forward exchange discount or premium. Like the PPP, the IRP permits the cost of capital (interest rates) to be equal across all nations. If interest rates are higher in one nation versus another, you would think that the demand for this higher interest rate would attract so much capital that the currency would have to appreciate. Under most practical circumstances, this is exactly what happens in the short run; however, the interest rate parity condition suggests that the currency of the nation with the higher interest rate should devalue versus the other nation's currency. Arbitrage forces the IRP equation into parity, thereby permitting the most nimble currency traders to profit handsomely. However, the most popular explanation of why IRP may not hold in the short run concerns government interactions. Monetary policies of federal banks have been known to use interest rates to appreciate the valuation of their currency.

Mathematical Notation

$$\text{IRP} = \frac{1 + \text{Int (foreign)}}{1 + \text{Int (domestic)}} \times \frac{\text{Futures (or forward) exchange rate}}{\text{Spot rate}}$$

Example. The 1-year interest rate in Italy is 10%, and in the United States it is 4%; the lira is currently at a spot rate of 3000 lira to $1. The currency is correctly priced at 3173.07 lira on the futures market.

$$\frac{1.10}{1.04} = \frac{x}{3000}$$

The value of *x*—the price of the currency on the futures market—is 3173.07.

Quick Math Method

The percentage difference between the forward rate and the spot rate is approximated by the interest rate differential.

As in the preceding example, the interest rate differential of 6% approximates the devaluation of the lira:

3000 lira × 1.06 = 3180 lira.

Interest Rate Arbitrage

To understand the method by which a currency trader may expect to profit given an inequitable (non-parity) condition between two nations, consider the following example of riskless interest arbitrage (also called covered interest arbitrage).

Example. Assume that IRP is not holding and that the current spot rate is UK£ = $1.80 or .5556£ per 1 US$. Furthermore, the 1-year interest rates between the nations are:

U.S. rate = 6%   U.K. rate = 5%

Whereas the currency is trading on the futures exchange at:

$1.81/1UK£ (or .5525 pounds per $1)

Hence, a careful examination of the IRP equation would suggest that IRP is not currently holding because the future's price should be $1.8172/1£ (or .5503£/$1).

The math:

$$\frac{1.05}{1.06} = \frac{x}{.5556£ / \$1}$$

The value of x (the value of the exchange rate on the futures market) should be .5503£/$1, but it is trading at $.5525£/$1. The exchange rate on the futures exchange has not correctly (according to IRP) valued the British pound versus the dollar; it is trading at a discount to the value perceived by the IRP.

Quick Math Method

The United States is paying more interest than the United Kingdom, therefore, if IRP holds, the U.S. dollar should depreciate versus the pound by the equal amount of the difference between the rates (1%) to remain in parity. This would assign a value of approximately $1.818 (or .5501£ per $1), but as indicated $1.81/£ is not enough depreciation to make parity (which is 1.8172 or .5503£/$).

So how do the most nimble of currency traders take advantage of the situation? Consider the following steps:

1. Borrow 100£ in the United Kingdom (at 5% interest rate due in 1 year), because the cost of borrowing is less than that of the United States. The total due in 1 year is 105£.

2. Convert 100£ to US$ at the current rate of $1.80 per pound, which is $180, and invest this for 1 year at 6% to have total receipts of $190.80 in one year.

3. But we will still need to pay back the U.K. loan in pounds next year and therefore you would want to hedge this currency exposure by locking in next year's exchange rate today using the futures market. At $1.81 per pound would give you a locked-in number of pounds in one year:

$$\frac{\$190.80}{1.81} = 105.41£$$

4. All you need to pay back is 105£ so your risk-free profit per 100£ is .41£ (or .0041 per pound)

With this type of action prevalent in the foreign currency markets (probably the most liquid and intensely monitored financial market), arbitrage would force into parity any conditions that would permit a riskless profit. The point to take home from this exercise is that the foreign exchange markets, due to their strong interlinking with the futures market, are very efficient and only the most nimble currency speculator can achieve superior results. That is not to say that a currency investor cannot profit—for the difference between a speculator and an investor revolves around the fact that the speculator has "placed a bet" and is not risk averse, whereas the investor might have mountains of research supporting his trade and is committed to a defined expected time horizon and expected return bogey.

PROBLEM SET
INTERNATIONAL PARITY CONDITIONS

Question 1

The £/$ exchange rate (the number of Irish currency per U.S. dollar) is currently (spot) 0.720£/$1, where the Irish inflation rate is 7% and the American inflation rate is 5%. Where ("at what price") should the futures on this exchange rate trade?

Answer

The purchasing power parity equation is calculated as follows:

$$\frac{1.07}{1.05} = \frac{x}{.720}$$

Algebraically, we solve the equation in the following manner:

$1.07\ (.72) = 1.05\ (x)$ Multiply the factors on a diagonal basis

$.7704 = 1.05\ (x)$

$.7704/1.05 = x$

$x = .7337£$ per $1

This makes sense because the interest rate differential points to an approximately 2% decrease in the punt versus the dollar. If you multiply 1.02 (2% increase in the number of punts per dollar or a 2% decrease in the value of the punt versus the dollar) times .72, the answer is .7334.

Question 2

Suppose that:

1. Spot dollar/KR (Denmark) exchange rate is $.39/KR.
2. The futures market for this currency is quite liquid and efficient, and 1-year futures contract is trading at 2.60KR/$.
3. The U.S. 1-year risk-free rate is 4%.
4. The Denmark 1-year risk-free interest rate is 7%.

Describe how an investor can profit without taking on any risk.

Answer

The method would be interest rate arbitrage. The math works out as follows:

First calculate the IRP equation to understand where a futures contract should be trading for the exchange rate.

$$\frac{1.07}{1.04} = \frac{x}{2.5641KR}$$

$$2.7436 = 1.04(x)$$

$$x = \frac{2.6381KR}{\$1}$$

So, the futures contract to be in parity, should be traded at 2.6381KR/$ for delivery in 1 year. But, as in the given example, the futures contract for KR/$ exchange rate is trading at 2.60KR/$. Therein lies the opportunity to profit:

1. Borrow $100 in the United States. In 1 year, the debt owed is $104 ($100 + 4% interest).
2. Convert the $100 to Krone at the current spot rate (2.5641KR/$) for a total of 256.41KR.
3. Invest these proceeds in Danish interest rate market (at 7%), yielding 274.358KR in 1 year.
4. If the futures contract was in parity (IRP holds), then we would convert these Krone to dollars (274.358KR/2.6381KR/$ = $104)

to satisfy our $104 debt. But the futures contract is not trading in parity, and we are able to sell 274.358 Krone today, in the futures contract, for 2.60KR/$, which would yield $105.52 in 1 year.

5. Pay the loan of $104, resulting in a risk-free profit of $1.52.

Question 3

Given the following data, calculate the real interest rate:

Nominal interest rate = 7%

Expected inflation rate = 2%

Answer

According to the Fisher equation:

Nominal interest rate = (Inflation rate) (Real interest rate)

7% = 2% (Real interest rate)

7%/2% = Real interest rate

Real interest rate = 3.5%

Chapter

Investment Mathematics

In this chapter you will learn:

- ✔ The present and future value of money calculations.
- ✔ The methodology behind net present value equation.
- ✔ How annuities are valued.

The idea that money appreciates in value over time is one of the oldest tenets of investment finance. Even the earliest lords and barons realized that when capital (gold or some other means of exchange) was transferred between two persons (one being the lender, the other the borrower), an additional amount, above the transferred amount, came due as a fee—now referred to as interest. Interest can be thought of, in its simplest terms, as the amount of money that is gained by giving up one's capital in an investment.

Investment finance requires a comprehensive knowledge of the values of money, some of which are:

- ✔ Interest.
- ✔ Compounding effect.
- ✔ Reinvestment rate.
- ✔ Discount rate.

Understanding the time value of money makes the reciprocal relationship—present value—become rather rudimentary. The future value equation states: "The dollar ($) value at a compounded rate of 10% for 5 years will be worth the future value"; while the present value asks the question "What is the dollar value ($) in 5 years at 10% per year worth today?"

The net present value (NPV) equation is the quantification of a cash flow diagram illustrating each movement of capital over time. In essence, the NPV is the calculation of the present value of the entire stream of movements. The following diagram should help in the understanding of this investment construct:

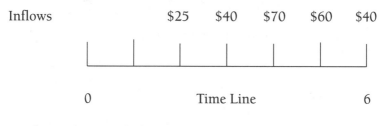

Inflows $25 $40 $70 $60 $40

0   Time Line   6

Outflows $100 $50

As illustrated, this hypothetical project (ranging from a company's campaign exercise in market share penetration through acquisition to a real estate venture) has an initial cost (cash outflow) of $100 and a subsequent (year 1) outflow of $50 (many projects require a continued cash outflow in the early years) and inflows (years 2–6) as described.

Typically, the corporate budgeting and finance departments of large firms use advanced versions (with decision trees and probability analysis) of the NPV diagram to determine whether a proposed project has viability. If the NPV is positive (the magnitude is not as important) then it is assumed that the project has merit for inclusion among the firm's new opportunities; however, all this depends, as it often does in finance, on the discount rate used in the diagram. If a project has a positive NPV and does so using a very conservative discount rate (meaning a high rate), this would mean that the project would have a consequently higher rate of return and thereby include more risk. The higher the risk in a given project, the higher the rate of return that must be incorporated in the project.

An annuity is a financial contract that guarantees a certain, absolutely defined cash flow. One can think of an annuity as an NPV diagram where all the payments are outflows (after an initial inflow or investment) of equal amounts.

This chapter will identify, explain, and demonstrate some important mathematical terms. Because the novice investor can learn this material much more effectively through detailed examples than from pages of theory, this chapter will emphasize examples and problem sets.

Just a word on the Present/Future Value and Annuity Tables (see Appendix B). Although these tables are used in every financial text and are an accepted methodology for solving these problems, today's practitioner should become far removed from this antiquated methodology. A few, hard-earned dollars and a rainy afternoon should permit, under normal circumstances, a foothold into the understandings of a financial calculator. There are few things more imposing than an investor who sports a scientific calculator while discussing an investment portfolio with his financial services provider, whose oversized metallic blue calculator looks more like a new toy than an important tool. Perhaps you can check this financial planner's work by simply "plugging and chugging"; wouldn't it be an exhilarating feeling to catch him making an error: *Now who is the advisor?*

In the problem set to follow and throughout this book, I rely on (as I do every day) the Hewlett-Packard (HP) 12C financial calculator. For the record, in no way, shape, or form do I receive any benefit in endorsing this excellent tool, except for the fact that I believe it will make any practitioner's job that much more efficient. As mentioned, a major commitment is not required to master this instrument—probably the most difficult facet is adjusting oneself to the reverse notation that is the hallmark of these calculators. It is this notation (four [4], enter, five [5], times [×]— would yield the requisite "20") that is like a secret handshake or password that only VFIIs are aware of and able to decipher. So pick one up today and begin to impress your friends with your superb understanding of this often confusing idea of future value of money (compound interest, present value, etc.).

FUTURE VALUE OF MONEY

If an investor commits $1000 of capital to an account that will pay an annual rate of interest of 7%, his first year's account balance will be $1070 or ($1000 × .07) = $70 worth of interest plus the principal balance of $1000. Assume the investor leaves this investment account alone (no withdrawals or deposits) for another year (at 7%). The balance at the end of year 2 becomes $1144.90 or $1070 plus $74.90 worth of interest. In summary, our investor has profited by $144.90 over 2 years, in the following manner:

Year 1: $\$1000 \times 7\% = \$70$ interest

Year 2: $\$1000 \times 7\% = \$70$ interest

$\$70 \times 7\% = \$4.90$ interest on interest

Total $= \$144.90$

The lender receives $70 interest from the borrower for his commitment of capital; the interest-on-interest ($4.90) is due to compounding, the single factor that separates the notions of simple interest from compound interest.

If our investor kept earning 7% for a total of 7 years, the account balance would be $1,605.78; this amount is known as the future value. With the future value amount, the interest-on-interest or compounding factor is embedded in the calculation. The mathematical equation for future value is denoted as follows:

$\$1000(1.07)^7$ or Principal amount $(1 + \text{interest rate})^n$

There are three methods by which one could calculate the future value of a principal amount (given the rate and number of periods):

1. Using the equation as previously shown.
2. Using a scientific calculator's (HP12C) future value (FV) function.
3. Using the future value tables (see Appendix B).

The first two methods are simplified through the use of a calculator, whereas the third method utilizes the "present value factors" tabulated for several rates (1%–15%) and for many numbers of periods. Let's attempt to solve our example using this table.

We want the Future Value Factor for 7% and 7 periods—so we search the table (using the coordinates for n periods and $X\%$) for the corresponding factor -1.6058 and then multiply this factor by the stated dollar amount to calculate the final future value:

$\$1000 (1.6058) = \$1605.80$

As it is already obvious, the factors on the future value table are each equal to the equation:

$(1 + \text{rate})^n =$ future value factor (FVF) for n periods

PRESENT VALUE OF MONEY

"Hey Mac, I'll give you $62.27 today for $100 in 7 years; you'll earn a 10% rate on your money." This proposition is flawed because the we know the interest rate that makes $62.27 into $100 in 7 years is only 7%. Algebraically, we can calculate the future value factor as:

$$FV/PV = (1 + i)^n$$

$$100/62.27 = 1.6059 \text{ so } 1.6059 = (1 + i)^n$$

$$1 + i = 1.07 \text{ and then } i = 7\%$$

Present value is what someone will pay today for a cash flow sometime in the future. This cash flow can either be a lump sum (i.e., balloon payment) or a cash flow stream spanning many periods (an annuity). Either way, the methodology is the same—what absolute dollar amount compounded at a designated rate for a certain time would equal the future value amount?

PROBLEM SET
FUTURE VALUE AND PRESENT VALUE

Question

Calculate the following amounts:

A. The FV of $1000 in 19 years compounded at 5% per year.

Answer

$$FV = PV \{(1.05)^{19}\}$$

$$= 1000 \{2.527\}$$

$$= \$2,527$$

B. The PV of $643 in 3 years compounded at 11% per year.

Answer

$$PV = FV / (1.11)^3$$

$$= 643/1.3676$$

$$= 470.17$$

C. If $300 is invested at a rate of 6%, how many years will be needed to generate an ending value of $600?

Answer

$$(1.06)^n = FV/PV$$

$$(1.06)^n = 600/300$$

$$n = 12$$

Note in the preceding example it would be advised to either use the trial and error method (see Figure 7.3) or a financial calculator. The keystrokes for the HP12C, for this example, are as follows:

$600 = FV$

$-300 = PV$ (PV is always inputted as a negative value)

$6 = i$

$0 = PMT$

$n =$ the calculator will yield the answer as "12"

D. Find the value of $100 invested for 5 months at a rate of .8% per month.

Answer

$$FV = 100 \, (1.008)^5$$

$$= 100 \, (1.0406)$$

$$= \$104.06$$

NET PRESENT VALUE AND INTERNAL RATE OF RETURN

In these cash flow problems we examine an investment with a specified diagram of the inflows and outflows of money to determine the net result or the net present value (NPV). As mentioned, this process is very useful in the evaluation of certain types of investments (real estate, bonds, and in its most basic sense—equities) as well as specific projects.

Example

A real estate project has the following cash flows (an investment is considered an outflow); is it a recommended project given the required rate of return of 10%?

Initial investment	$(1500)
Year 1	$(3000)
Year 2	$(1200)
Year 3	$ 4900
Year 4	$ 8500

Graphically,

($1500)($3000)($1200)

NPV = (1500) + (3000)/1.10 + (1200)/(1.10)^2
    + 4900/(1.10) ^3 + 8500/(1.10) ^4

= (1500) + (3000)/1.10 + (1200)/1.21 + 4900/1.33
    + 8500/1.46

Note. The denominators in this equation could also be found by taking the reciprocal (i.e., 1 divided by) of the future value factor (FVF) corresponding to the *n* periods and 10% rate on the Future Value Table. The preceding equation is equivalent to multiplying each dollar value by the corresponding present value factor rather than dividing by the future value factor. Stated empirically, PVF = 1/FVF. Getting back to the preceding equation,

= (1500) + (2727) + (991) + 3684 + 5805

= +4271

As the example demonstrates, the resulting present value is positive and therefore is recommended for investment. It may also be useful in determining the maximum initial amount that could be invested and still expect a positive NPV. In this case it would be $5771 (simply add $1500 and $4271).

This NPV framework is used in many other areas besides real estate, but the premise is always the same: today's value of a stream of inflows and outflows given a specific capitalization rate. But assume you are given the beginning cash flow and the ending cash flow as well as all the cash flows in between and are asked to calculate the capitalization rate that would make the NPV equal to zero. In other words, you must calculate the expected return over the life of the investment (project); this rate of return is known as the internal rate of return (IRR). The following example is a means to understand the IRR.

Example

A stock is expected to pay a dividend of $1.00, $1.50, and $2.00 in each of the next three years, respectively. At the end of the third year, the stock is expected to sell at a price of $40. The stock is currently priced at $30. What is the expected return over the next three years to an investor who buys the stock?

First dissect the problem by diagramming a cash flow table:

Year	Cash Flow
0	(−$30.00) (This represents the initial investment in the stock)
1	$1.00 (Dividends represent positive cash flow)
2	$1.50 (Same—positive cash flow)
3	$42.00 (Sale of the stock is a cash inflow or receipt plus the $2 dividend received)

Graphically the above would translate as follows:

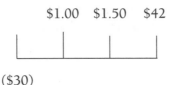

$1.00 $1.50 $42

($30)

To calculate the net present value (NPV), the following equation would be employed:

$$NPV = \frac{CF0}{(1+i)^0} + \frac{CF1}{(1+i)^1} + \frac{CF2}{(1+i)^2} + \ldots + \frac{CFn}{(1+i)^n}$$

In this equation, the NPV is the dollar amount resulting from the above discounting of cash flows. The internal rate of return (IRR) is the interest rate that allows the cash flow, when discounted at that rate, to be equal to a zero NPV. In some circumstances, IRR can also be known as the required rate of return, the discount rate, or the capitalization rate.

The next step is to determine the interest rate that, upon discounting each cash flow (years 1–3), would permit a positive value of $30 to thereby offset the negative value of $30 (year 0) and make the net present value equal to zero. Two methods are used to calculate this rate: (1) trial and error and (2) a financial calculator.

In the first method, we are forced to calculate each cash flow's present value using different rates to determine the rate at which the NPV is equal to zero. In our example, we initiate the calculation at 10%:

Year	Future Value	Present Value Factor (Table B.10)	Present Value
1	$ 1.00	.9091	$ 0.91
2	1.50	.8264	1.24
3	42.00	.7513	31.55
Total			$33.70

Using the 10% rate, we have calculated a positive NPV (−$30 minus $33.70 = $3.70) that, in its simplest terms, reflects a profitable transaction. But we are searching for the internal rate of return (IRR) and therefore we now need to adjust the discount or interest rate to decrease the NPV to zero (an increase in the rate will decrease the present value factors and thereby decrease the NPV). An interest rate equal to 14.5% (the present value table only shows those factors for whole numbers; therefore, it is necessary to calculate the factor using either extrapolation/trial-and-error techniques or the present value factor equation shown earlier) works out to be the internal rate of return (the rate at which the NPV is equal to zero) and is therefore the rate that is embedded in this project.

If you use a financial calculator, the keystrokes are quite simple (a rudimentary understanding of the notation used is all that it takes) and would yield the same answer (14.5%). However, the user is cautioned to make sure that the signs of the cash flows are accurate; that is, the first cash flow must be a negative value (it is an outflow) while all other cash flows are positive. The keystrokes are as follows:

$$-30cf_o; 1cf_j; 1.50 \ cf_j; 42cf_j; IRR \ldots 14.5\%$$

As mentioned, this capitalization rate takes into account the risks associated with the project and would therefore be higher (to compensate the investor) for those projects with greater risk and lower for those with less. Intuitively, one could assume that this capitalization rate may change throughout the life of the project at hand; risk is higher in the early going and then tends to decrease as the project becomes more viable. These changing inputs—both the amount and the direction (inflow or outflow) of the cash flows and the capitalization rates—make the NPV framework unique.

ANNUITIES

In an annuity, the cash flows and the capitalization rate are the same for the life of the investment. To value an annuity, the investor needs to discount each cash flow at the same capitalization rate to arrive at a present value. This exercise may be familiar to anyone who has been offered the choice of a lump sum or annuity payout on a retirement plan (or lottery ticket!); the choice becomes whether the investor expects to be able to invest the lump sum at a higher rate (over the period) than is assumed in the annuity.

Example

Assume that an annuity of three payments, each equal to $100 is made annually, at the end of each year. (Most annuities are assumed to be "ordinary annuity" or "in arrears," where the cash flow payment is assumed to come at the end of the period. An adjustment should be made in calculating annuity with payments received in the beginning of the period.) Once received, each payment is invested to earn an interest rate of 10%. How much will the total value of the resulting sum be worth at the end of the third year?

Here again, as with any of these cash flow problems, we begin by diagramming the cash flows:

Year	Amount	Future Value Factor	Future Value
1	$100	1.21	$121
2	100	1.10	110
3	100	1.00	100
Total			$331

The first year's $100 payment will receive 2 years' (the full 2nd year and third year) worth of interest and is therefore awarded the highest future value factor, while the last payment does not receive any interest (received at end of year 3 when the annuity stops earning interest).

The future value of this annuity (as shown) is simply the sum of these three calculations. Generalized, this calculation can be written for n payments (let i = interest rate and PMT = cash flow):

$$FV = PMT [(1 + i)^0 + (1 + i)^1 + (1 + i)^2 + \ldots + (1 + i)^{n-1}]$$

The arithmetic in the equation has by now grown to be somewhat intuitive. There certainly must be a better way to calculate an annuity, as I am sure you are asking yourself right now. Well there is—the Future Value (and Present Value) of an Annuity tables (see Appendix B, Tables B.9–B.12).

Before tackling the eye-distorting annoyance of those tables, it is first essential to understand the algebra behind those columns of tiny figures:

FVFA = Future Value Factor of an Annuity

$$FVFA = [(1 + i)^n - 1/i]$$

So now we solve our future value problems with the following equation:

FV = Annuity PMT [FVFA]

Redoing the previous problem using this new formula:

$$FV = \$100 (3.31) = \$331$$

Note. The FVFA can be found either on Table B.11 or simply through the following algebra:

$$FVFA = [(1.10)^3 - 1/.10]$$
$$= (3.31)$$

Now look at the annuity problem for the other side, that is, present value. It can be quite advantageous to an investor to understand the value (in today's dollars) of some future, periodic, equal cash flow payments. Assume that a somewhat naive NFII is told by a more than slightly pedantic VFII that the previously illustrated annuity stream (a $100 "ordinary annuity" for 3 years at 10% per year) could be purchased today for $248. Before accepting a *sounds-too-good-to-be-true* investment, NFII asks VFII to illustrate the annuity investment in a more detailed format (this particular NFII happens to be a lawyer, just our luck, who is somewhat versed in the area of proper due diligence):

Year	Annuity PMT	PV Factor	PV
0	What we are attempting to calculate		
1	$100	.9091	$ 90.91
2	100	.8264	82.64
3	100	.7513	75.13
Total			$248.68

So, in this case, the VFII continues, "an investor need only pay $248.68 for this annuity to achieve an internal rate of return of 10%." The professorial VFII then goes on to illustrate the algebraic methodology behind the numbers:

PVFA = Present Value Factor of an Annuity

PVFA = $\{1- (1 + i)^{-n}/i\}$ or alternatively PVFA = $\{1/i - 1/i(1 + i)^n\}$

In our case, the PFVA works out to be (can also be found in Table B.10):

$$PVFA = \{1 - (1.10)^{-3}/.10\}$$
$$= 2.4869$$

Once armed with this factor, the balance of the problem becomes rudimentary (simply apply the following equation):

PV (of annuity) = PMT (PFVA)

"Now for good ol' plugging and chugging" says the now becoming somewhat bombastic VFII:

PV (of annuity) = $100 (2.4868)

= $248.68

PROBLEM SET
INVESTMENT MATHEMATICS

PRESENT VALUE AND FUTURE VALUE

Question 1

Find the future value of $100 invested for 5 years at a 6% interest rate.

Answer

Using Appendix B, Table B.9, find the Future Value Factor (FVF) for a 6% interest rate (horizontal axis) for 5 years (vertical axis). This factor, 1.3382, is then multiplied by investment amount, $100, to calculate the total future value—$133.82.

Question 2

Find the present value of $500 to be received in 4 years using 8% as a discount rate.

Answer

Using Appendix B, Table B.8, find the Present Value Factor (PVF) for an 8% interest rate for 4 years. This factor, 0.7350, is then multiplied by the investment amount, $500, to calculate the total present value—$367.50.

Question 3

What would $100 in 10 years be worth today assuming a discount rate of 11%?

Answer

This problem also calls for the use of Table B.8. The PVF is 0.3522 (on the table given the vertical and horizontal values) and is then multiplied by $100 (as per the "given" of the table) to get a present value today of $35.22.

Question 4

This problem requires a scientific calculator and is for illustration purposes only.

A. Find the rate of return that turns $200 into $300 over 5 years.

B. Estimate (without using a calculator) the rate of return that turns $100 into $200 in 10 years.

C. Again, without using a calculator: If $300 is invested at a rate of 6%, how many years will be needed to generate an ending value (FV) of $600?

Answer

Using HP12C or similar calculator:

A. Enter the following:

−200 PV (this is the present value and is shown as a negative to represent an outflow).

300 FV (the future value or the amount expected in the future).

5 n (the number of periods or in most cases, years).

0 PMT (there have been no additions or subtractions to this stream).

i (this represents the interest rate).

You may see "running" go across your calculator.

The answer should show as 8.447% (this represents the internal rate of return).

B. Rule of 72: a rough estimate of the number of years it takes to double. In this case, the investment doubled in 10 years; therefore, the estimate of the average annual rate of return is 7.2% because by dividing 72 by 10 you get 7.2 percent.
C. Using the Rule of 72, we can estimate that it will take about 12 years for this investment to double (72 divided by 6 is 12 years).

ANNUITIES

Question 1

Find the future value of a 5-year annuity consisting of payments of $100 per year invested at an interest rate of 6% per year.

Answer

Using Table B.11, find the Future Value Factor of Annuity (FVFA) for 5 years at 6%. This FVFA is 5.6371; multiply this factor by the investment amount to ascertain the value of the cash flow stream (annuity). The future value is $563.71. The intuitive approach of simply adding five contributions of $100 each is not correct because of the interest each year on an increasing principal amount.

Question 2

Find the present value of a $100 per year, 10-year annuity discounted at an 8% rate.

Answer

Using Table B.10, find the Present Value Factor of Annuity (PVFA) for 10 years and 8% interest rate. This PVFA is 6.7101; simply multiply the investment amount (in this case, $100) by this factor to ascertain the present value of this cash flow stream—$671.01.

Question 3

(For illustration purposes only.) For $10,000, one can buy a 7-year annuity that will pay $2,000 per year. What is the rate of return on their annuity?

Answer

Using a scientific calculator, plug in the following data:

> −10000 PV; 7 n; 2000 PMT, 0 FV; i . . . 9.19%

Question 4

An investor is putting $2000 per year into a mutual fund that averages a return of 9% per year. How many years will these payments have to be made before the fund will be worth $100,000 (rough estimate only)?

Answer

Using Table B.12, first ask yourself what factor would we need to multiply by $2000 to get $100,000. This factor is about 50; how many years at 9% do we need to get a factor of about 50? By going down the 9% column we see that at about 20 years we get a 50 FVFA.

Question 5

(For illustration purposes only.) A person takes out a $200,000 mortgage loan to be paid monthly over the next 360 months at an annualized interest rate of 8% compounded monthly. Find the monthly payment.

Answer

Using a scientific calculator, plug in the following data:

> −200,000 PV; 0 FV; 8% divided 12 i; 360 n; PMT . . .
> "running" . . . $1467.53

NET PRESENT VALUE AND INTERNAL RATES OF RETURN

Question 1

An investment has the following cash flow, calculate the NPV (assume a 10 percent discount rate):

Year	Cash Flows (CF)
0	−$3000
1	−$5000
2	$2000
3	$4000
4	$6000
5	−$1000

Answer

$$NPV = -3000 + \frac{(5000)}{(1.10)} + \frac{2000}{(1.10)^2} + \frac{4000}{(1.10)^3} + \frac{6000}{(1+10)^4} + \frac{-1000}{(1.10)^5}$$

$$NPV = -3000 + (4545.45) + 1652.89 + 3005.25 + 4098.08 - 620.92$$

$$NPV = 589.85$$

Question 2

An investment that costs $10,000 produces a cash flow of $3000, $4000, and $6000 in each of the next 3 years. To find the internal rate of return, a cash flow diagram needs to be examined. Then, one could solve for the IRR using a scientific calculator.

Answer

Using a scientific calculator, plug in the following data:

−$10000 CF0; 3000 CF1; 4000 CF2; 6000 CF3 . . . IRR . . .
running . . . 12.71% is the answer.

Chapter

Quantitative Analysis

In this chapter you will learn:

1. Basic statistical constraints.
2. Regression equation analysis.

In the Chapters 1 through 3, we studied the tools that were, for the most part, solely tied to the investment field. This final chapter, in Part One, focuses on the scientific art of quantitative analysis. Quantitative analysis has its roots in statistics and its branches reach far into many scientific disciplines. In the investment field, the use of statistics and other more specific tools of quantitative analysis have become a critical part of the work of financial analysts. Whether your interests are merely basic investment planning or more intensive analysis, proper portfolio management and investment result presentation require the use of quantitative analysis.

In quantitative analysis, as in most mathematical fields, each piece of the discipline builds on some basic tenets. Statistics is the foundation on which we build our quantitative analysis structure.

BASIC STATISTICS

Measures of Central Tendency

The use of statistics enables us to summarize data accurately without overwhelming the user in numerical minutia. Each of us, in our own profession, have probably come across a numerical task that leaves us fiddling with the basic arithmetic and missing the big picture. Statistics permits the user the ease of seeing the big picture and then moving along to the task at hand. In the simplest of examples, consider the hypothetical company (ABC Products, Inc.) that produces widgets. ABC has several different product lines for specific market niches (each with their particular unit price) that present a confusing database for effective analysis. Note the following example.

ABC Company, Inc.—Product Analysis		
Product	Unit Price ($)	Profit Margin (%)
Consumer product	20	20
Commerical product	40	15
Government product	10	10
International product	50	30

What does the data tell us, besides the niche diversification, about the business of ABC Products, Inc.? Can we use the figures to analyze the business? Are we able to make some forecasts about future business?

When confronted with the task of quantitative analysis, the first step is to summarize the data using some basic statistical constructs. Before continuing with the ABC Product's data, it is necessary to understand some of these basic constructs.

Arithmetic Mean. This is usually referred to as an average of a set of numerical values. The mean is the most commonly used measure of return (not compounded) in investment finance. Although its mathematical notation can seem a little frightening to those not familiar with such notation, its definition and application are understood by most third graders. We simply add all the observations together and divide by the number of observations.

Mean Equation in Scientific Notation

$$\frac{\sum\limits_{i=1}^{N} X_i}{N}$$

The mean is the sum Σ (sigma) of all observations of X from the first (X_i) to the Nth divided by the population size (N). (Note if it was a sample size, use $N - 1$.)

The underlying concept implied by the use of an average is that all the observations (figures) in a specific database (population) are of equal significance and are therefore represented equally by this calculated average. This is the most misleading use of the mean; a highly diverse group of data cannot be represented by a single average that does not take into account the particular vagaries and nuances of each value.

For example, it is simple to calculate the average unit price of the widgets produced by ABC Company:

$20 + 40 + 10 + 50 = \$120$

$120 divided by 4 = \$30$

Therefore, $30 per unit is the average unit price.

What is the average profit margin for ABC?

$20\% + 15\% + 10\% + 30\% = 75\%$

75% divided by $4 = 18.75\%$

Therefore, the average profit margin for ABC is 18.75%.

But ABC sells most of their product (more than 85% of revenues) to the government. The average unit price of $30 and the average profit margin of 18.75% is certainly not representative of the true economic value of this segment of the company's business. These averages overstate the actual average unit price and profit margin. It should now be obvious, if it wasn't already, how dangerous it can be to rely on strict averages without understanding their economic derivations.

Geometric Mean (Average). The main use of the geometric mean in investment analysis is to average changes over time. Once again, the

mathematical notation can be quite intensive for even the most mathematically sophisticated investor:

Geometric Mean

$$[(1 + X_1)(1 + X_2)\ldots(1 + X_n)^{\frac{1}{n}} - 1]$$

The basic meaning behind the geometric mean is the law of compounding
and therefore it is typically seen in the calculation of the compounded annual growth rate (CAGR).

In the case of ABC Products, the geometric mean of the profit margins (assuming each product is sold in subsequent years; i.e., consumer
products are sold only in 1990, commercial products only in 1991, government products only in 1992, and international products only in 1993)
can be calculated as follows:

$$= \{(1.20)(1.15)(1.10)(1.30)\}^{.25} - 1$$

$$= \{1.9734\}^{.25} - 1$$

Note. We use the decimal value of 1/4 (.25) in the calculation of the
exponent. In calculating this equation, simply enter .25 and then the y^x
key (using HP12C calculator).

$$= 1.1852 - 1$$

$$= 18.52\%$$

Therefore, the annual compounded profit margin is 18.52%.

The geometric mean is expected to be less (slightly) than the arithmetic mean, due to the essence of compounding. This fact becomes important to the investor who is evaluating the returns of a given investment
opportunity—the CAGR removes some of the volatility inherent in arithmetic average calculation.

Median. The median is middle value in a stream of observations aligned
in increasing numerical order. It is the value that divides the stream exactly in half; one half will lie above the median and the other half below.

$$\text{Median} = \frac{X \text{ smallest} - X \text{ largest}}{2}$$

In the ABC Products example, the median would be $30. Unit prices are aligned in increasing order, from smallest to largest value (10, 20, 40, 50), and the median represents the middle value.

Mode. This statistic represents the most frequently occurring observation in a given database. It is less sensitive to extreme values in the database (outliers) than either the mean or the median.

In the ABC Products example, the mode is undefined because there is no repetitive value in either the unit cost or profit margin databases.

Measures of Dispersion

The preceding statistical constructs center around the notion of *central tendency.* Central tendency describes the behavior of data, specifically the tendency to cluster or group along a particular value. Mean (arithmetic and geometric), median, and mode all describe this clustering effect, although each has its own measurement format. This section in the basic statistics discussion focuses on the dispersion of a specific piece of data from its central value (be it mean, median, or mode). When describing the effects of dispersion on data, we turn to the following constructs:

Range. This refers to the distance between the lowest and the highest data value. The range can be disrupted by extreme or unusual values; these *outliers* are often ignored to provide a remedy to this problem.

Turning to our simplistic example of ABC Products:

The range for unit prices is reflected by {$10, $50}.

The range for profit margin is reflected by {10%, 30%}.

The use of range can tell us very little about the actual dispersion around a central value given a specific data set. Therefore, we must introduce another statistical construct that becomes crucial in the study of finance, to more accurately describe the dispersion or variation in a data set. The following three measures of dispersion are most commonly used in investment finance.

Variation. The difference between each value (observation) and the mean of the data set is its variation. The following notation describes this constant mathematically:

Variation Equation

$$\sum_{i=1}^{n}(X_i - \overline{X})$$

The total variation in a data set is always summed to zero: Each positive variation is canceled out by an exact negative variation in the data set. For example, consider the following simple set of observations: 10% (Observation 1) and 5% (Observation 2). From this, we can see that the variation of +2.5 (10% – the mean of 7.5%) exactly offsets the variation of –2.5 (5% – the mean of 7.5%). Because of this characteristic, the variation measure is not very useful except to allow a foundation for the easy calculation of other measures.

Variance

Variance Equation

$$\frac{\sum_{i=1}^{N}(X_i - \overline{X})^2}{N}$$

Variance is the sum (sigma) of all X observations minus the mean $(\overline{X})$, squared and then divided by the population size (N) or if a sample size $N - 1$.

This measure is calculated in the exact manner as variation, except that in variance the variation between the observed value and its mean is squared. By squaring the individual variations, all negative values are eliminated, thereby permitting a total variance value greater than 1. It is important to note that the total variance (before being divided by the population size or N) does not equal 0 as in the case of variation where the signs are positive and negative. An important interpretation feature to variance is that the higher it is the more disperse is the population. Furthermore, we now are able to use this dispersion value to some statistical significance. Or are we? (Implementing a simple spreadsheet program facilitates the number crunching.) The ABC Products data (see box at top of page 95) can serve as an example.

Although the math in the preceding statistical summary is correct, what about the interpretation? How does one describe the units in the

Unit Price	Mean	Variation	Variance
20	30	−10	100
40	30	10	100
10	30	−20	400
50	30	20	400
Total Variation: 0			
Total Variance: 1000			
Variance: 1000 divided by N (or 4) = 250			

variance value—dollars squared? So while the variance equation is help-ful in the calculation of dispersion by eliminating the problematic effects of the negative variation values, it introduces a new problem: definable units of measurement. However, our statistical friends also worked around this units of measurement problem—they took the square root of the variance in order to yield a more unit-sensitive value called *standard deviation*.

Standard Deviation. Simply the square root of the variance, standard deviation was developed to provide a more realistic and definable unit of measure (it is measured in the same units as the average). A major advan-tage in using the standard deviation (as well as the variance) to quantify the dispersion in a data set is that it takes every value into account, not just the highest and lowest (as in the range). The following represents the standard deviation equation:

Standard Deviation—Scientific Equation

$$\sqrt{\frac{\sum_{i=1}^{N}(X_i - \overline{X})^2}{N}}$$

Standard deviation is the square root of the variance. In other words, take the sum of all the X observations minus the mean, squared and then divide by the population (or sample size minus 1) size and then take the square root.

Confidence Limits

With the standard deviation measure, we can apply probability constraints, although only when the distributions are normally distributed (that is, mean equal to 0 and standard deviation equal to entire distribution). Normally distributed data sets (or populations) are similar to a standardization—formulating the data in such a way that it conforms to a particular template so that its information may be studied under certain parameters.

Symmetrical distributions are those where the mean, mode, and median are all equal and thereby the distribution would resemble the curve in Figure 4.1. The normal distribution represents a certain kind of symmetrical relationship in which the mean is equal to zero and its standard deviation is equal to the entire distribution.

The following normal distribution curve describes the probabilistic inferences drawn from a typical data set:

✔ There is a 68% probability that an item in a population will have a value that is within one standard deviation on either side of the mean.

✔ There is a 95% probability that an item in a population will have a value that is within two standard deviations on either side of the mean.

✔ There is a 99% probability that an item in a population will have a value that is within three standard deviations on either side of the mean.

Example. If earnings per share are expected to be $5 (therefore, by definition, $5 is the mean) with a standard deviation of +/– $0.50, then we can state that:

✔ There is a 68% chance that the actual earnings per share will be between 4.50 and $5.50:

1 standard deviation ($.50) plus observation value ($5) is equal to $5.50.

1 standard deviation ($.50) minus observation value ($5) is equal to $4.50.

Confidence Limits (Continued)

✔ There is a 95% chance that actual earnings per share will be between $4 and $6:

2 standard deviations ($1.00) plus observation value ($5) is equal to $6.00.

2 standard deviations ($1.00) minus observation value ($5) is equal to $4.00.

✔ There is a 99% chance that actual earnings per share will be between $3.50 and $6.50:

3 standard deviations ($1.50) plus observation value ($5) is equal to $6.50.

3 standard deviations ($1.50) minus observation value ($5) is equal to $3.50.

The standard deviation measure can also be used in the understanding of investment portfolio risk or volatility. If a portfolio is said to have an average rate of return of 13% (e.g., over a 5-year period), with a standard deviation of 20%, then we could state the following:

✔ There is a 68% chance that the returns will fall between −7% (that is, the average return minus one standard deviation, or 13% − 20%) and +33% (that is, the average return plus one standard deviation, or 13% + 20%).

✔ There is a 95% chance (or stated differently—with a 5% confidence) that the returns will fall between two standard deviations, or −27% (i.e., 13% − 2 × 20%) and 53% (i.e., 13% + 2 × 20%).

✔ There is a 99% chance that the returns will fall between three standard deviations, or −47% (i.e., 13% − 3 × 20%) and 73% (i.e., 13% + 3 × 20%).

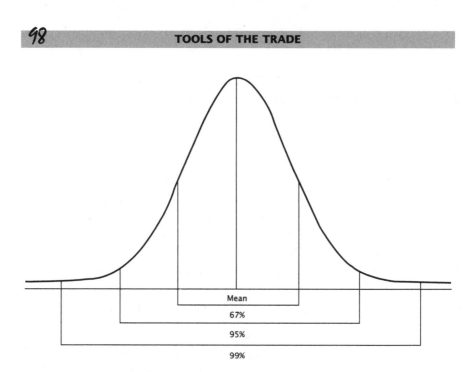

FIGURE 4.1 Typical normal distribution curve.

PROBLEM SET
BASIC STATISTICS

Question 1

Consider the following set of numbers:

4, 23, 12, 7, 14, 7, 11, 20, 1, 25, 4, 13, 7, 2, 15

Calculate the following:

The mean: _____

The median: _____

The mode: _____

The range: {_____}

The variation: _____

(*Note.* The sum of the individual variations is always 0.)

The variance: _____

The standard deviation: _____

The first step is to calculate the set of summary statistics for the above sample:

Summary Statistics		
X	(X-mean)	(X-mean)²
4	–7	49
23	12	144
12	1	1
7	–4	16
14	3	9
7	–4	16
11	0	0
20	9	81
1	–10	100
25	14	196
4	–7	49
13	2	4
7	–4	16
2	–9	81
15	4	16
Total	165	0	778
N	15		
Mean	11		

Now we can use this data to answer the questions at hand (see below) as well as to extrapolate inferences into the future (see Regression Analysis appendix).

Answer

Mean: 11
Median: 11
Mode: 7
Range: {1, 25}
Variation: 0 (as per definition)
Variance: 51.86 (units are undefined)
Standard Deviation: 7.20

Question 2

What is the geometric mean (compounded annual growth rate), arithmetic mean, variance, and standard deviation of the following set of return figures?

1992	9%
1993	21%
1994	11%
1995	−3%
1996	29%

		X	(X-mean)	(X-mean)^2
	1992	9%	−4.4	19.36
	1993	21	7.6	57.76
	1994	11	−2.4	5.76
	1995	−3	−16.4	268.96
	1996	29	15.6	243.36
Total		67	0	595.20
N	5			
Mean		13.4		

Answer

Geometric mean: 12.87%   Variance: 119.04 (units undefined)

Standard deviation: 10.91%   Mean: 13.4%

APPENDIX—REGRESSION ANALYSIS

Regression is the analysis of the relationship between one variable and some other variable(s). In essence, regression is the means by which data (as discussed in this chapter) and the variation in that data are used to help make predictions. In regression, there are two types of variables: the dependent variable (explained variable, endogenous variable, or the predicted variable) and the independent variable (the explanatory variable or the exogenous variable). The dependent variable is thought of as the variable whose value depends on the other variable(s), and the independent variable is the variable that is being used to explain the dependent variable.

Linear regression is the technique used to determine the extent of a change in one variable (dependent variable) resulting from a change in another (independent variable). Because of the linear assumptions of regression, it is critical to first express the relationship between variables in a linear equation:

$$y = \alpha + \text{ß}x$$

where:

> y = the value of the dependent variable ascertained by the equation
> α = the y axis (vertical) intercept; referred to as alpha
> x = the values of the independent variable
> ß = a measure of covariance (relationship) between the two variables; referred to as beta

It is essential to first understand that regression revolves around the variation the data (the independent variable) has around the mean and then to use that variation to explain the variation in another variable (the dependent variable). This "variation analysis" is the very first step with regression where we formulate a set of summary statistics to use throughout our analysis. The example below may help shed some light on this area.

Assume that we want to see the effect of air pollution (measured in "toxic" particles per 1 millionth of cubic inch of air) during the winter (in New York City) months on sales of precipitators (electrical devices that remove air particles). Precise Precipitators, Inc. has provided the following data:

Precise Precipitators, Inc.		
	Pollution (Particles/0.000001) X	*Sales Revs ($000s)* Y
Nov. 92	4,500	$ 95
Dec. 92	3,200	78
Jan. 93	7,500	141
Feb. 93	11,000	290

TABLE 4.1	Precise Precipitators, Inc.—Summary Statistics						
	Data		Variation		Variance		Covariance
	X	Y	(X-mean)	(Y-mean)	x^2	y^2	xy
Nov. 92	4,500	95	-2,050	-56	4,202,500	3,136	114,800
Dec. 92	3,200	78	-3,350	-73	11,222,500	5,329	244,550
Jan. 93	7,500	141	950	-10	902,500	100	-9,500
Feb. 93	11,000	290	4,450	139	19,802,500	19,321	618,550
Total			0	0	36,130,000	27,886	968,400
Mean	6,550	151					
Total Variance					9,032,500	6,972	

Note. The dependent variable is always X and the independent variable is always Y. Due to the small number of observations, the degrees of freedom was 0 ($N = 4$).

The first thing to do is to calculate the data's summary statistics (see Table 4.1).

Mean of pollution (X):	6550
Mean of precipitator sales (Y):	151
Sum of variation from mean for each x variable:	0
Total variance in X:	9,032,500
Sum of variation from mean for each y variable:	0
Total variance in Y:	6,972
Standard deviation of X:	3005.41
Standard deviation of Y:	83.49

Once the summary statistics are in place, we can proceed onto the calculation of some more defined statistics.

Covariance

This is a measure of correlation between sets of variables:

1. Multiply each variable's variation from its mean by the other variable's variation from its mean.

   That is: $[(X_i - \overline{X})(Y_i - \overline{Y})]$

2. Add each of the preceding products to get total variation.

That is: $\sum_{i=1}^{N}[X_i - \overline{X})\,(Y_i - \overline{Y})]$

3. Divide (2) by $N - 1$ (number of observations) to get covariance.

$$\text{Covariance (between } X \text{ and } Y) = \frac{\sum_{i=1}^{N}[X_i - \overline{X})\,(Y_i - \overline{Y})]}{N-1}$$

As the preceding equation indicates, some statistics need to be adjusted by the number of observations minus 1 (instead of dividing by N). This adjustment is not of a critical nature (without it one would yield a very similar estimate) but it should be noted that the amount subtracted from N increases with an increased number of estimates (as in multiple regression). This is referred to as degrees of freedom.

Correlation

This measures the goodness of fit of a regression relationship.

$$\text{Correlation} = \frac{\text{Cov}X_1Y}{(\text{Stan dev } X)\,(\text{Stan dev } Y)}$$

Correlation coefficients range between -1 and $+1$.

✔ -1 is perfectly negatively correlated.
✔ 0 is no correlation.
✔ $+1$ is perfectly positively correlated.

Note. The extremes $+1$ and -1 are not normally observable and therefore are said to not exist. A perfectly negatively correlated hedge between two assets represents a perfect inverse relationship. The same holds true for the correlation of $+1$ which would represent a perfect direct relationship. Although much time and effort are devoted to achieving these perfect hedges (through a heavy commitment to quantitative models and financial engineering using derivatives) it seems apparent that transaction costs and liquidity premiums (spreads between buy and sell prices) make it impractical and therefore relegated to the annals of theory.

Coefficient of Determination (or R-squared): This statistic calculates the amount of variation (in %) of the dependent variable (Y variable) that is explained by the regression equation. The higher the R-squared, the stronger the regression equation.

R^2 = Correlation squared

Simple Regression Example

Note. This example is used for simple illustration purposes only. Due to its simplicity, this example serves as an excellent illustration of the basics of regression analysis. However, the reader is cautioned that the implications of this example may be flawed in a strict statistical sense. Due to the high correlation between the variables, this regression may suffer from multicollinarity which would dilute the model's statistical significance. This notwithstanding, the example serves as a template to the functioning and procedure involved with regression.

As a hardware store owner, Mr. Jones wanted a better way to forecast how many snow shovels he might need for the upcoming winter season. Because snow shovels are a seasonal item and are quite cumbersome to Mr. Jones' small retail space, he felt it was critical to attempt to ascertain the very best estimate so that the store would not be burdened with storing the shovels during the off-season.

In discussions about this project with his business manager, Jones agreed that there must be some relationship between snowfall (in his area) and demand for snow shovels. This was quite obvious; but how can Jones quantify the relationship to permit a forecast? Jones's business manager suggests regression analysis. He explains that by using previous years' data of snowfall and snow shovel sales they could extrapolate the relationship which would allow forecasting. Once the coefficients of the equation are calculated, the anticipated snowfall for the upcoming season can be inputted and an estimate for sales will be calculated. Jones realizes that the variability of weather cannot be truly estimated, but feels confident in the written forecasts (for snowfall) of the *Farmer's Almanac*.

Therefore the business manager completed the following analysis:

1. The regression equation is $Y = \alpha + ßX$.
2. Alpha (α) represents the *y*-intercept, or the amount of snow shovel sales if there were 0 inches of snowfall.
3. Beta (ß) represents the slope or the ratio between the change in snowfall and the change in sales of shovels.

Using the data in Table 4.2 we first must calculate the following (note we are using the sample size calculation of $N - 1$):

Variance of X:	$221.60/9 = 24.62$
Standard deviation of X:	Square root of $24.62 = 4.962$
Variance of Y:	$1606010/9 = 178445$
Standard deviation of Y:	Square root of $178445 = 422.42$
Covariance of X and Y:	$16496/9 = 1832$
Correlation coefficient:	$r = 1832/(4.962)(422.42) = 0.8740$
Coefficient of determination:	$R^2 = (0.8740)(0.8740) = 0.7639$ or 76.39%

TABLE 4.2 Jones Hardware—Regression Data and Summary Statistics

Month-Yr.	X: Snow (Inches)	Y: Shovel Sales ($)	x	y	x^2	y^2	xy
Nov. 92	12	$1,020	3.8	$153	14.44	23,409	581.4
Dec. 92	15	1,300	6.8	433	46.24	187,489	2,944.4
Jan. 93	11	1,500	2.8	633	7.84	400,689	1,772.4
Feb. 93	13	1,000	4.8	133	23.04	17,689	638.4
Mar. 93	3	700	-5.2	(167)	27.04	27,889	868.4
Nov. 93	6	500	-2.2	(367)	4.84	134,689	807.4
Dec. 93	2	300	-6.2	(567)	38.44	321,489	3,515.4
Jan. 94	11	1,200	2.8	333	7.84	110,889	932.4
Feb. 94	8	900	-0.2	33	0.04	1,089	-6.6
Mar. 94	1	250	-7.2	(617)	51.84	380,689	4,442.4
Total	82	$8,670	0	$0	221.60	1,606,010	16,496.0
Mean	8.2	867					

Let: x = variation from mean
y = variation from mean
x^2 = squared variation from mean
y^2 = squared variation from mean
Variance X = $\Sigma x^2/n - 1$
Variance Y = $\Sigma y^2/n - 1$
Covariance XY: COVxy = $\Sigma xy/n - 1$

Regression Equation: $Y = \alpha + \text{ß}X$
Let: α = alpha or y-intercept
ß = beta coefficient or slope
Y = dependent variable
X = independent variable

Now that we have calculated the summary statistics, we can move on to the coefficients of the regression equation:

Beta is calculated by the following equation:

COV/var x, which would be $1832/24.62 = 74.41$.

Alpha is calculated by the following equation:

$\alpha = \text{Mean}Y - \beta(\text{mean } X)$

$\alpha = 867 - (74.4)(8.2)$

$\alpha = 256$

Our regression equation is now $Y = 256 + 74.4X$

By inputting anticipated snowfall in inches for any given month (X), we can calculate an estimate of snow shovel sales (Y). For example, the almanac forecasted 10 inches of snowfall for the December 1996 month, which would be equal to sales of $996 for that month. From this information, it is assumed that Mr. Jones can estimate the need for snow shovels.

While this example is simplistic, the outcome is significant for investment analysis—the use of regression analysis to calculate the effect of one (or more—known as multiple regression) variable on another. The investor could certainly use regression analysis in his interpretation of an investment scenario: What would be the effect of a decrease in interest rates on new home sales? The number of high school graduates on personal computer sales? The population of 49-year olds (in the United States) on the S&P index? (For the last example, one is suggested toward Harry Dent's work, *The Great Boom Ahead*.) Due to the ability of regression analysis to forecast future trends, its use has been widespread in the investment analysis practice. While a powerful tool in its own right, regression analysis also needs to be coupled with several other factors (i.e., strong data, identifiable relationships, sensible economic framework) to avoid the many problems that can plague the regression equation (multicollinearity, autocorrelation, etc.).

PROBLEM SET
REGRESSION ANALYSIS

Question 1

The standard deviation of the independent variable is 20%. The standard deviation of the dependent variable is 12%. The covariance between these 2 variables is 0.0096. The correlation between the variables is:

    A. 0.40.

    B. 0.29.

    C. 0.12.

    D. None of the above.

Answer

    A. The covariance (0.0096) divided by the product of the standard deviations $(0.20)(0.12) = 0.40$.

Question 2

The R^2 of a simple regression of two factors, A and B, measures the:

    A. The insensitivity of changes in A to changes in B.

    B. Statistical significance of the coefficient in the regression equation.

    C. The standard error of the residual term in the regression equation.

    D. The percent of variability of one factor explained by the variability of a second factor.

Answer

    D. The R^2 measures the percent explained by the independent variable.

Question 3

Tom Sayles is the President of Southwest Steel Products, a nail wholesaler in the home construction industry. Tom believes that there is a relationship that can be estimated through regression analysis between nail sales and housing starts. He calculates the following through the regression equation

$$Y = \alpha + \text{ß}X \text{ (Sales} = 5.37 + .76X),$$

where:

    Y = Nail sales, in thousands (the dependent variable)
    α = Intercept (alpha)
    ß = Beta estimate
    X = Housing starts, in thousands (the independent variable)
    $R^2 = 0.56$

The regression statistics presented above indicate that during the period under study, if housing starts were 17 (actually 17,000), the best estimate of nail sales is:

    A. $18290.
    B. $22290.
    C. $58290.
    D. $137000.

Answer

    A. Nail Sales = 5.37 + (0.76)(17) = 18.29 or $18,290.

Question 3

The preceding regression information indicates that for the period under study, the independent variable (housing starts) explains approximately % of the variation in the dependent variable (nail sales).

    A. 56.
    B. 29.
    C. 33.
    D. 12.

Answer

    A. The definition of R^2.

PART TWO

───────

FUNDAMENTAL FINANCIAL SECURITY ANALYSIS

Now that we have labored through the bricks and mortar of this journey we can progress to the next phase—the valuation of securities. Utilizing the tools learned (and practiced) in the first part, we can now learn the methodologies behind the valuation of financial securities. In Chapter 5, *Equity Analysis and Valuation,* we are exposed to the many disciplines behind today's valuation processes. First, we need to reduce a security to its basic blocks—those individual components that make up the value of each individual security. Once again careful attention must be paid to the trends and industry nuances that differentiate each company.

While focus is given to the fundamental analysis methods (dividend discount methods) of equity security valuation, the practitioner is cautioned to note that there exists many other methods (and many more still yet identified) that may be used to value the particular equity. The fundamental methodology is chosen because it is built on previously discussed tools, in addition, it has a time-tested record of reliance. Although the markets will move from extreme to extreme over any given period, the basic tenets of the fundamental methodology will always be useful.

Credit analysis is as crucial to the investment practitioner as equity analysis. Credit analysis focuses on the ability of a company to pay on its debts. Any company that may have difficulty in this area can worry even the most steadfast investor. With credit analysis, we are thrown into a new set of ratios and quantitative constructs that are expected to yield any potential yellow flags. We will meet Myron, our faithful credit analyst, whose briefcase of specific credit analysis tools is jam-packed with those quantitative equations based on the teachings in Part One of this book.

Once the quantitative formulation is developed, the equity and credit analyst then turns his attention to the qualitative measures that are critical to the valuation of all securities. This is the proverbial "kicking-the-tires" routine that is tantamount to the valuation process and requires the practitioner to keep an open mind and a skeptical eye at the same time. While this anatomical feat may take many years (or several market cycles) to master, without qualitative measures the true measure of a security's value can never be fully calculated.

The two chapters that follow each have a problem set or case study to increase your understanding of these often confusing areas.

Chapter

Equity Analysis and Valuation

In this chapter you will learn:

✔ Fundamental equity analysis—The ROE equation.

✔ Industry and qualitative factors evaluation.

✔ Growth rate estimation.

✔ Investment valuation techniques.

Definition

An investment is the current commitment of capital for a period of time in order to derive future payments that will compensate the investor for (1) the time the funds are committed, (2) the expected rate of inflation, and (3) the uncertainty of the future payments.

The preceding definition breaks the investment equation into its three basic "needs." Any investment valuation process would require a careful quantification of each part. However, before we can do this, we first must analyze an equity investment as a business.

The performance measurement of any business begins with a detailed, empirical analysis of the company's operating levers—those ratios that clue the analyst into the performance measurement of a particular firm. These levers can be thought of as a multilevel control panel by which its financial managers report the workings of a company to maximize return. Perhaps at a particular juncture in a firm's life cycle, it should leverage its business (either to achieve a larger market share or take advantage of a specific event in the industry). Accurate financial analysis would be able to detect this increased leverage and consequently evaluate the managers' decision. Therefore, the financial ratios (levers) that comprise performance and operating parameters such as return on equity (ROE) serve as a means to monitor and evaluate the performance of a company's financial management and ultimately its business. In addition, the return-on-equity equation will highlight the financial manager's use of assets—*Are assets being utilized in the most efficient manner?* As well as operating margins—*Are other companies in the industry achieving higher gross margins?*

The ROE equation will provide a clear picture of the eventual disposition of the asset in question, namely, *Is it a buy, sell, or hold?*

Poor financial management does not, necessarily, mean an underperforming business and poor future prospects. There are certainly examples of fine businesses that on orchestrating a successful management turnaround begin to show strong empirical (i.e., "in the ratios") performance. This is a testament to the power of top-notch management. Because these are highly subjective issues, their adequate evaluation may be extremely difficult. In this chapter, we will discuss other elements that indicate a truly excellent management team.

The performance of a business within its industry also deserves the attention of the financial analyst. The knowledge of competitive pressures within a particular industry will aid in evaluating the performance of a particular company. Questions can range from concerns over the trends in raw material (input) prices to the current (environmental, regulatory, etc.) barriers to entry. The work of Michael Porter (Harvard University) serves as an excellent foundation for a careful evaluation of a particular industry's competitive forces as well as strategies to better position a company within its industry. Porter defined five competitive forces that influence the industry as a whole, each of which is broken down into its definable inputs and defining characteristics. We will go into these five forces in detail later in this chapter.

After completing the empirical detective work, the investor can then turn attention toward the question of valuation. (Okay, now that we know the performance measurements of Company XYZ, how do we value its equity or share price?) This discussion revolves around the basic mathematical underpinnings of the bond market, namely the value of the discounted (to the present day) future cash flows of a particular financial instrument. In a nutshell: What is the current value of next year's (and the following year's . . .) cash flow to equity (net earnings for stocks and coupon payments for bonds)? In addition, we must introduce the concept of growth and its implications to the valuation process. No company will grow at the same rate forever (Industrial Lifecycle Model) and will, eventually, seek its sustainable growth rate. The process is not complete, however, until a risk assessment of the probability of receiving those cash flows can be estimated. This is a unique (to the particular venture) risk that is captured through adjustments to the Capital Asset Pricing Model's (CAPM) required rate of return (k) estimate. Market risk—the risk that cannot be diversified away—is captured through the statistical construct known as Beta (the covariance between the return of the specific share and the return of the market as a whole).

Many valuation models in financial analysis have their own particular set of strong points and drawbacks. Analysts need to determine one best suited for the valuation of a particular security, or the midpoint value among many different valuation methods. The latter often permits the formation of a "valuation-matrix," a tool that can illustrate the range (under specific circumstances) of values over the spectrum of valuation methods.

After bringing all this work together, the investor must decipher the nagging question on all investors' minds—*buy or sell?* The answer of fair value may not be so easily summed up with an endorsement of one transaction or another. Fair value (or undervalued or overvalued) can depend on a long list of extenuating circumstances. As this book stresses, investment analysis is not an exact science. Even though it may be deeply lodged in the quantitative formats, financial analysis still requires a good deal of the "human touch," for it is the study of a business, not the numbers on a financial statement.

RETURN ON EQUITY (ROE)

The DuPont Derivation Equation

$$\frac{\text{Net income}}{\text{Pretax income}} \times \frac{\text{Pretax income}}{\text{EBIT}} \times \frac{\text{EBIT}}{\text{Sales}} \times \frac{\text{Sales}}{\text{Assets}} \times \frac{\text{Assets}}{\text{Equity}}$$

$$\underset{\text{burden}}{\text{Tax}} \times \underset{\text{burden}}{\text{Interest}} \times \underset{\text{margin}}{\text{Operating}} \times \underset{\text{turnover}}{\text{Asset}} \times \text{Leverage}$$

Definitions (also see Chapter 1)

Net Income. The bottom line of the income statement. This figure takes into account all the expenses related to running the business (including: depreciation and amortization, taxes, interest charges).

Pretax Income. The amount of income before taxes are taken out. The corporate tax rate is levied against this amount to yield the income tax expense. Interest on debt payments (cost of debt financing) is tax deductible; it is removed from pretax income and therefore is not being taxed.

Earnings before Interest and Taxes (EBIT). The operational income of the business before any effects of leverage and taxes. This line item reflects the costs involved in operating a business (marketing expenses, cost of goods sold, salaries, fixed costs, etc.) but does not include such items as depreciation and amortization, taxes, and interest expense.

Revenues. The measure that combines all recorded sales within the firm. Sales are considered to be the inflow of capital resources to the firm from the disposition of goods or services. There are several nuances to the major methods of revenue recognition (percentage of completed and completed contract methods); however, each must follow the underpinnings of the *Statement of Financial Accounting Concepts (SFAC) 5,* "Recognition and Measurement in Financial Statements of Business Enterprises." SFAC 5 calls for the satisfaction of the following two conditions for revenue recognition to be realized:

1. The completion of the earnings process (in addition to a measure of the costs needed to complete a given project).
2. A quantification of the amount of revenues (or other benefit) expected to be received.

Assets. The balance sheet's "Total Assets" amount (combines both current and noncurrent assets). An asset is anything having commercial or exchange value that is owned by a business, institution, or person.

Equity. Also a balance sheet item reflecting the firm's net worth. It is calculated with the simple arithmetical notation: Assets − Liabilities = Equity. In an investment sense, equity refers to the ownership interest possessed by shareholders in a corporation.

Before the advent of this derivation, financial executives at major industrial companies were, more or less, at the mercy of the "machine." Although the machine provided for their livelihoods, it would give no details to how it might be run more efficiently. No sense of where (what division) or when it would need more oil (liquidity) or more fuel (leverage). The machine just ran its course and the financial management team was there only to put out fires when they arose. However, with the derivation of the return-on-equity ratio, the financial executives at Du Pont (in the mid-1950s), and later many industrial firms, were able to fine-tune the performance of the company and its operating divisions by adjusting the individual levers to achieve maximum efficiency and profitability. This "tweaking" of the company's financial ratios gave rise to the importance of financial managers who were able to quantify their expertise and rationalize their commitment. No longer would excuses like "cyclical downturns in the industry" satisfy the board of directors, and later the shareholders. They demanded more statistics:

> If the economy (or industry) is slowing, perhaps we should reduce our leverage so as not to compound the slower revenue pace? Or, given the demise of our largest competitor, perhaps now is the time to increase leverage so as to capture market share?

The correct answer? It depends; in some circumstances either strategy would yield the desired return. With the ROE, however, the investor can perform *what if* testing. We can estimate growth (or lack thereof) that would, given some other assumptions, yield the targeted ROE. This exercise practically resembles the composition of a symphony, where each note, placed in sequence with others, will result in a different sound. If we, as conductor, strive for a certain harmony, achieving it may take several permutations of the same instruments. A little tweaking here and there can surprise even the most musically inclined.

Investment practitioners (yes, I mean you!) can use the ROE derivation to seek further information about the company's performance in comparison with its peers. If Company A has a larger asset turnover than its peer group, one could hypothesize that the firm is being managed at a higher efficiency level. Why would this company yield a higher amount of sales for a given unit of assets than another company in the industry? Perhaps management of Company A has striven for a higher level of productivity from its asset base and therefore, yields a higher amount of sales for given unit of assets or perhaps a company just hired 50 new salespeople. Each of us, in our personal peer group (of equally earning friends and relatives), could think of a person who seems to get so much more assets out of his earnings than the rest of us (*How does my brother-in-law afford all those* luxuries?). In our peer group, however, debt (leverage) may be (incorrectly) seen as an asset when it is not; again, the importance of the equity portion of ROE equation.

This industry analysis is also aided through the use of *common-size financial statements*. These financials permit easy analysis of each contributory item to total revenues and assets:

TABLE 5.1 Company ABC (Common Size Statement) (shown in percentages)				
Income Statement	12/31/9x	Balance Sheet	12/31/9x	
Revenues	100.00	Cash and equivalents	7.41	
Cost of goods sold	65.00	Trade receivable	16.7	
Gross profit	35	Inventory	28.23	
Operating expense	25.31	Other	3.38	
Operating profit	9.69	Current assets		55.72
Other expenses	3.15	Fixed assets (net)	44.28	
Profit before taxes	6.54	Intangibles	0	
Tax expense	2.33	Other	0	
Net income	4.32	Total assets		100.00
		Notes payable	12.27	
		Current portion LTD	0	
		Trade payables	11.22	
		Income tax payables	0.39	
		Other	5.44	
		Current liabilities		29.32
		Long-term debt	15.87	
		Deferred taxes	0	
		Other noncurrent liabilities	0	
		Total liabilities		45.19
		Equity		54.81
		Total liabilities and equity		100.00

These statements can be used when doing industry comparisons or trend analysis.

The following paragraphs provide a more detailed look at each of the five components of the ROE equation.

Tax Burden. This is the percentage of pretax income which falls to the bottom line as net earnings; therefore, 1– tax burden = tax rate paid by company. Well-established firms expect a nonvolatile tax burden; however, with loss carryforwards and related tax-shielded policies, many small firms witness a volatile tax burden. The prudent analyst must be aware of a small firm with seemingly high ROE but a rather high tax burden (therefore a low tax rate): What will happen to ROE when the tax advantages are fully exhausted?

Interest Burden. This lever indicates the financial strain on the company caused by the costs of leverage. Although debt has its advantages, they are not without costs; debt service can become a stifling obligation to even the strongest firm. Like the tax burden, the interest burden also provides a figure that is not quite a "burden," but rather an additive to ROE. The interest burden's calculated value is the percentage of EBIT that flows down to the pretax income line; 1– interest burden is the true drag to the company due to the costs of leverage.

Operating Margin. This ratio evaluates the company's operating margin or the company's effectiveness at minimizing costs. This ratio measures the true efficiency of the management at running the company. By using Earnings Before Interest and Taxes (EBIT) (instead of net earnings, where the ratio would be known as the net profit margin), we get a true read on the firm's operating efficiency without the effects of leverage or taxes.

Asset Turnover. This measures the asset utilization efficiency of the firm. How many times do the assets need to be turned to produce the level of sales? This lever will certainly differ dramatically between industries; an airline manufacturer (capital intensive and therefore greater amount of assets needed to produce a sales amount) will definitely have a lower ATO than that of a janitorial supplies firm given a similar level of sales.

Leverage. The ratio between total assets and equity (assets minus liabilities) provides the analyst with the ability to recognize the firm's position on leverage. A firm growing at x% without debt (no leverage) could certainly grow at a faster rate than x given an initial (or increased) amount of debt. Be wary of too much leverage, especially in a cyclical firm, for it could lead to financial distress. What is the optimal amount of debt that a company should undertake? The answer to this hypothetical question is not so easily obtained (although the academic work of Miller & Modigelani has made strong progress in this area). However, suffice it to say optimal leverage depends upon many factors (industry outlook, current business operations, cash-flow constraints), each of which need to be investigated carefully by management before an increased leverage scenario could be endorsed.

Industry Average Return on Equity

The following industry groups allow an investor to identify those companies within a particular industry that have a particular advantage (in ROE) over their peer group. The values are calculated using the average equity (beginning period equity + ending period equity divided by 2) of the individual companies composing a particular industry group. In addition, the ROE values are weighted by market capitalization of the companies in the industry group.

Industry Group	Group's Average ROE (1991–1996)
S&P 500	*15.5%*
Chemicals	13.8
Oil Services	9.5
Banking	17.4
Semiconductor	25.1
Airlines	7.1
Tobacco	36.7
Household Products	20.3
Entertainment	11.5
Medical Devices-Small Cap	15.6
Beverages	38.1
Automobile Manufacturers	5.0

Now that the ROE derivation is firmly in memory, it is time to consider derivations of the equation that are often seen in the work of the financial analysts. For example:

The Return on Assets (ROA)

$$\frac{\text{Net income}}{\text{Sales}} \times \frac{\text{Sales}}{\text{Assets}}$$

or

Profit margin × Asset turnover

As shown earlier, this statistic can isolate the efficiency of a company in the use of its resources. This ratio includes debt as an asset (inasmuch as it does not reflect the assets as net, i.e., after debts) whereas the ROE equation does reflect these net assets.

Net Return on Equity

$$\frac{\text{Net income}}{\text{Sales}} \times \frac{\text{Sales}}{\text{Assets}} \times \frac{\text{Assets}}{\text{Equity}}$$

or

Net profit margin × Asset turnover × Leverage

Here we are only losing the "burden ratios" (Tax and interest burdens) and thereby combining the first three levers into one.

With the preceding derivations as well as the other ROE-related levers at one's disposal, the proactive investor is able to simply (yes, I mean simply) "plug and chug" to achieve the desired result. As the examples make obvious, the equations are all "chain-linked," so that pieces cancel out and the entire equation collapses into a more simplified model. As mentioned, the ROE (and ROA, etc.) derivation provides a more detailed look into the company's performance and financial management practices.

QUALITATIVE ANALYSIS

When exploring a company's prospects, an investor should be quite concerned about the management—those who are at the helm. Today's investors must feel comfortable in speaking with (and even inquiring of) top management about the future prospects of the enterprise (that is where the money is; discounted value of future cash flows). As equity owners, investors have a vested stake in the way the company is managed. With effective management in a good operating environment, any company should have many positive net present value (NPV) projects. As discussed earlier, positive NPV projects translate into achieving the required rate of return, which in turn permits an efficient valuation.

Management plays an important role in the growth sequence of a firm. But how does one evaluate management? Is there a quiz that all members of the management team must pass to be considered effective? Besides the empirical analysis of the firm, are there other methods we can employ to value solely the management team's efforts?

In most cases, the investor can get a "gut feeling" about the people who run a particular company. Relying on such a subjective methodology to analyze performance, however, comes with potential pitfalls. Perhaps the president and his three vice presidents were all top in their B-school class? Or they are very wealthy and therefore must (a tenet of finance?) work for a great, high growth company? Even though this gut-feeling approach to management analysis is most prominent among seasoned analysts, additionally, they often pepper their comments with the work of Tom Peters. Peters, a well-known and respected author (*In Search of Excellence: Lessons from America's Best Run Corporations*, Thomas J. Peters and Robert H. Waterman, 1982) enumerated several characteristics that all top companies should have in common. After a painstaking search through the ranks of more than 60 U.S. corporations for the behavioral traits that contribute to excellence, Peters and Waterman identified the following attributes:

- ✔ Doing it, not just talking about it.
- ✔ Customer friendly.
- ✔ Endorsing an empowered workforce—entrepreneurship.
- ✔ People management—getting the most from your employees.
- ✔ Operating a hands-on and value-driven.
- ✔ Sticking to the basics.
- ✔ Simple form, lean staff.
- ✔ A defined management hierarchy.
- ✔ Innovative, cutting-edge products (often, a high R&D expense is clue).

As described by Peters and Waterman, an excellent company is known to all who visit it in a very short period of time. This visitor may first recognize the morale of the staff or the efficiency by which they do a seemingly mundane task. The employees are quite vocal about their successes and failures, choosing not to hide behind emotions but rather to work as a team to achieve 150% of their goals. Energy (the hum of the office or plant) flows within a well-run company. An excellent company is not a proverbial den of slaves with the manager constantly cracking the whip; instead, it sponsors a symbiotic atmosphere that motivates every worker to strive to do what is best for the common good. All of this might sound utopian, but any CEO would only hope that all companies were so organized.

But these characteristics do not ensure strong investment performance. As a matter of fact, the excellent companies in 1981 witnessed "declines in asset growth rates, decline in equity growth rates, drop in market-to-book ratios, lower average returns on total capital, lower ROEs, and lower average returns on sales" (Clayman, 1987) over the 4-year period ending in 1985. This is a clear example of regressing toward the mean (over time, investment returns will seek to align themselves with the long-term average); the companies that had been deemed excellent became less so during the same period that the mediocre companies became excellent.

In addition, this can serve as a reminder of the importance for investors to possess adequate and fair expectations for their return benchmark (i.e., the utility fund is not going to average a return of 35%).

INDUSTRY ANALYSIS

Once we have a handle on the somewhat nebulous concept of qualitative evaluation, we need to turn to the evaluation of the industry in which a particular company competes. This industry competition is synonymous to the soil conditions that a farmer would be subject to in cultivating a crop. If the land is hilly and the soil is full of rocks, the farmer certainly needs to evaluate his crop-growing scenario to maximize his output. Similarly, the corporation needs to evaluate its environment to maximize the profit that can be generated. This evaluation consists of surveying the competition within the industry, regulations which can impact the profitability of a firm within an industry, and the potential substitutes that can wreak havoc on even the most established firms.

Michael E. Porter reigns as the czar of industry analysis. His five competitive forces serve as a template for the evaluation of the environment in which firms conduct their business. Porter's competitive forces are detailed in the following schema:

1. Bargaining power of buyers.
2. Bargaining power of suppliers.
3. Threat of new entrants.
4. Threat of substitute products or services.
5. Rivalry among existing firms.

These five forces interact to determine the profitability conditions within a particular industry. An analyst would be expected to survey the industry in which a specific firm is operating to identify how these forces are affecting (or may affect) the ability of the firm to continue growing. If a firm is in a monopolistic strategy, its market share would be far less penetrable by competitors unless a substitute product has been introduced. The company which brings this substitute product to market can employ a strategy of undercutting the leader to gain market share. However, the monopoly would be expected to retaliate (and should have the margin advantage or staying power to permit a concerted retaliation effort) to force out this threat. Technological advantages take an important role in this competition; if a substitute product is more efficient or provides greater utility, then it is likely that it will survive the pressures of the monopoly.

Company Life Cycle

No company can grow at the same rate indefinitely, but rather, goes through a growth cycle. Many companies may go through this cycle several times throughout their history. The cycle has five stages as shown in Figure 5.1:

1. *Start-Up or Development Stage.* In this stage, the market for the company's products is small and sales growth is modest. The profit margin and net profits are typically very small or even negative (losses) due to the incurring of major development costs.

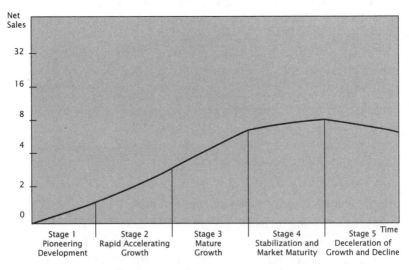

FIGURE 5.1 Life cycle of an industry.

2. *Rapid Growth.* Here the market for the company's products is developing with little to no competition. Sales growth is usually quite rapid while there is excessive demand for the company's products. Profit margins are typically very high, and growth in net income could be as high as 100% per year.

3. *Mature Growth.* The market for a company's products in this stage is maturing; supply now meets demand and competition has entered the market. Sales growth is above normal but not accelerating. Earnings and profit margins have decreased or stabilized due to the increase in competition.

4. *Stabilization and Market Maturity.* In this stage, which is typically the longest phase, the company's product market matches that of the aggregate economy/industry. Earnings growth varies by industry and by firm, and profit margins have decreased due to further increases in competition.

5. *Decline.* In this final stage, a company's product market witnesses a shift in demand due to growth in substitutes. Sales growth declines as do profit margins (could actually be negative) and earnings growth. Companies in this stage are usually candidates for restructuring and possibly takeover candidates for corporate raiders.

PROBLEM SET

Question 1

The financial statements for Parrot Computers Inc. (see Appendix B, Tables B.3 and B.4) are to be used to compute the following ratios for 1994.

    A. Return on assets.

    B. Return on common shareholders' equity.

    C. Leverage ratio.

Answer

    A. Return on Assets: Net income/Avg assets

        ROA = 960/2400

        ROA = 40%

B. Return on common shareholders' equity: Net income – Preferred divs/Average common equity

ROE = 960/1750

ROE = 54.86%

C. Leverage ratio: Average assets/Average common equity

Leverage = 2400/1750

Leverage = 1.37%

Question 2*

The Coca-Cola Company (KO) and PepsiCo, Inc. (PEP) are the leading companies in the worldwide market for soft drinks and snack foods. Return on shareholders' equity is a prime measure of management's performance and can be analyzed using turnover, leverage, profit margin, and income tax rate. Use the ratios and company data provided in Tables B.7 and B.8 to calculate and return on average common equity for KO and PEP for the 2 years 1977 and 1983.

Answer

		Tax Burden Net/Pre	Interest Burden Pre/EBIT	Return on Sales EBIT/Sales	Asset Turnover Sales/Assets	Leverage Assets/ Equity
Coke	ROE					
1983	19.6% =	.56	.933	15.9%	1.33	1.78
1977	21.3% =	.54	1.0	17.5	1.59	1.41
Pepsi	ROE					
1983	16.6% =	.58	.762	8.4	1.75	2.56
1977	22.8% =	.55	.896	11.0	1.83	2.31

The trends for both companies have been negative from the 1977 levels. While ROE has declined for both companies, the decline is particularly severe for PEP.

---

*CFA Exam question. Reprinted with permission.

Question 3

Use the data on Parrot Computers (Tables B.3 and B.4) as reference to solve the following problems. Compute the following ratios:

Fixed asset turnover.

Debt to equity.

Answer

Fixed asset turnover = Sales/Fixed assets = 6000/1200 = 5x

Debt to equity = 250/1750 = 14.29%

Question 4*

Using the Analyst Notes (AN) for Mento Machines (below), evaluate the competitive structure of the router industry based the analysis of the 5 competitive forces. For each of these forces, cite three items of evidence from the Analyst Information Package that justify your evaluation.

Mento Machines—Analyst Notes:

1. Network environments are very complex due to the hardware and software technology and the lack of common standards. Routers are needed to connect computers with diverse operating systems ("languages"). The two industry leaders' routers accommodate 25–30 such "languages" whereas newcomers' routers support five or fewer.

2. The two industry leaders have substantial research and development budgets, patents, and technology and design expertise.

3. The two industry leaders have extensive direct sales and service organizations.

4. Theoretically, routers would not be needed if all computers had compatible systems and could communicate easily with each other.

---

*Industry Analysis CFA 1994 Level 2 Exam. Copyright 1994 by AIMR. Reprinted with permission.

5. New research and development and the adoption of universal "languages" may eventually eliminate the need for routers, but that is not expected to happen for many years.

6. Other pieces of equipment frequently perform some functions of routers, but this is not yet significant nor is it anticipated that they will be able to duplicate all the functions of today's routers.

7. The cost of routers is a small percentage of the total cost of a computer network.

8. A high quality router can significantly increase the efficiency of a network system relative to the router's cost.

9. Customers prefer a single supplier of routers.

10. Customers who switch to another supplier's routers face high costs related to the change.

11. Router industry leaders subcontract the manufacturing of their products to companies whose services are plentiful and commodity-like.

12. Routers are assembled mostly from commonly available electrical components.

13. Some of the components used to assemble routers are proprietary to a single supplier but these are currently insignificant.

14. 80% to 90% of sales of the two router industry leaders are to repeat customers.

15. Competition in the router industry is based on product features. Price is secondary. The two industry leaders have different sets of product features.

Answer

The five competitive forces within the industry structure as detailed by Michael Porter are as follows:

Threat of new entrants.

Threat of substitutes.

Power of buyers.

Power of suppliers.

Rivalry among existing firms.

In the Mento Machine problem, the following serves as an answer:

Threat of New Entrants

Barriers to entry are high and rising because of the unique nature of the router market. The two industry leaders have established significant leads in understanding complex customer needs, developing technology, building a highly trained sales and service staff, and building reputations for proven product liability (AN 1, 2, 3). Any new entrant will have difficulty overcoming any of these factors alone and extreme difficulty overcoming all of them at once. The threat of new entrants is, therefore, low as a result of the extensive skill sets required at the outset to compete effectively.

Threat of Substitutes

This threat is currently low, mainly because of the lack of unifying protocol (AN 4, 5), but it is rising somewhat because of the selective provision of some router functions by other pieces of equipment (AN 6). Longer term, the threat of complete substitution may come in the form of a unified protocol rendering a router obsolete.

Power of Buyers

Buyer power is low and will remain low because of the high costs to switch (AN 10). Preferences for a single vendor (AN 9), the low cost of routers relative to whole systems (AN 7), and the importance of increasing overall network efficiency (AN 8).

Power of Suppliers

Supplier power is low as a result of the commodity-like nature of the components and required manufacturing capabilities and the multiple vendors of each supplier (AN 11, 12, 13).

Rivalry among Existing Firms

Rivalry does not seem too intense; the two main suppliers do not even compete for 80%–90% of their sales (AN 24, 29). When they do compete, they compete on a basis other than price and are known for different product sets (AN 30).

VALUATION OF EQUITY SECURITIES

The previous section focused on measuring and evaluating the financial levers that make up the return on equity equation. These levers hold the keys to many of the financial facets within a specific firm. However, before moving to the next step, equity valuation, we must first formulate a measurement process for those important inputs—risk and growth.

Evaluating Risk

Any discussion of risk in investment finance should focus on the study of the required rate of return. This is the rate that the risk measure, known as beta, will incorporate. Beta represents the covariance between the returns of an individual security and the market. A beta of 1 would perfectly correlate with the market, whereas a beta of 2 would mean that the particular equity would be twice as volatile (if the market increased or decreased by 10%, then this equity would increase or decrease by 20%). An investment that would be perfectly negatively correlated with the market (beta = −1) represents a perfect hedge and is not possible under practical circumstances. Consequently, this search for a perfectly negative correlation between assets has spawned the derivatives market to create a synthetic hedge that approaches such a correlation.

The required rate of return (also referred to as the discount rate or capitalization rate) will serve as the discount rate that represents the required rate of return for an investor in this particular equity. This discount rate incorporates the risk of that particular equity security (measured in the context of the market) as well as the risk-free rate available in the market. The model that permits the derivation of this rate is the Capital Asset Pricing Model (CAPM) calculated by the following formula:

$$k = r_f + ß\,(r_m - r_f)$$

where:

ß = Beta (the covariance of returns between that particular equity and the market portfolio)

r_f = risk-free rate (typically represented by the Treasury rate)

r_m = the return on the market portfolio

Once the required rate of return (k) is calculated we can utilize it as a discount-rate mechanism in the valuation exercise of the present value of future cash flows. Although before we discuss valuation lets first practice the calculation of "k" using the CAPM equation.

CAPM—Sample Problems

What is the required rate of return for the following equities given the following data:

U.S. Treasury bond yield = 7% and Historical market return = 12%

SEC Corp.   Beta = 1.45 $k = 14.25\%$
IRS Corp.   Beta = .85 $k = 11.25\%$
FBI Corp.   Beta = 1.00 $k = 12\%$

Evaluating Growth

In addition to understanding the derivation of the rate by which an equity security's cash flows will be discounted to arrive at a present day valuation, it is necessary to consider other critical input in valuation—growth.

Although there are probably many methods to measure growth in a company (growth of net income, growth of sales, employee growth, market share, etc.), the method that is most often employed in fundamental equity analysis is as follows:

Growth = Return on equity × Retention ratio

$$g = ROE \times b$$

where the retention ratio (b) is calculated as follows:

Retention (plowback) ratio = 1 − Dividend payout ratio

$$b = 1 - p$$

This equation for growth makes some intuitive sense—ROE is the return on the book assets of a firm and the retention ratio is the amount of those earnings (return) that is not paid out to shareholders, but rather retained and "plowed back" into the firm for growth (positive net present value) projects. The following example illustrates this important financial tenet:

> Company A posts net income of $500,000. The Board of Directors decides to pay $100,000 in dividends to shareholders. Therefore Company A's dividend payout ratio is 20% (100,000/$500,000) and the retention ratio or plowback ratio is 80% (400,000/$500,000).

Net income:	$500,000	% of net income:	100%
Dividends paid:	100,000	% of net income:	20 (dividend payout ratio)
Retained earnings:	400,000	% of net income:	80 (retention ratio)

This growth product (g) is often referred to as sustainable growth (g^*) for the simple fact that dividend payout policy is typically unlikely to be volatile (*Note.* Sticky dividends and the signaling effects of dividend changes reduce volatility). Although this tenet is probably more couched in convenience than theory by analysts seeking a simplistic dividend discount model rather than the more intense life-cycle models (2-stage H model or multistage model). No matter its derivation, sustainable growth certainly plays an important role in the financial management process by permitting corporate officers to develop critical firm strategies. For example, if Company X has a sustainable (calculated) growth rate of 12% but has an actual growth rate (in sales or in earnings) of 15%, then Company X's financial management would need to develop strategies to raise capital or decrease (yes, decrease) actual growth (for not doing so could lead to a severe cash crisis—the demise of many financial managers at fast-growing companies).

Consider the following:

> *If sustainable growth is less than actual growth ($g^* < g$):* First, management needs to determine how long the situation will continue. If the company's growth rate is likely to decline in the near future as the company reaches maturity, the problem is only a transitory one that can probably be solved through increased borrowing.

If, however, the situation is expected to continue and is not an industry-wide phenomenon, then the firm needs to adopt one or more of the following strategies:

1. *Sell new equity.* This strategy is usually considered to be on the more expensive side of the spectrum; furthermore, it is not available to many (smaller or nonpublic) companies. Consider that most corporate executives feel that the stock market usually underprices their firm's shares (hence the large amount of insider purchases) and thereby wouldn't want to sell new equity at those discounted prices. In addition, the costs of an offering (advisory fees, selling concessions, "dog and pony shows," etc.) can be seen as prohibitive. Finally, the increased number of shares outstanding might have a dilutive effect on earnings. In a market that hammers a firm's shares when they "only" meet earnings expectations, it would seem obvious that a firm's managers could be sensitive to this potentially dilutive effect.

2. *Increase leverage.* As mentioned, this often comes with an increased risk (of financial distress). This increased risk translates to an increased risk-premium associated with the shares' cost of capital going forward.

3. *Reduce payout ratio.* Although theoretically this would seem to be the best (least expensive and most efficient) method to raise capital, most companies are reticent to decrease dividends due to the negative reaction from shareholders. This signaling effect suggests that investors would see a decreased dividend as a signal that something is awry within the firm and subsequently sell their holdings. Ironically, this decrease in dividends may be due to increased prospects for growth projects within the company's business and thereby a positive for the shares.

4. *Profitable pruning.** This is the corporate strategy that purports a sale of marginal operations to plow the capital back into the remaining businesses. Profitable pruning reduces sustainable growth problems in two ways: It generates cash directly through sales of marginal businesses and it reduces actual sales growth by eliminating some of the sources of growth.

5. *Increase pricing.* It may become necessary for a firm to increase their prices (on goods or services sold) to reduce the growth of the business (note the obvious inverse relationship between price and revenue).

Now, consider the other side of the growth paradigm:

If sustainable growth is greater than actual growth ($g^* > g$): First determine whether this situation is temporary or longer term. If temporary,

---

*R. L. Higgens, *Analysis for Financial Management* (Burr Ridge, IL: Business One Irwin, 1992), pp. 127–131.

management can simply continue accumulating resources in anticipation of future growth. If longer term, the issue then becomes whether the lack of growth is industry-wide (natural result of maturing market) or company-specific. If the latter, the company needs to do some soul-searching to identify and remove the internal constraints on company growth. This can be a painful exercise resulting in organizational restructuring as well as decreased developmental expenses.

When a company is unable to generate sufficient growth from within, it has three options:

1. *Ignore the problem.* This could leave the company open to a corporate raider seeking an opportunity to dismantle the company by selling the company's "crown jewels"—the hidden value of certain divisions. The market value of a conglomerate's divisions may be significantly below that of their nonconglomerate (or pure-play) peers due to small net benefit impact one division would have in a very large corporation. In addition, the market has a tendency to award higher valuations to pure plays versus conglomerates (the idea here is that if an investor chooses to diversify he could do so with individual companies and therefore not have a need for a large, ineffective conglomerate).

2. *Increase dividends.* Although some investors may argue that higher dividends are good for stocks, fundamentally speaking, this tenet seems to be flawed. By paying more dividends (which results in greater income flow), the actual result becomes simply returning more money to shareholders. Remember that the equity investor has placed funds in this enterprise to participate in the expected increase of good fortune that the enterprise promises. If the investor wanted a cash flow, why didn't he buy a bond? Furthermore, the problem of taxation arises, inasmuch as all dividends are taxed as current income (rates as high as 39%). This double taxation constraint certainly would prevent a highly compensated, tax-avoidance investor from investing. There is, of course, the investor who wants both income (to cushion declines in stock price) and equity (to participate on the upside).

Dividend signaling is the corporate finance tenet that discusses the negative impact on equity prices due to an announcement of a reduction in dividends. As this theory postulates, a share price will decline a moderately significant amount whenever a company has announced a reduction in current dividends because of the typical stability one expects from a dividend. The dividend policy is like an unwritten contract between the board of directors and the investors that offers a continued cash flow to equity owners as long as management can expect to generate it. So one can expect a reduction in dividends to mean that the company is undergoing a contracting business cycle or possibly something worse (financial distress? or company-specific problems?) because the dividend is sacred and the board would only cut it if things were getting rough.

However, I offer the following scenario as means of disputing this dividend signaling effect. Assume that the company in question is experiencing slow growth in its business and is therefore finding few positive net present value projects to reinvest the cash flow from operations; the retention (plowback) ratio is low and declining. So if this company has a surplus of cash and nowhere to invest it strategically for the desired return, it decides to return it to shareholders in the form of dividends; therefore, the payout ratio is increasing. Assume further that this sequence of decreasing retention ratio and increasing payout ratio continued for some time before a new, constant level was achieved. Furthermore, this new level of dividend payout stays on for several periods. Then the business begins to turn and this company is on the forefront (seeing the cycle turn before any other player in the industry) with a perfect opportunity to capture significant market share and other positive NPV projects. However, capital (to invest) is needed quickly to lock in these projects before any other players capture them. There are many different sources available to the public company seeking capital, but the most efficient and fundamentally valid (but hardly used) source is the retention ratio. It would make sense (least expensive method, most direct, should provide equity investors their desired growth) to increase what you retain from the business (or reduce your payout ratio) when growth opportunities present themselves.

This theory notwithstanding, the market still discounts equities in companies that reduce their dividend. Evidently, investors (or anyone else for that matter) do not want to lose something they have come to expect.

3. *Buy growth.* The attempt to diversify into other businesses is the quintessential modus operandi of a corporate raider, who would come into a company sell off any marginal (or nonprofitable) businesses to raise funds to purchase a growth operation. However, this buying of growth strategy does not need to take place in a sick company. A company may be throwing off too much cash from operations and not have enough growth prospects which to invest. In this case, the company needs to either buy back its shares (thereby increasing equity value by decreasing shares outstanding) or buy a growth business.

PROBLEM SET
EVALUATING GROWTH

Question 1

The following are selected financial data (growth rate in sales represents end-of-year data; all else is beginning-of-year policy data) for the Widget Corp., a New Jersey based retailer of specialty products for the engineering market:

	1986	1987	1988
Profit margin (%)	1.77	1.65	1.16
Retention ratio (%)	91	90	81
Asset turnover (x)	2.51	2.35	2.38
Financial leverage (x)	2.36	2.72	2.72
Growth rate in sales (%)	10.04	14.54	7.28

A. Calculate Widget's sustainable growth rate in each year.

B. What is Widget's payout ratio for each year?

C. Comparing the company's sustainable growth rate with its actual growth rate in sales, what growth problems does Widget appear to have faced over the 1986–1987 period?

D. In 1988, what strategy did Widget seem to employ to remedy the growth problem highlighted in Part c?

Answer

A. The sustainable growth rate for the following periods:

1986	1987	1988
9.55%	9.49%	6.08%

B. The payout ratios for the following periods:

1986	1987	1988
9%	10%	19%

C. During this period Widget's actual sales growth is greater than its sustainable growth rate and it seems to be increasing at a fast rate. Widget Corp. is growing too fast; to sustain this growth, management would need to adjust the company's financial "levers." In 1987, management seems to begin this task by decreasing the asset turnover ratio, net profit margin ratio, and retention rate. However, the significant increase in financial leverage more than offsets these decreases and the ensuing increase in actual sales is again greater than the sustainable growth rate.

D. In 1988, management again toyed with the financial levers of Widget Corp. in order to permit a more sustainable growth strategy. A significant decrease in the net profit margin and the retention ratio coupled with only a slight increase in asset turnover ratio and a flat leverage ratio yielded a sharp decrease in actual growth that was much closer to the sustainable growth rate. In subsequent years, further fine-tuning of these levers should permit the Widget Corp. strong, sustainable growth without the problems that too much growth can bring.

EQUITY VALUATION

We have analyzed the equity investment on the grounds of performance (with the ROE equation), risk (under the construct of the CAPM), and growth prospects (the concept of sustainable growth rate using the retention ratio); now it is time to pull all this together and value the equity.

How is an equity security valued? This is the ultimate reason we study fundamental equity analysis—to determine the financial security's "true value." The following methods are used in typical valuation analysis:

- ✔ Dividend discount method—also known as Gordon's constant growth model.
- ✔ H model.
- ✔ Multistage (2-Stage) model.
- ✔ Price to sales.
- ✔ Earnings and book value ratios.

It is important to define the inputs in each model:

P_0 = Price today (in time zero)

DIV_1 = Dividend in next period (in time 1)

k = Required rate of return calculated by CAPM

g = Growth rate (of earnings, dividends, or sales)

Earnings = Posted net income of the company

Sales = Posted revenues of the company

Book value = Value of net total assets

For each of the discounted cash-flow methods (constant growth, H model, and multistage models) the intuition is the same—calculating today's value of a future cash-flow stream given a rate of growth and discount rate. The cash-flow stream in the classical case represents dividends; but what about non-dividend-paying equities? Other cash-flow streams used are free cash flow (defined as net earnings + depreciation and amortization charges – changes in working capital and – maintenance capital), earnings, and cash flow to debt holders (this is often used in the analysis of a hybrid security).

The following represents the mathematical notation for each of the models:

Constant Growth Model

$$P_0 = \frac{DIV_0 (1+g)}{k-g} = \frac{DIV_1}{k-g}$$

H Model

$$P_0 = \frac{D_0(1+g_n)}{k-g_n} + \frac{(D_0)(H)(g_a - g_n)}{k-g_n}$$

P_0 = Price today

D_0 = Today's value of dividends

g_a = Initial, abnormally high, growth rate

g_n = Long-run growth rate

H = Number of years it is expected that the abnormally high growth rate will last. (*Note.* We use H, half of 2H, in our calculation because we expect this abnormal growth rate to slow linearly over that period.)

Multistage (2 Stage) Model:

$$P_0 = \Sigma \frac{DIV_0(1+g_{1-5})^t}{(1+k)} + \frac{P5}{(1+k)^t}$$

where:

P_0 = Today's value of the shares
Σ = Sum of notation
DIV_0 = Current period's dividend
g_{1-5} = Dividend growth rate for the periods 1 through 5
g_{long} = Growth rate from periods 6 on
t = Time period (year)
k = Capitalization rate
P_5 = Period 5 value of the shares; incorporates the use of the long-term growth rate (g long)

where:

$$P_5 = \frac{DIV_6}{k-g} = \frac{DIV_5(1+g_{long})}{k-g_{long}}$$

Equity Valuation—Sample Problems

Given the preceding data (from the CAPM problem set) in addition to the following information, calculate the intrinsic value of each security:

1. SEC Corp.

   Current dividend = $2.50

   Long-term growth rate = 12%.

   Intrinsic value = $2.50 (1.12) divided by (.1425 – 12) = $124.44

2. IRS Corp.

   Current dividend = $1 and is expected to grow at 5% per year for next 2 years and then settle down to a long-term growth rate of 9%.

   $$\text{Intrinsic value} = \frac{\$1(1.05)}{1.1125} + \frac{1(1.05^2)}{1.1125^2} + \frac{DIV_2(1.09) \text{ divided by } .0225}{1.1125^2}$$
   $$= \$44.98$$

CASE STUDY: EQUITY VALUATION

*Merck & Company**

The valuation of equity securities is a process that takes into account all we have learned up to this point. It is not a science for the fainthearted; it requires devotion to diligence, a keen and skeptical sense for the truth, and an indefatigable spirit to uncover an unknown value. The proactive investor needs to understand the macroeconomic indicators that revolve around our economy to accomplish a top-down analysis as well as the profitability measures utilized in the ROE equation. Be it the seasoned investor or the novice, good investment decisions always seem to come down to one thing—the quality of the homework. In the following case study, much of the preliminary detective work has been forgone to focus on the procedure, practicality, and overall methodology behind the valuation process. This is not an endorsement for the "quick and dirty" method witnessed in this case study, only a means of illustrating this important function in financial analysis.

The following list summarizes the data provided in the tables for this case study:

- ✔ Current dividend amount: $DIV_0 = \$1.00$ (or earnings amount or cash flow).
- ✔ Growth rate (g): estimated through methodology that employs basic business statistics.

  g_{1-5} = Range of 5-year growth rates estimated by analysts (see Table 5.2).

  g_{long} = Represents analysts' estimates of long-term growth rates; that is growth rates beyond the initial 5-year period (see Table 5.2)

- ✔ Capitalization rate (risk-adjusted discount rate): $k = 14.24\%$ or .1424 (see Table 5.1 for derivation).

Note. Although one can estimate the capitalization rate (k) by either Capital Asset Pricing Model (CAPM) or the alternative Arbitrage Pricing Theory

---

*Excerpted with permission from *Merck & Company: A Comprehensive Equity Valuation Analysis.* Copyright 1996, Association for Investment Management and Research, Charlottesville, VA. All rights reserved.

(APT); it is assumed, for the purposes of this example, that the CAPM equation will provide a more straightforward approach despite its drawbacks.

Company Profile (Adapted from Value Line, November 6, 1992).
Merck & Company is a leading manufacturer of human and animal health care products and specialty chemical products. Important product names include Vasotec, Prinivil (angiotensin converting enzyme (ACE) inhibitor agents for high blood pressure and angina); Mevacor, Zocor (cholesterol reducing agents); Primaxin, Mefoxin (antibiotics); Pepcid (antiulcer agent); Recombivax HB (hepatitis B vaccine); and Prilosec (gastrointestinal acid inhibitor).

Business Analysis

✔ International business: 46% of sales and 18% of pretax profits.

✔ Research and development: 11.5% of sales.

✔ Labor costs: 32%.

✔ 1991 depreciation rate: 4.7%.

✔ Estimated plant age: 8 years.

✔ Corporate headquarters: PO Box 2000 (R32–43) Rahway, NJ 07065

✔ Number of employees: 37,700.

✔ Number of shareholders: 91,100.

✔ Stock ownership: Directors own 1%.

The first step in the valuation process is to ascertain which valuation technique is most appropriate given the problem at hand and the data given. It is expected that we should use a form of the discounted cash-flow model. This is the most commonly utilized technique in security analysis and would be appropriate given the data provided. In this case, we will employ a version of the dividend discount model which describes a technique to value a company growing at different rates for certain periods of time. The Multistage Method is more rational (considering the industrial lifecycle) but is also quite difficult to estimate due to the additional level of assumptions needed (forward ROE, retention ratios, etc.).

For this method, a growth matrix (see Table 5.2) is developed that spans the ranges for the growth rates in different stages. The first growth rate covers the growth in the first 5 years (ga = abnormal growth rate used in the 2-stage model to estimate intrinsic value. This rate pertains to a level of growth that does not seem to be sustainable for very long into the future. Typically, this growth can be related to an industry-wide event that has a short-lived impact on the industry) while the second rate focuses on the long-term rate of growth (gs = normal or sustainable growth rate is the growth rate that is estimated through the Return on Equity). The additional growth rate (outlier) is used to capture the possibility that changes in the industry will bring significantly lower growth than predicted by the range of analysts (worse case in the growth scenario).

Armed with the growth rate matrix as well as the other inputs we can begin the process by pursuing the company's intrinsic value. We start with the value of the discounted sixth year's (the first year under the new growth rate) earnings. To this value we adjust for the value of each year under the nonsustainable growth rate to yield the desired total value. The following notation illustrates this model:

$$P_0 = \Sigma \frac{DIV_0(1+g_{1-5})^t}{(1+k)^t} + \frac{P_5}{(1+k)^t}$$

Where the price today (P_0) is equal to the sum of the dividend amounts, increased each year by applying the growth rate, discounted by the respective discount rate for that period. The second part of this equation, as indicated, is the value of the sixth year's dividend discounted at the appropriate discount rate to arrive at the share value in year 5 (P_5), which is again discounted to the present value to achieve P_0. One could think of this 2-stage equation as having a body and a tail; the body is the first few years' worth of discounting and the tail is the infinite portion of the equation.

Financial Data—Merck & Company

TABLE 5.2   Capital Asset Pricing Model

CAPM equation: $k = R_f + ß(R_m - R_f)$

Inputs: Risk-free rate (R_f) = 7.44% (30-yr. Treasury rate)

Historical average equity market risk premium ($R_m - R_f$) = 6.80%

Beta coefficient (value line) = 1.00

Capitalization rate (k): = 0.0744 + 1(0.068)

= 14.24%

TABLE 5.3 Analyst Estimates for Growth				
	High	Mean	Low	Outlier
5 Year	19%	17.1%	14%	10%
Long-term	12	10	8	

TABLE 5.4   Discounted Cash Flow Valuation and 2-Stage Model Inputs: Most Likely Scenario

Initial (5 yr.) growth rate: $g_{1-5} = 17.10\%$

Long-term growth rate: g long $= 12\%$

Expected price in 1997 (Value line projections): $92.50

Current dividend: $DIV_0 = \$1.00$

Current market price: $43.25

Calculating Merck's Intrinsic Value

The Multistage Model. The notation of the Multistage Model:

$$P_0 = \Sigma \frac{DIV_0(1+g_{1-5})^t}{(1+k)^t} + \frac{P_5}{(1+k)^t}$$

Where:

P_0 = Today's value of the shares

Σ = Sum of notation

DIV_0 = Current period's dividend

g_{1-5} = Dividend growth rate for the periods 1 through 5

t = Time period (year)

k = Capitalization rate

P_5 = Period 5 value of the shares; incorporates the use of the long-term growth rate (g_{long})

The following calculations should be used as a means of understanding this valuation method:

Assume, for reasons that would be detailed in the analyst's report (i.e., current political pressure on pharmaceutical companies, Merck's long-term market share strategy, competition from generic drug manufacturers, etc.) that the growth rate for periods 1–5 is 19% and the long-term growth rate (periods beyond 5 years) is 10%. (That is, according to Table 5.2, the high estimate for the 5 years growth rate and the mean estimate for the long-term growth rate.)

Furthermore, our analysis has pinpointed (using the CAPM methodology) a discount rate for Merck's shares as 14.24%. Lastly, Merck's current dividend per share is $1.00.

Step 1. Now we can begin to input values into the equation and calculate the results ("plug and chug"). Using your calculator, figure the following:

$1 ($DIV_0$) multiplied by 1.19 ($1 + g$) is equal to $1.19 ($DIV_1$). Then DIV_1 is divided by 1.1424 ($1 + k$) to equal the first year's contribution to the equation, or 1.0417.

Next, calculate year 2's cash flow—$1.19 multiplied by 1.19 (19% growth rate) is a dividend in year 2 of $1.4161 ($DIV_2$), which is then discounted (divided) by 1.1424^2 ($1 + k^2$) or 1.3051 to arrive at the second year's value of 1.0851.

The third year (and subsequent 2 years) are calculated the exact same way:

$1.4161 ($DIV_2$) × 1.19 ($1 + g$) = $1.6852 ($DIV_3$)

$1.6852 divided by 1.1424^3 = 1.1303

The fourth year is

{$2.0054 ($DIV_4$ or DIV_3 multiplied by 1.19) divided by 1.1424^4} = 1.1774

The fifth year is

{$2.3864 ($DIV_5$ or DIV_4 multiplied by 1.19) divided by 1.1424^5} = 1.2265

We now simply sum the first 5 years' worth of contribution to yield the "body" portion of this 2-stage equation:

1.0417 + 1.0851 + 1.1303 + 1.1774 + 1.2265 = 5.6610

Step 2. In the next step of this method, we begin by ascertaining the value of the sixth period's dividend (DIV_6). This dividend is crucial to our analysis for it is the first year where a new growth rate is being applied (g_{long}).

The following equation is used to calculate P_5:

$$P_5 = \frac{[Div_0(1+g_{1-5})^5](1+g_{long})}{(k-g_{long})}$$

As discussed, this would represent the "tail portion" of the 2-stage equation.

The fifth period's dividend ($\$2.3864$ or DIV_5) multiplied by 1.10 (1 + g_{long}) to calculate the sixth period's dividend ($\$2.625$ or DIV_6). Then DIV_6 is discounted using the constant growth methodology (employed when calculating a share price that has an infinite growth lifespan):

$\$2.625$ divided by 14.24% minus 10% ($k - g$) or 4.24% which equals $\$61.9113$ and can be thought of as P_5 or the price of the equity in period 5.

The following matrix summarizes values of P_5 ($P_5 = DIV_6/k - g$) under the following assumptions:

		g_{1-5}			
		.19	.171	.14	.10
	.12	$119.32	$110.09	$96.27	$80.52
g_{long}	.10	61.91	57.12	49.95	41.78
	.08	41.30	38.11	33.32	27.87

The value of P_5 does us little good (unless we wanted to know the expected value of the shares in year 5) because we are interested in the present value of these shares. Therefore, the next step discounts this P_5 value back to P_0 by using the very same methodology used in the "body portion" of the equation—divide P_5 by 1.1424^5 to get a present value of stage 2: $\$61.9113$ divided by 1.1424^5 (*Note.* This is not the sixth power because constant growth method provided us a value in the fifth year and thereby a "$n = 5$" is used in the discount rate calculation), which equals the tail portion contribution of $31.8185.

Step 3. The final step is to simply add the contributions from the two stages to calculate the present value of these shares—$5.6610 + $31.8185 = $37.47.

Practitioners of this method would view Merck as being overvalued because the current price ($43.25) is a good deal more than 10% above the calculated value ($37.47). Perhaps there were some inputs that were not effectively estimated? Maybe the practitioner (analyst and investor alike) has underestimated the company's growth rate?

Many subscribers to this method would develop a matrix of ending values (see following example) in attempting to pinpoint the two growth rates (for periods 1–5 and long term) that is "assumed" by the present value developed through the 2-stage calculation.

Present Value Matrix				
			g_{1-5}	
		.19	.171	.14	.10
	.12	$66.98	$61.97	$54.45	$48.85
G long	.10	37.48	34.74	30.64	25.94
	.08	26.89	24.97	22.09	18.79

From the preceding, it is obvious that under a 10% long-term average growth rate and a 19% growth rate for the early years, Merck has an intrinsic value of $37.48—just as calculated earlier. But would a long-term growth rate of 12% and a 10% growth rate for the periods 1–5 be more in line with the calculated value ($48.85 vs. a current value of $43.25)? Perhaps we need to reevaluate the short-term growth rate? Could this well-established, highly capitalized company in such a very competitive industry actually grow at 19% per year for the next 5 years? Although the answer to this rhetorical question could easily be an affirmative, the financial analyst would be cautioned to support his case very carefully.

Note. From the preceding matrix, it is apparent that a higher long-term growth rate is much more additive to present value than the same increase in the short-term growth rate. One would see this as quite intuitive:

The long-term growth rate lasts longer and therefore should have a much more pronounced effect on the present value. This is the lesson to be learned: The portion of the 2-stage equation that is more difficult to develop a growth rate for (because things can change quite dramatically going out further into the future) has the bigger effect on the present value. So, to steal a battle cry from a popular TV police drama: "Be careful out there!"

Chapter

6

Credit Analysis

In this chapter, you will learn:

- ✔ Traditional credit analysis.
- ✔ The methodology behind credit ratings.
- ✔ Fixed income securities.

Credit analysis, for the exclusive purpose of making loans, is one of the oldest arts in investment finance. As an example, assume that centuries ago, benevolent overlords (yes, they did exist, albeit, in the minority to their tyrannous brethren) would determine whether a minor lord was deserving enough (Did he work hard? Was he knowledgeable about his craft—be it artisan or agrarian? Did he possess any collateral?) for a loan. This loan was to be used by the minor lord to produce goods that could be later sold to earn enough currency (or other goods) to repay the loan with interest. The credit analysis function didn't really take form during these early years for the simple reason that brutal force and cruel punishment prevented any serious defaults.

The concept illustrated by this somewhat far fetched example is important for our discussion on credit analysis—the relationship between the two "investment parties" (lender and borrower) is very different from the relationship shared by equity owners and the company. With the equity relationship, the players seek a mutually beneficial outcome: the capital growth of the firm and consequently the increase in the share price.

Therefore it is in the best interests of the shareholder (who has no claim to the assets of the company, but rather only the future growth prospects) to hope and even assist (perhaps this is a bit utopian—shareholders promoting the company's prospects; or is it?) in the future growth of the company. In the case of the bondholder and the company, however, the relationship is not as mutually synergistic because the bondholder simply desires (read: is only entitled to) the stated interest payments on a timely basis and the eventual repayment of principle at maturity. Therefore the agency relationship that exists between bondholder and company is more consistent with the relationship between a company and its raw material supplier (just pay me for my goods promptly and we will be satisfied). It is important to realize that a bondholder (as well as the equity holder) is also a supplier to the company—a supplier of capital. But because the bondholder is "entitled" to the assets of the firm upon default (depending on the covenants embedded in the bond issuance) he is less interested in any future growth and more concerned about current net worth and business policies.

In early modern times, the analysis of lending practices was *the* investment science. Only over the past 100 years or so has equities entered into the analysis. Proponents of this "paper financing" could easily value its worth; they would charge an exorbitant fee for their compensation to outweigh any risks of forfeiture. As you probably can guess, this fee was renamed to the more euphemistic "debt service" or "interest." In addition, the early covenants of these loans granted the lender many rights and liberties (perhaps the takeover of a business, the sale of assets, or a management reorganization) to such a degree that the sheer power rendered by these financiers could force the reconciliation of any outstanding loan.

As the financial markets became more standardized and regulated, these financiers were forced to succumb to more realistic interest terms. In addition, with the advent of equities, firms in need of capital could now seek it without submitting to unfair practices by the lending financiers. Hence the birth of the formal study of credit analysis. Lenders needed to make up for the "margin squeeze" created by these external forces. If the amount that was being charged to borrow capital was under pressure (decreasing), then it stands to reason that the "default cushion" that the lenders had enjoyed was also diminishing. Therefore, the need grew for a more prudent methodology to assign default rates. Because the lenders needed to become more discriminating, they employed the analysts to scrutinize a borrower's current business, industry position and trends, current financial picture (ratio analysis), and collateral (assets) before considering the holding of any bonds (granting credit). Furthermore, the analyst would attempt to rationalize the reason the company was seeking credit:

> Was the company's expansion plans warranted? Did the planned acquisition make economic sense given the current environment?

In addition, the analyst would be concerned about the company's balance sheet:

> Does the company have any noncurrent assets held at book value that have a significantly higher market value? How about the liability side of the balance sheet—what is the amount (percentage of pension assets) of unfunded pension liabilities? What assumptions (assumed rate of return; wage inflation; workforce attrition/growth rate) are being incorporated in valuing this unfunded pension liability? What is the company's current debt level?

These are the musings of a credit analyst; they have certainly come a long way. And, they indicate what the savvy potential investor should look for.

THE TOOLS OF CREDIT ANALYSIS

Although many of the tools used by the credit analyst have already been covered in Chapter 5, certain tools are used primarily, if not exclusively, by those seeking to justify the purchase of credit instruments. Now let's meet Myron—our stereotypical green-eyeshaded credit analyst. Myron is gainfully employed (although he seems to spend most of his money on computer games, Spiderman comics, and lettuce for his pet rabbit) at a major commercial bank's credit department. So what does Myron do all day at work? Let's open his briefcase (or toolbox if you will grant me this license) and see what is inside.

Ratio Analysis

The analysis of fundamental ratios is the hallmark of the credit analysis function. Several ratios are used in credit analysis, each with its own set of intricacies and circumstances. The credit analyst will employ these ratios to get a handle on the structure of the company in question and its ability to pay the debt service embedded in the covenant of the fixed income security. As the following describes, the underlying theme of ratio analysis is an attempt to get a handle on the company's financial flexibility. Financial flexibility is critical to the company because of the eventual downturn that any company will be subject to and the negative implications that come along with such a downturn. Can the firm manage to weather such a storm? Do they have the flexibility to continue to pay their debt? Will they miss market share opportunities because of any forced retrenchment? These are real potential problems, not just for major corporations but for small companies and even individual borrowers. Assume for a moment that you are a lending officer at a local bank (not the most pleasant daydream I know, but bear with me) and you are deciding which application to approve for a $10,000 loan (assume you can only approve one):

- ✔ *Applicant A.* Has a sales position within the fast-growing telecommunications industry in which he has attained a high degree of recent successes:

  Average taxable income of $100,000 over the past 2 years ($80,000 in the first year and $120,000 in the second).

  Household debt (credit card balances, student loans) of $35,000.

  Home value (recently assessed) is $235,000 (floating rate mortgage of $200,000).

  Investment and savings (net of retirement accounts) accounts balances are $3,500.

- ✔ *Applicant B.* Has a middle management position (recently promoted) in a large conglomerate, which he has held for several years:

  Average taxable income of $60,000 over the past 2 years ($55,000 & $65,000, respectively).

  Household debt of $1,000.

  Home value (recently assessed) of $150,000 (with a fixed-rate mortgage of $95,000).

  Investment and savings (net of retirement accounts) account balances of $3,000.

Although an argument could be made for either of these applicants, the more obvious candidate for a loan would be Applicant B. Applicant B has more fiscal restraint (less debt and more modest tastes) and therefore, a greater level of financial flexibility. Although, Applicant A has grown his earnings at a faster pace than Applicant B, he is also in a more volatile position (sales in a "new" industry). What would happen to A if his business contracted next year? Does he have the financial wherewithal to withstand this downturn? Assume, for argument sake, that his industry's sales are highly correlated (don't worry, we are not going to get into that regression stuff again) to the changes in interest rates. Doesn't that make some economic sense? Of course it does: A sells telecommunication equipment to large corporations (I don't think Mr. Jones, down the street, is going to buy many "core-satellite transformer units") and large corporations' expenditures on such items usually depend on economic conditions, namely, interest rates (i.e., if A's equipment is extremely expensive, most corporations would finance such purchases). So as rates increase, a corporation's propensity to borrow capital may diminish and consequently Applicant A would be expected to suffer an earnings decline.

Now back to Myron's briefcase. These ratios (or tools) come in four flavors each measuring a different part of the company. The first set of ratios measures how efficiently the company is employing their assets. In this category there are three ratios that enable Myron to gain a handle on the efficiency of the company. Like the asset turnover ratio in the return on equity equation (Chapter 5), these ratios measure the assets (in this case inventory and fixed assets) necessary to attain a particular level of sales. A company that can achieve a level of sales of "y" with only "5y" (an asset turnover ratio of .20) of fixed assets (machinery—plant and equipment, etc.) is more efficiently deploying those assets than a company that needs "10y" (an asset turnover ratio of .10) worth of fixed assets. As it may be clear to you already—the credit analyst is most interested in inventory, accounts receivable, and fixed assets is because they are typically the most expensive for the company and therefore would impact its financial flexibility the most.

Note. It is critical for the discussion in this chapter to recall the importance of not relying on the single value of any ratio but rather to look at a trend over time as well as within an industry group or historical average. For example, it does not suffice to state that the company's credit should be downgraded because of a reading of 4 times ("4 times" or a "turnover ratio of 4") in the inventory ratio without seeking the trend over the past several quarters as well as the same quarter last year (allowing for seasonality). In addition, the analyst needs to be sensitive to differences between industries—supermarket companies and airplane manufacturers would differ greatly with regard to inventory turnover ratios.

Asset Utilization/Efficiency Ratios

Inventory Turnover (ITO) = Cost of goods sold (COGS)/Avg. Inventory.[1] The inventory turnover ratio (ITO) explains the number of times the inventory amount (on average) is produced and sold during the period. This ratio, probably more than most, is dependent upon the industry in which the company is operating.

Fixed Asset Turnover = Sales/Fixed Assets. In this ratio, we are seeking the amount of sales that can be generated (or as mentioned, the amount of fixed assets necessary to achieve a level of sales) from a given level of fixed assets. A company that desires to increase the level of sales by $x\%$ needs to increase the amount of fixed assets by a comparable amount to keep the fixed asset turnover equal to its trend value. What could be a reason for not having to increase the level of fixed assets to achieve an increase in sales? You got it—efficiency increases. If the fixed assets can be utilized more efficiently (perhaps an inexpensive overhaul or cleaning would do the trick), then the company wouldn't need to increase the amount of fixed assets.

Accounts Receivable Turnover = Net Credit Sales/Average Account Receivables.[2] In this ratio, we first need to estimate the percentage of sales that are credit sales; in other words, how much of our sales are owed to us? This ratio is not speaking to the average consumer's use of credit cards because in that case the merchant has a relatively quick receipt of the funds (net any user fee) from the credit card company. This ratio refers more to the large manufacturer that grants credit to customers. Think of a construction company that is purchasing a truck load of lumber from a local supplier. The lumber is billed to the construction company (now this sale is an account receivable on the books of the lumber company) via an invoice with certain terms detailed (e.g., "net 30 days") that the construction company now posts this invoice to his account payable account. A company with a consistent Account receivable turnover would illustrate strong credit policies and solid relationships with customers; if you are satisfied with a company's product and service, then you are more likely to pay for their goods on time.

---

[1] Average inventory is estimated by: Beginning inventory + Ending inventory/2.
[2] Average account receivable is estimated by: Beginning A/R + Ending A/R/2.

The financial flexibility or liquidity measures (the next step of ratios) are most important to the credit analyst. Working capital (defined as current assets minus current liabilities) is the primary measure of financial flexibility: The stronger a company's liquidity, the better able it will be to weather a downturn in its business or cash flow generation.

Liquidity Ratios/Financial Flexibility: Major Ratios

Working Capital = Current Assets – Current Liabilities. As discussed, this is the true measure of a company's financial flexibility. Be careful to use only the current assets and liabilities in this calculation. Furthermore, a skeptical eye should be cast toward inventories (see acid test)—How liquid are these inventories? Do they deserve to be classified as current assets?

Current Ratio = Current Assets/Current Liabilities. This ratio provides an inkling of the current leverage situation at the company. Current assets and liabilities are those that are readily converted to cash, therefore this ratio quantifies a snapshot of the short-term borrowing capacity of the company. Once again, the importance to the credit analyst is gaining an edge on the financial flexibility issue: Can the company increase its short-term borrowing if the market opportunity exists to capture market share or expand a production facility?

Cash Ratio = Cash + Cash Equivalents/Total Current Assets. Here we are getting an idea of the amount of cash that is currently on the balance sheet. Cash is always king.

Acid Test = Current Assets – Inventory/Current Liabilities. This ratio is often referred to as the *Quick Ratio,* due to its "down-and-dirty" way of getting at the heart of the liquidity issue.

Minor Ratios

Days' Sales in Cash = Cash/Sales per Day. This ratio reflects the amount of liquidity that a company has in relation to the amount of sales (in $) made per day. Can the level of cash support the level of sales per day? If the sales per day are increasing a rapid pace, the company will need to expend capital to keep the amount of resources high enough to support such sales.

Days to Sell Inventory = 360 Days/ITO. How many days will it take to sell the inventory, given the current ITO? It is clear why this ratio is considered a liquidity measurement.

Accounts Receivable Collection Period = 360 Days/Account Receivable Turnover.[3] Similar to the previous ratio, the accounts receivable collection period illustrates the number of days it is expected to take in order to collect all the outstanding accounts receivable. Any deficiency (versus the trend) in this ratio would be a yellow flag to the analyst for it can point to lax collection policies, poor service, and strained relationships with customers.

In the next category of ratios, we resort to some of the tenets described in Chapter 5. For the purposes of credit analysis, the ROE (return on equity) equation could be simplistically calculated, whereas the equity analyst requires a much more in-depth analysis. In credit analysis, the performance measures, both ROE and ROA, permit the credit analyst to develop a trendline growth for the particular company in question. A company that demonstrates consistent, strong growth of these ratios would certainly receive a more favorable review than one that does not, right? Well, not exactly, for in the words of a colleague and glib attorney, "It depends."

Credit analysis attempts to get a handle on the company's ability to service its debt, not its growth prospects. The performance (remember that net income is used in these ratios as a measure of performance) of a company has its place in the formulation of a credit analysis, but as shown with the Loan Applicants A and B example, growth of net income is not the most important measure of credit quality. The major reason for this seemingly hard to believe tenet of credit analysis is due to the basic qualities of net income. Net income is often (and totally within the guidelines of USGAAP) manipulated by management policies. We have already covered the effects of inventory methods (see Chapter 1 LIFO Versus FIFO) on the reported net income of a company. Management's hand can mold reported numbers in other areas such as depreciation methods, unfunded pension liability recognition, and revenue recognition.

Performance Ratios

ROE = Net Income/Equity. Remember to use total equity in your calculation. Also it wouldn't hurt to do a complete Du Pont-style breakdown to gain some additional knowledge of the company's strengths and weaknesses.

---

[3] Can also be derived from the following equation: Accounts receivable/Sales per day.

Positive Accounting

There exists an accounting theory (positive accounting—bonus plan hypothesis) (see Chapter 1) that when executive compensation is greatly enhanced by stock options, management will have a vested interest in optimizing the company's reported numbers.

> A bonus plan does not always give managers incentives to increase earnings. If in the absence of accounting changes, earnings are below the minimum level required for payment of a bonus, managers have incentives to reduce earnings this year because no likely bonuses are likely to be paid. Taking such an "earnings bath" increases expected bonuses and profits in future years.
>
> *Watts and Zimmerman,* "Positive Accounting Theory:
> A Ten-Year Perspective," *The Accounting Review*
> (January 1990, p. 139)

Does this type of corporate power strike you as unfair, inequitable, even illegal; well it shouldn't because the knight in shining armor is standing ready to keep the markets as efficient as possible. This knight (actually a cadre of knights) is known as the analyst. Investors can rest assured knowing that he is seeking out any improprieties, misconceptions, and questionable tactics so that the market can remain as efficient as possible. Are there situations that this cadre (membership requires only diligence of study, a somewhat open mind, and a financial calculator) may miss? Of course, that is what makes security analysis interesting (and profitable).

Don't confuse the positive accounting theory with a strict condemnation of the utilizing of stock options as employee incentives. Rewarding employees with ownership in *their* company can make a good company into an exceptional one. As discussed earlier, an investor would want to search for companies that have high insider ownership and a culture of personal overachievement for the common good of the company.

ROA = Net Income/Assets. The same suggestions apply as for the preceding ratio. Also be careful to include all assets, not just current assets.

The following ratios are extremely important to the credit analyst for they measure not only the long-term solvency of the company but its ability to meet their obligations. This ability is often looked at as the best way to measure a company's credit quality.

Leverage Ratios and Coverage Ratios

Debt-to-Equity = Debt/Total Equity. Here we looking at a snapshot of the total capitalization of a company—how much is made up of debt and how much of equity. A debt-to-equity ratio of 3 to 1 illustrates a company that is leveraged (has debt that is "historically" valued) to the tune of three times its equity's current market value). Herein lies an irony (and significant importance) of intensive credit analysis—the equity is marketed daily (with the movement of stock prices) whereas most liabilities (subject to FASB 115) are held on the balance sheet at historical cost. The credit analyst would be wise to reprice (to market) the company's outstanding debt to get a more realistic picture of the debt to equity ratio. How does one mark-to-market the debt of a company? By comparing the value of the debt currently to what it would cost if it was to be issued today. As the interest rate environment changes, so will the required price that the market demands for the debt. For example, an AA corporate 10-year bond may have needed a yield of 10% when issued, but only an 8% yield is currently required in the marketplace. Therefore the issuer would be able to save by refinancing this debt 200 basis points (2%) annually in debt service. The importance to credit analysis should be obvious: By repricing the debt, the analyst can get a better idea of what the borrowing power of the company may be and therefore, gain a better handle on its financial flexibility.

In the empirical sense, assets equal liabilities plus equity. Debt is part of capitalization just as much as equity, only the relationship between the investor (of the capital) and the company is quite different (agency frictions).

This ratio can take many forms:

✔ Long-term debt/Total equity.

✔ Total debt/Total equity.

✔ Total debt/Total capital.

Times Interest Earned = EBIT/Interest Expense.[4] This ratio gives the analyst an idea of the ability of the company to handle its debt. The more times the company can cover its interest expense, the better it is for the holder of the debt. It is important to use a measure that is not affected by the perverse tax rules that often manipulate net income; hence a cash flow measure is typically utilized in this ratio.

---

[4] EBIT = Earnings before interest and taxes; a measure of operating income.

This ratio also is calculated in different ways:

$$\frac{\text{Times interest}}{\text{earned}} = \frac{(\text{Pretax income} + \text{Interest expense})}{\text{Interest expense}}$$

In addition, we could use other measures that are organized in similar fashion but that use different inputs:

$$\frac{\text{Cash flow coverage of}}{\text{fixed charges}} = \frac{\text{Pretax operating cash flow} + \text{Fixed charges}}{\text{Fixed charges}}$$

Operating cash flow (OCF) = Pretax income + Depreciation/Amortization
+ Deferred income taxes + Minority interest income
− Undistributed earnings from subsidiaries − Increase in receivable
− Increase in inventories + Increase in accounts payable
− Decrease in accrued taxes

QUALITATIVE ANALYSIS

Now that we have discussed the quantitative side of credit analysis, we can move on to the qualitative side. Like equities (see Chapter 5), bonds also have a nonquantitative side to their analysis. Although the agency relationship between the bond investor and the issuing company is quite different from that of an equity investor, the basics of business analysis are still critical to the understanding of the enterprise at hand. After all, once the means of financing—equity, bond, option, and so on—is removed from the equation, what remains is a business. It is the analysis of this enterprise that is central to financial analysis. Whether it be a local grocer, newsstand, or a multinational conglomerate, a careful and skeptical eye must be cast on the actual business not just the financial reports of this business. The study of this side of the financial analysis equation is referred to as qualitative analysis (which should not imply that there is no quality in quantitative analysis).

Economic Cyclicality

A qualitative analysis of the future prospects of an enterprise relies on the underlying function of the entire economy. As mentioned in Chapter 2, a boom-and-bust cycle to the economy permits certain industries to capitalize on the strength of the economy. Cyclical is the term typically used to identify these industries. Industries sensitive to the economic cycle are capital goods, heavy industry manufacturers, and financial intermediaries.

Getting back to credit analysis—by tracking the trend of the economy, our credit analyst friend, Myron, forecasts the industries most likely to experience an increase or decline in cash flows. A company's cash flow is critical to credit analysis for it speaks directly to the heart of financial flexibility. A company with an expected increase in cash flow is more likely to be able to maintain interest payments without any significant impact to its bottom line.

The following facets could be thought of as "red flags": These are areas to be carefully monitored by the wary-eyed analyst using the qualitative approach to credit analysis.

Future Growth. Now that we have addressed the importance of economic cycles, we need to turn our attention to the specific company:

> Is the growth (measured by financial data, market share, or product impact) of the company expected to increase and be maintained at a high level or is a stable, no-growth scenario forecasted?

In a fast-growth company, the analyst needs to calculate whether the capacity needed to meet product demand can be easily financed is, without any serious impact to the company's financial flexibility. Whereas in the slow-growth company, the question then becomes: "Is there a movement toward industry consolidation and diversification?"* The company in the fast-growing condition is more likely to experience a credit improvement than one in a slow-growth condition.

Industry Analysis. Once again, as we saw in equity analysis, the work of Michael Porter (1985) is very critical to the understanding of the industry environment in the credit analysis arena. How competitive is the industry in question? Are the players out to gain market share at the expenses of profits? Is the industry trending toward oligopoly (consolidation)—small company's vulnerability to large company's appetite fueled by notions of economy of scale?

Vertical Integration. A company that controls its factors of production has a major competitive advantage within the industry. This control is

---

* F. Fabozzi, *Handbook of Fixed Income Securities* (3rd ed.), (Homewood, Il: Irwin, 1991).

typically witnessed in companies that are vertically integrated, that is, in control of the costs of production inputs. Also companies that are not self-sufficient (with regard to input factors) but are sufficiently powerful in its industry to pass along increased costs are in a strong position.

Regulatory Environment. The threat of regulation within an industry can ruin the management's best-laid plans. The investor needs to ascertain the direction (trend) of the regulatory environment and the subsequent effect of this regulation on the profitability of the particular company. In some instances, it may prove to be an interesting strategy to be ahead of the curve with regard to regulatory affairs. Using the example of environmental legislation, a company could receive a valuation premium for socially conscious behavior as well as the market realization that the company is a "clean" leader in the industry.

Quality of Earnings

Earnings quality could be seen as a proxy for conservatism within the reported earnings of a company. The following are considered to be factors that an investor would deem as being the characteristics required in a company's earnings report for it to be seen as of high quality:

- ✔ Use of LIFO inventory accounting if prices are increasing.
- ✔ Bad-debt reserves that are high relative to past credit losses.
- ✔ Use of accelerated depreciation methods and short lives so that the noncash expense is exhausted quickly thereby not affecting earnings for any lengthy period.
- ✔ Rapid write-off of goodwill and other intangibles.
- ✔ Expensing (rather than depreciating) start-up costs of new operations.
- ✔ Conservative assumptions (employee attrition rate, pension plan asset growth, new hiring growth, etc.) used for employee benefit plans.
- ✔ Established adequate reserves for lawsuits and other contingencies.
- ✔ Conservative revenue recognition methods.
- ✔ Clear and adequate disclosures.

Source: G. I. White, A. C. Sondhi, and D. Fried, *The Analysis and Use of Financial Statements* (New York: Wiley, 1994), p. 1127.

Accounting Practices. Here we are looking for the unusual—the questionable accounting technique—to determine the type (liberal or conservative) of accounting management that could be expected going forward. When applying the Generally Accepted Accounting Procedures (GAAP) standards, each company has a margin within it which it can report its accounting data. A company that reports on the more conservative side of this margin is expected to receive a premium from the analyst when judging the financial wherewithal; consequently, the company that reports on the more liberal side is expected to receive a discounted value. This premium and discount speaks directly to the issue of quality of earnings—the idea that the company on the conservative side is more likely to be forthright with management, report consistently better financial data, and have stronger operating cash flow (earnings before interest, taxes, depreciation, and amortization).

RATING AGENCIES

The primary rating agencies—Standard & Poor's (S&P) and Moody's—have (separately) developed their own rating definitions (Table 6.1) to provide investors with an insight to the overall creditworthiness of a particular company (throughout this section the entity referred to as the "company" could also be considered to be a municipality or related agency). Creditworthiness is typically defined as the possibility that a company would default on its interest or principal payments given the probability that adverse business or industry conditions could result in financial difficulties. Credit is a two-way street; one needs to evaluate not only the ability of a specific company to pay its bills, but also the probability that some outside forces could impact this ability.

    Five rating agencies provide credit ratings on debt issues: Standard & Poor's Corporation, Moody's Investor Service, Duff & Phelps, Inc., Fitch Investors Service, and McCarthy, Crisanti & Maffei, Inc. Moody's and Standard & Poor's dominate the industry with each representing approximately 2000 companies. Four of the five credit agencies use letter rankings to designate their respective credit ratings. S&P and Fitch utilize the AAA rating to reflect the highest rating and D for their lowest rating (currently in default). Moody's letter rankings are a bit different (I guess they want to differentiate themselves, eh?) ranging between Aaa (highest rating) to C (lowest) whereas Duff & Phelps' (changed from a numerical ranking system in June 1989) ratings range between AAA to CCC.

THE RATING PROCESS

The process of getting a credit rating begins as you might think it would—someone (a buyer) requires the services of another (the seller) and will be charged a price for such services. In the case of credit analysis, the buyer is the company looking for a credit rating on new issuance of debt from the provider of such services, namely the credit agency. If a company desires a credit rating on an issue, they apply to the rating agency, which in turn will assign a cadre of their analysts to investigate the entire company, its industry (competitive position, etc.) and the possibility of different economic scenarios affecting the company's ability to service its debt. The agency would levy an initiation fee (similar to a retainer) of between $5,000 and $20,000 for which the company would have the issue reviewed periodically during its life (until maturity or call) and at least one formal review annually. It is important to realize that the fee charged by the credit rating agency pertains to only a specific issue and not to the company itself. It stands to reason, however, that a company rated AA for an issuance today would carry the same rating several weeks later (for a new issuance), unless something changes within the company's operating structure and business.

Once a company has contracted a rating agency, it then becomes the job of the agency to have their analysts examine the company's operations, personnel, and competitive strategy as well as financial statements. In addition, the company's forward-looking business statements (projections and pro forma statements) are most critical in the credit analysis field. Getting a feel for the ability of management (are they overly optimistic or more conservative with their projections?) would allow the credit analyst a strong leg up with the task ahead.

The rating agencies have always suggested that their credit ratings are more a function of the professional judgment of their analysts than of some mechanical, mathematical equation. If you think about it, this makes a lot of business sense; if credit rating was a simple exercise of number crunching then who would really need an expensive analyst's recommendation—companies could simply calculate the ratios themselves. By keeping the credit rating process a mystery (the actual criteria are not disclosed), the rating agency can maintain the comparative advantages of their business operations.

Now, assume that the company doesn't agree with the rating agency's opinion; the company has the option to appeal the rating. This appeal process would incorporate the issuer, rating agency as well as the underwriter (their fee is dependent on getting the deal done) in a negotiation process.

During this negotiation process, changes would be offered to permit the rating agency's improved rating. These changes would mostly be focused on alterations to the actual offering memorandum (terms of the offering) with special attention paid to payment terms and restrictive covenants. In a successful negotiation process, was the changes suggested and agreed by both (issuer & underwriter) parties satisfy the rating agency so as to allow a favorable rating.

Why does a company desire a credit rating? In a perfect world (to finance theorists, a world where all information is readily available and fully digested or understood by the investing public), there would be no need for credit ratings because investors would be fully aware of a company's prospects. This theory is not entirely practical, however, and therefore corporations require this "third party endorsement" to entice capital investment. In addition, other benefits of credit ratings are the breadth of the coverage and the easy access to the ratings as well as their near universal acceptance. Ultimately, the reason for a credit ratings is that other issues carry a rating and therefore, each company needs to compete for this "pool" of capital on a level playing field. From an individual investor's point-of-view, the first question a fixed income investor would often ask would concern the issue's credit rating. Control of this pool of capital is tied to the underlying credit rating of a particular issue; hence the bane of existence for the rating agencies.

The threat of a credit rating downgrade is not a couched threat but quite a real one with major implications for the company. If an issue is downgraded, its market price is sure to be negatively affected, and consequently, the issuing company's debt service of subsequent debt offerings will be increased. This increase in debt service can impede a company's financial situation as well as its level of flexibility. A downgrade below the investment grade dividing line of BBB- or Baa3 (Moody's), may find the corporation without the all-important institutional market for its paper (downward pressure on the debt's price could be demonstrated due to institutional selling). Some institutions and fiduciary funds are prohibited, either by policy or legal constraints, from participating in non-investment-grade investments thereby removing this major buyer of debt from the pool of capital of a non-investment-grade issuer. Less demand for a good or service will, invariably; lead to a lower price; in this case, the lower price is reflected in higher yield that the issuer must pay to attract capital.

As in the portfolio management decisions of the Treasury market for the timing of bond purchases due to anticipation of future interest rates (i.e., to buy when there are expectations of decreasing interest rates and to sell with expected increases in rates), the corporate bond market also has a specific methodology. This methodology, while also partially dependent on interest rate forecasts, has the further constraint of anticipating changes in credit quality. Corporate bond investors would make a forecast of credit quality trends within a specific sector (e.g., industrial, consumer non-durable, financial) and therefore quantify the consequent spreads deserved above their risk-free Treasury counterparts. For example, if the yield spread (between 30-year Treasury) of a current 30-year, BB-rated financial sector bond is 165 basis points (the Treasury may yield 7% and the corporate bond 8.65%, or a difference of 1.65%), but the sector has a historical spread of 120 basis points, then it could be rationalized that this bond would be inexpensively priced. To complete this analysis, however, the specifics of the industry and the particular issue need to be examined carefully. Essentially, tight (versus historical averages) spreads imply strength in the sector and consequently a favorable outlook, while wide spreads would indicate an unfavorable outlook.

How Can Investor Keep Apprised of Potential Changes in Credit Ratings?

The rating agencies have recently engaged in the dissemination of rating change information through the practice of issuing a "watch list"—a compilation of securities that the agency is currently reviewing, for either upgrade or downgrade due to newly released external information. For example, if ABC Corp. was rated AA+ by S&P and last night the company announced a major acquisition that is expected to significantly increase their debt amount as well impact their current cash flow, the rating agency would be expected to post ABC on the watch list as a possible downgrade. This possible downgrade release is made to the public and is readily available to all investors.

Brokerage companys also fill the gap in the area of fixed income research. Most major companys as well as boutiques pride themselves on their research capabilities and performance records. Several annual surveys (Institutional Investor's All Star List being most prominent) rank the best individual analysts in particular fields as well as the company with the greatest tally of these "All Star Analysts." The competition among the research departments of the major companies is intense, each attempting to vie for the high spot on the survey. Bidding wars have broken out between companies attempting to buy the employment contracts of top-notch analysts who begin to feel more and more like baseball free agents than capitalistic detectives. I recall one instance a few years ago where a highly respected analyst jumped ship to a competitor only to jump back the very next day for his old company's counteroffer. As the story goes, the previous company's research director waited outside the analyst's new office building to present the counteroffer. Upon accepting the offer, on the street outside the building, the analyst proceeded directly back to his old company's building sending for his briefcase and personal belongings a week later.

While much of this fixed income research is provided to the company's institutional clientele (those are the biggest buyers of fixed income debt), it is obtainable for the asking through your representative at the company. This suggests an important commentary on the freedom of information currently available to investors: "If it is out there it can be gotten."

BASICS OF BONDS

Definitions

As the nomenclature suggests, a fixed income security, is just that—a security that generates a fixed cash flow. The following definitions attempt to organize the quantitative factors found in a fixed income security.

> **Coupon.** This represents the percentage paid to the security owner as a periodic (typically semiannually) cash flow. This cash flow is calculated by multiplying the stated coupon and the bond's par amount. For example, if a bond is offered (in the market) at $1020 (quoted as 102) with a coupon of 8%, the annual cash flow that is generated would be $80; (note: a bond's par amount is typically $1000).
>
> **Price.** A bond's maturity price is usually $1000 and this price will fluctuate according to market conditions. The inverse relationship between a bond and its yield is best described by the actions of a seesaw—as the price goes up, the yield goes down and vice versa. This makes sense: The more money you need to pay up front (to buy the bond) the more that price will reduce your return (known as yield).
>
> **Current Yield.** This is simply the cash flow generated divided by the price paid for the bond. This ratio is reflected as a percentage and permits the buyer of the security to evaluate the cash flow generation.
>
> **Yield to Maturity.** Unlike the current yield, the yield to maturity calculation calculates the fixed income security's return using the

security's maturity value as an ending cash flow. The yield to maturity (YTM) calculation is simply an internal rate of return (IRR) equation, where the price paid for the bond is the initial, negative outflow, the coupon cash flows represent the periodic inflows, and the maturity value is the final value at termination.

What Is a Bond?

A bond, in its vernacular form, is an agreement between two persons and this agreement, in its financial form, relates to the repayment of borrowed money at some future date (maturity date). So a bond, just as it sounds, is one person's promise to do something (repay borrowed funds) within a given amount of time.

This agreement is detailed in a legal document known as an *indenture,* which defines the rights and obligations of the borrower and the lender with respect to a bond issue. The credit analyst would carefully examine the indenture as part of his credit review searching for any provisions that would make the issue more likely to be paid on a timely basis. These provisions, seen as safeguards to the lender, can cover such areas as additional debt issuance (the lender would want to limit the borrower's ability to increase their outstanding debt until their bond is extinguished), sinking fund requirements (moneys escrowed by the borrower to assure future repayments), and sale and leaseback transactions (protects the lender from the borrower's sale or lease of assets that would be viewed as security to the lender).

Types of Bonds

The following represents a brief list of some of the more popular types of bond issues currently available in the market.

High Yield Bonds. The notoriety of these previously described "junk bonds" has somewhat waned since the healing of the Drexel and Milken era, and now these bonds are seen more as an investment than as the medium of choice of corporate raiders and takeover specialists. Typically, bonds that are rated below a "B" are considered in this category although some investors may prefer a simpler delineation—investment grade, those rated AAA to BBB-; and high yield, those rated below BBB-. Diversification, among industries as well as specific issues, is the most critical element in high yield bonds investing. With a well-diversified portfolio, the investor is less subjected to the vagaries of a specific industry and the potential default risk, as well as the liquidity issues that exist in smaller, less frequently traded offerings. Due to the heavy emphasis on the potential turnaround of the company in question, high yield bonds are more often analyzed as an equity issue than as a bond. The typical high yield bond analyst would need to focus on the equity fundamentals instead of the credit analysis.

Municipal Bonds. This type of fixed income security permits the issuer (municipality, agency of government; highway, bridge, mass transit, or tunnel projects) to raise capital at a lower rate due to the tax-free cash flow generated. Because of this government subsidy, investors (especially those in high tax brackets) have enjoyed a higher after-tax return than otherwise may be available (on an after-tax basis) on taxable securities. To evaluate between these different securities, an investor needs to calculate the taxable equivalent yield (TEY):

$$TEY = \frac{\text{Tax free yield}}{(100\% - \text{Tax bracket})}$$

Convertible Bonds. A convertible is a hybrid security, somewhere between an equity and a bond. The holder of a convertible receives a periodic cash flow (represented by the coupon) as well as the ability to exchange the bonds into common stock at some given exchange rate (number of shares per bond).

Example

Consider the following convertible bond issue:

Coupon:	7%
Maturity:	10 yrs.
Current market price/bond:	$1050
Current market price of common:	$55
Conversion ratio:	15.75
Dividend on common/share:	$1.00

The conversion ratio represents the number of shares of common stock that each bond can be exchanged for within the given period of the bond (maturity date). The premium (or discount) that the convertible bond is currently selling at is calculated by simply multiplying the conversion ratio by the current stock price (to ascertain the current value of conversion) and comparing this value to the bond's current price. If converted, each bond would result in 15.75 shares of common, each valued at $55 per share for a total value of $866.25, which is a $183.75 discount to the current value of the bond. Furthermore, the bond issue is currently providing a higher amount of current cash flow (7%) versus the common stock (1.82%). In dollar terms, the cash flow generated on the bond is currently $70 per bond, whereas the common stock would only generate $15.75 per each bond converted. It would seem imprudent and unjustified for an investor to convert his bond holdings at this time (while shares are trading at $55).

TABLE 6.1 Standard & Poor's Corporate and Municipal Rating Definitions

DEBT

A Standard & Poor's corporate or municipal debt rating is a current assessment of the creditworthiness of an obligator with respect to a specific obligation. This assessment may take into consideration obligators such as guarantors, insurers, or lessees.

The debt rating is not a recommendation to purchase, sell or hold a security, inasmuch as it does not comment as to market price or suitability for a particular investor.

The ratings are based on current information furnished by the issuer or obtained by Standard & Poor's from other sources it considers reliable. Standard & Poor's does not perform an audit in connection with any rating and may, on occasion, rely on unaudited financial information. The ratings may be changed, suspended or withdrawn as a result of changes in, or unavailability of, such information, or based on other circumstances.

The ratings are based, in varying degrees, on the following considerations:

I. Likelihood of default-capacity and willingness of the obligator as to the timely payment of interest and repayment of principal in accordance with the terms of the obligation;

II. Nature of and provisions of the obligation;

III. Protection afforded by, and relative position of, the obligation in the event of bankruptcy, reorganization or other arrangement under the laws of bankruptcy and other laws affecting creditor's rights.

(continued)

TABLE 6.1 (Continued)

AAA Debt rated "AAA" has the highest rating assigned by Standard & Poor's. Capacity to pay interest and repay principal is extremely strong.

AA Debt rated "AA" has a very strong capacity to pay interest and repay principal and differs from the higher rated issues only in small degree.

A Debt rated "A" has a strong capacity to pay interest and repay principal although it is somewhat more susceptible to the adverse effects of changes in circumstances and economic conditions than debt in higher rated categories.

BBB Debt rated "BBB" is regarded as having an adequate capacity to pay interest and repay principal. Whereas it normally exhibits adequate protection parameters, adverse economic conditions or changing circumstances are more likely to lead to a weakened capacity to pay interest and repay principal for debt in this category than in higher rated categories.

BB, B, CCC, CC, C Debt rated "BB," "B," "CCC," "CC," and "C" is regarded, on balance, as predominantly speculative with respect to capacity to pay interest and repay principal in accordance with the terms of the obligation. "BB" indicates the lowest degree of speculation and "C" the highest degree of speculation. While such debt will likely have some quality and protective characteristics, these are outweighed by large uncertainties or major risk exposures to adverse conditions.

BB Debt rated "BB" has less near-term vulnerability to default than other speculative issues. However, it faces major ongoing uncertainties or exposure to adverse business, financial, or economic conditions which could lead to inadequate capacity to meet timely interest and principal payments. The "BB" rating category is also used for debt subordinated to senior debt that is assigned an actual or implied "BBB"—rating.

B Debt rated "B" has a greater vulnerability to default but currently has the capacity to meet interest payments and principal repayments. Adverse business, financial, or economic conditions will likely impair capacity or willingness to pay interest and repay principal. The "B" rating category is also used for debt subordinated to senior debt that is assigned an actual or implied "BB" or "BB"—rating.

CCC Debt rated "CCC" has a currently identifiable vulnerability to default, and is dependent upon favorable business, financial, and economic conditions to meet timely payment of interest and repayment of principal. In the event of adverse business, financial, or economic conditions, it is not likely to have the capacity to pay interest and repay principal. The

TABLE 6.1 (Continued)

"CCC" rating category is also used for debt subordinated to senior debt that is assigned an actual or implied "B" or "B"—rating.

CC The rating "CC" is typically assigned to debt subordinated to senior debt that is assigned an actual or implied "CCC" rating.

C The rating "C" is typically applied to debt subordinated to senior debt which is assigned an actual or implied "CCC"—debt rating. The "C" rating may be used to cover a situation where a bankruptcy position has been filed, but debt service payments are continued.

C! The rating "C!" is reserved for income bonds on which no interest is being paid.

D Debt rated "D" is in payment default. The "D" rating category is used when interest payments or principal payments are not made on the date due even if the applicable grace period has not expired, unless S&P believes that such payments will be made during such grace period. The "D" rating also will be used upon the filing of a bankruptcy position if debt service payments are jeopardized.

Plus (+) or Minus (–): The ratings from "AA" to "CCC" may be modified by the addition of a plus or minus sign to show relative standing within the major categories.

NR Indicates that no public rating has been requested, that there is insufficient information on which to base a rating, or that S&P does not rate a particular type of obligation as a matter of policy.

Debt Obligations of issuers outside the United States and its territories are rated on the same basis as domestic corporate and municipal issues. The ratings measure the creditworthiness of the obligator but do not take into account currency exchange and related uncertainties.

Bond Investment Quality Standards: Under present commercial bank regulations issued by the Comptroller of the Currency, bonds rated in the top four categories ("AAA," "AA," "A," "BBB," commercially known as "Investment Grade" ratings) are generally regarded as eligible for bank investment, in addition, the Legal Investment Laws of various states may impose certain rating or other standards for obligations eligible for investment by savings banks, trust companies, insurance companies and fiduciaries generally.

Source. Standard & Poor's Bond Guide. Reprinted with permission.

TABLE 6.2 Standard & Poor's Corporate & Government Bond Yield Index—by Rating

Weekly Averages / Monthly Averages

	*Treasury	INDUSTRIALS AAA	AA	A	BBB	BB+	*ELECTRIC AA	A	BBB	**U.S. GOV'T LONG TERM	INTER-MEDIATE	SHORT TERM	MUNI-CIPALS
Weekly Averages 1997													
August 26	6.59	7.07	7.19	7.36	7.58	8.32	7.33	7.35	7.69	6.73	6.40	6.02	5.50
August 19	6.41	6.89	7.00	7.17	7.40	8.11	7.10	7.14	7.46	6.62	6.25	5.91	5.45
August 12	6.61	7.08	7.20	7.36	7.58	8.24	7.27	7.34	7.67	6.72	6.37	5.99	5.51
August 5	6.42	6.88	6.99	7.16	7.39	8.08	7.02	7.09	7.39	6.54	6.22	5.94	5.41
Monthly Averages 1997													
August	6.51	6.98	7.10	7.26	7.49	8.19	7.18	7.23	7.55	6.65	6.31	5.96	5.47
July	6.44	6.92	7.02	7.19	7.45	7.88	7.07	7.13	7.42	6.56	6.21	5.92	5.41
June	6.70	7.20	7.29	7.47	7.73	8.23	7.39	7.42	7.72	6.86	6.49	6.16	5.60
May	6.89	7.40	7.48	7.67	7.93	8.52	7.62	7.63	7.98	7.04	6.71	6.51	5.71
April	6.98	7.48	7.56	7.74	7.99	8.57	7.75	7.76	8.12	7.17	6.85	6.68	5.88
March	6.81	7.13	7.39	7.57	7.84	8.38	7.60	7.62	7.97	7.05	6.68	6.29	5.78
February	6.48	7.00	7.06	7.25	7.54	8.17	7.25	7.27	7.63	6.81	6.37	5.98	5.63
January	6.66	7.17	7.24	7.43	7.73	8.30	7.45	7.48	7.85	6.93	6.40	5.90	5.72
1996													
December	6.36	6.91	6.98	7.17	7.50	8.08	7.14	7.19	7.63	6.70	6.17	5.73	5.62
November	6.29	6.82	6.88	7.06	7.39	7.94	7.00	7.07	7.53	6.58	6.03	5.61	5.59
October	6.64	7.16	7.23	7.42	7.72	8.35	7.42	7.47	7.91	6.92	6.38	5.85	5.71
September	6.96	7.49	7.55	7.77	8.07	8.67	7.77	7.84	8.30	7.19	6.68	6.15	5.66
August	6.72	7.25	7.34	7.54	7.87	8.46	7.48	7.58	8.02	6.98	6.46	5.90	5.72
July	6.95	7.49	7.58	7.78	8.11	8.68	7.75	7.82	8.25	7.14	6.69	6.16	5.91
June	7.05	7.56	7.67	7.86	8.21	8.77	7.87	7.92	8.34	7.25	6.76	6.24	6.03
May	6.87	7.39	7.52	7.72	8.08	8.62	7.72	7.78	8.20	7.09	6.53	6.03	5.98
April	6.70	7.22	7.39	7.58	7.95	8.47	7.60	7.66	8.14	6.98	6.39	5.93	5.93
March	6.41	6.95	7.10	7.29	7.70	8.13	7.38	7.44	7.91	6.75	6.11	5.67	5.82
February	5.96	6.51	6.61	6.76	7.10	7.71	6.95	6.99	7.52	6.37	5.58	5.10	5.45
January	5.79	6.30	6.43	6.62	6.99	7.71	6.68	6.75	7.29	6.12	5.45	5.13	5.42

Annual Ranges

	*Treasury	INDUSTRIALS AAA	AA	A	BBB	BB+	*ELECTRIC AA	A	BBB	**U.S. GOV'T LONG TERM	INTER-MEDIATE	SHORT TERM	MUNI-CIPALS
1996 High	7.12	7.63	7.74	7.93	8.29	8.84	7.91	7.99	8.42	7.36	6.86	6.29	6.14
1996 Low	5.71	6.11	6.21	6.31	6.62	7.22	6.60	6.66	7.20	6.08	5.32	4.84	5.32

Annual Ranges (continued)

	*Treasury	PUBLIC UTILITY A	BBB	INDUSTRIAL AA	A	BBB	BB+	BB	B	COMPOSITE AA	A	BBB	**U.S. GOV'T LONG TERM	INTER-MEDIATE	SHORT TERM	MUNI-CIPALS
1995 High	8.55	8.72	9.32	8.44	8.54	8.91	9.46	10.40	11.74	8.54	8.81	9.39	7.98	7.82	7.75	6.68
1995 Low	6.60	7.97	8.11	8.59	8.64	7.69	7.83	10.86	10.49	6.82	6.94	7.97	6.11	5.52	5.28	5.40
1994 High	8.75	8.87	9.53	8.46	8.64	9.01	9.69	10.41	11.82	8.69	8.94	9.60	8.22	7.83	7.64	7.03
1994 Low	7.26	7.82	8.21	8.66	8.19	7.82	8.06	10.06	10.06	7.23	7.89	8.14	6.15	4.90	3.90	5.27
1993 High	8.34	9.03	8.77	8.12	8.21	8.60	9.03	9.88	11.19	8.23	8.63	8.82	7.35	6.14	4.57	6.22
1993 Low	7.28	7.99	7.65	8.16	8.21	7.48	7.35	10.37	10.37	7.26	7.73	7.50	5.75	4.63	3.63	5.23
1992 High	9.02	9.24	9.32	8.69	8.86	9.38	9.50	11.52	12.53	8.94	9.31	9.39	8.07	7.45	6.03	6.71
1992 Low	8.40	8.63	8.70	7.89	8.08	8.49	8.82	9.84	10.94	8.28	8.56	8.82	7.07	5.53	3.65	5.88
1991 High	9.54	9.75	9.99	9.14	9.55	9.89	11.83	12.58	20.53	9.54	9.80	10.86	8.70	8.13	7.20	7.15
1991 Low	8.77	8.93	8.93	8.05	8.25	8.87	9.13	10.60	12.87	8.51	8.90	9.03	7.36	6.32	5.03	6.50

* The Corporate Bond Index was replaced by a new index with a much broader scope. Yields are based on some, 2,100 securities with maturities of 15 years. The indices are compiled by Standard & Poor's Fixed Income Research Bond Comp (212-208-1199). Reprinted with permission.
** U.S. Government numbers are based on Wednesday close.

TABLE 6.3   Relationship between Ratings and Financial Ratios

KEY INDUSTRIAL FINANCIAL RATIOS

Three-Year (1988–1990) Medians	*AAA*	*AA*	*A*	*BBB*	*BB*	*B*	*CCC*
Pretax interest coverage (x)	11.08	9.43	4.65	3.16	1.91	0.88	0.63
Pretax fixed charge coverage including rents (x)	5.46	5.10	3.00	2.18	1.54	0.94	0.69
Pretax funds flow interest coverage (x)	13.65	11.65	6.65	4.97	3.00	1.59	1.22
Funds from operations/total debt (%)	82.90	74.20	45.60	31.70	18.70	8.40	7.00
Free operating cash flow/total debt (%)	24.80	23.40	8.70	3.40	(0.50)	(3.40)	(4.20)
Pretax return on permanent capital (%)	26.20	21.10	16.70	13.00	11.10	7.40	8.10
Operating income/sales (%)	21.60	15.90	14.90	12.00	12.50	9.30	12.30
Long-term debt/ capitalization (%)	12.90	16.60	29.50	39.40	45.70	63.50	79.30
Total debt/capitalization incl. short-term debt (%)	25.10	27.60	37.30	48.00	54.80	73.70	85.50
Total debt/capitalization incl. short-term debt (including 8 times rents [%])	38.20	38.70	50.90	58.60	65.50	78.50	87.20

Source. Standard & Poor's. Reprinted with permission.

PROBLEM SET
CREDIT ANALYSIS

Question 1

Use the Parrot Computer data (Appendix B) as reference to solve the following problems. Compute the following ratios:

Debt-to-equity

Return on equity (ROE)

Return on assets (ROA)

Days' sales in cash

Payable period

Fixed asset turnover

Receivable collection period

Times-interest earned

Current

Acid test

Answer

Asset Utilization/Efficiency Ratios

Inventory turnover (ITO) = Cost of goods sold (COGS)/
Average inventory

$$= 4000/700 = 5.71x$$

Fixed asset turnover = Sales/Fixed assets = 6000/1200

$$= 5x$$

A/R collection period = Account receivables/Sales per day

$$= 200/(6000/365) = 12.16x$$

Performance Ratios

ROE = Net income/Equity = 960/1750 = 54.86%

ROA = Net income/Assets = 960/2400 = 40%

Liquidity Ratios

Days' sales in cash = Cash/Sales per day = 300/(6000/365)

$$= 18.25 \text{ days}$$

Payable period = A/P/Credit purchases per day

$$= 400/(4000/365) = 36.50 \text{ days}$$

Current ratio = Current assets/Current liabilities

$$= 1200/400 + 100 = 2.4$$

Acid test = Current assets − Inventory/Current liabilities

$$= 500/500 = 1$$

Leverage Ratios and Coverage Ratios

$$\text{Debt-to-equity} = \text{Debt/Total equity} = 250/1750 = 14.29\%$$

$$\text{Times interest earned} = \text{EBIT/Interest expense} = 1700/100 = 17x$$

Question 2

Assume the following matrix for credit rating:

	AAA	AA	A	BBB	BB
Debt-to-equity	9%	15%	25%	35%	50%
Current ratio	2	1.5	1	.81	.60
Inventory turnover	15x	10x	8x	5x	3.5x
Return on equity	55%	40%	25%	12%	8%

Based on the preceding information, make a recommendation for a credit rating for Parrot.

Answer

For each of the following ratios the expected rating, according the given matrix, is as follows:

Debt-to-equity	Between AA & AAA
Current	Between AAA
Inventory turnover	BBB
Return on equity	AAA

Out of the preceding, only the inventory-Turn Over-ratio is not in the AA range. The ROE ratio is an important profitability measure, a high level of volatility also is associated with this net income-based calculation. To this end, a prudent credit analyst may be inclined to further investigate the "meat" behind this ROE calculation. Was net income affected by a one-time gain? What has been the trend of growth in the company's top and bottom line? Is the company enjoying a less-than-normal tax rate due to some external factors? Based on the preceding data, a rating of "AA+" would seem most appropriate for Parrot Computers, Inc.

Question 3

The most critical aspect of a municipal revenue bond ratings is:

    A. The management of the agency seeking the financing.

    B. The demographic shifts occurring in the municipality.

    C. The cash flow expectations from the project being undertaken.

    D. The annual tax revenues of the municipality.

Answer

The correct answer is (c). The most important factor in a revenue (not a general obligation) issue is the expected cash flows that are expected from the project. This makes intuitive sense from the standpoint that the revenue bond does not carry any taxing authority and is a contract between the agency and the investor. Each of the other three choices can be considered factors involved in the evaluation of general obligation (GO) municipal bonds.

Question 4

A New York City General Obligation bond is currently trading at par and has a coupon of 7%. What is the taxable equivalent yield that an investor needs to receive (assume a 40% total tax rate) to be equally compensated?

Answer

The bond is trading at par which means that the market price is currently $1000 per bond and the cash flow generated is $70 per bond (7% coupon) making the yield 7%. The tax equivalent yield is calculated using the following equation:

$$TEY = \frac{\text{Tax free yield}}{(100\% - \text{Tax rate})}$$

So given the 7% tax-free yield, we would require a taxable yield (assuming the 40% tax bracket) of 11.67% (7% divided by 60%).

Question 5

Which one of the following typically is not true of an insured municipal bond?

A. Insured bonds yield less than uninsured bonds

B. The insurance company is obligated to make all payments of principal and interest in a timely fashion if the bond falls into default.

C. The insurance can be canceled in the event the issuer fails to meet certain standards.

D. Insured bonds trade at a higher price than those bonds of an identical uninsured issue.

Answer

The answer is (c). The insurance carried on a municipal bond is noncancelable and represents a one-time payment (premium) to the insurance company at the time of issuance. Insured bonds are higher priced (vs. uninsured issues) and therefore yield less than uninsured bonds (choices (a) and (d)). The duties described in (b) is typical of an insured bond issue.

Question 6

Myron was called into a meeting with the management's of Kraft and Philip Morris. It was recently announced that Philip Morris intends to acquire Kraft. What areas of interest should Myron be concerned with in order to ascertain a fair assessment of the qualitative factors affecting the credit standing of Philip Morris? (Adapted from Chartered Financial Analyst Level 2 Exam-1989; reprinted with permission.)

Answer

The framework that a credit analyst needs to examine when speaking to the management of a company in an acquisition mode is as follows:

1. *Economic cyclically.* How closely do the tobacco, food, and beverage industries track GNP? Is tobacco consumption more tied to

sociopolitical and regulatory factors than to economic ones? In Jane Howe's (1991) chapter on credit analysis in the *Handbook of Fixed Income Securities,* she states,

The economic cyclically of an industry is the first variable an analyst should consider in reviewing an industry. The growth in earnings per share (EPS) of a company should be measured against the growth trend of the industry. Major deviations from the industry trend should be the focus of further analysis. Some industries may be somewhat dependent on the general economic growth but be more sensitive to demographic changes. Other industries are sensitive to fluctuations of interest rates. In general, however, the earnings of few industries perfectly correlate with one economic statistic. Not only are industries sensitive to many economic variables, but often various segments within a company or an industry move countercyclically, or at least with different lags in relation to the general economy. Therefore, the performance of each of its segments must be compared with the performance of the subindustry.

2. *Growth prospects.* Are the businesses of Philip Morris growing at steady pace, or is growth slipping? Will European consumption of cigarettes begin to slow as they have in the United States due to no-smoking regulations? Related to the issue of growth, is there consolidation going on in tobacco, food, or beverages? Howe (1991) queries,

Is the growth of the industry projected to increase and be maintained at a high level, or is growth expected to be stable? Each growth scenario has implications for a company. In the case of a fast-growth industry, how much capacity is needed to meet demand, and how will this capacity be financed? In the case of slow-growth industries, is there a movement toward diversification and/or consolidation within the industry? A company operating within a fast-growing industry often has a better potential for credit improvement than does a company whose industry's growth prospects are below average.

3. *Research and development expenses.* R&D is not a big item in the tobacco, food, or beverage industries, although some dollars are spent on new product development. In general, it is safe to characterize

these businesses as having a stable product line that will not vary much over time. Howe (1991) states,

> The broad assessment of growth prospects is tempered by a third variable—the research and development expenditures required to maintain or expand market position. Although a company may be situated well in an industry, if it does not have the financial resources to maintain a technological lead, or at least expend a sufficient amount of money to keep technologically current, its position is likely to deteriorate in the long run. In the short run, however, a company whose R&D expenditures are consistently below industry averages may produce above-average results because of expanded margins.

4. *Competition*. How competitive are these industries? Are there players who are out to gain market share at the expense of profits? Is the industry trending toward oligopoly, which would make small companies in the industry vulnerable to the economies of scale the larger companies bring to bear? Howe (1991) states,

> Competition within an industry also directly relates to the market structure of an industry and has implications for pricing flexibility. An unregulated monopoly is in an enviable position in that it can price its goods at a level that will maximize profits. Most industries encounter some free market forces and must price their goods in relation to supply and demand for their goods as well as the price charged for similar goods. In an oligopoly, a pricing leader is not uncommon. A concern arises when a small company is an industry that is trending toward oligopoly. In this environment, the small company's costs of production may be higher than those of the industry leaders, and yet it may have to conform to the pricing of the industry leaders. In the extreme, a price war could force the smaller companies out of the business.

5. *Sources of supply*. Are these businesses vulnerable to the cost of production inputs? Or is it the market position of Philip Morris such that it can easily pass on the higher raw material costs? Howe (1991) states,

> The market structure of an industry and its competitive forces have a direct impact on the fifth industry variable—

sources of supply of major production components. (A company that controls its factors of production is in a superior position.) A company that is not self-sufficient in its factors of production but is sufficiently powerful in its industry to pass along increased costs is also in an enviable position.

6. *Degree of regulation.* Tobacco has faced some regulatory hurdles in the past, as has the food and beverage to a lesser degree. What does the future hold in this area? Howe (1991) states,

   The analyst should not be concerned with the existence or absence of regulation per se, but rather with the direction of the regulation and the effect it has on the profitability of the company.

7. *Labor.* Are these businesses heavily unionized? What is the status of labor-management relations? Howe (1991) states,

   The labor situation is also important in non-unionized companies, particularly those whose labor situation is tight. The more labor intensive an industry, the more significance the labor situation assumes.

8. *Accounting.* Do these businesses have any unique accounting practices that warrant special attention? Howe (1991) states,

   An analyst should become familiar with industry practices before proceeding with a company analysis. Also important is whether a company is liberal or conservative in applying the Generally Accepted Accounting Principles (GAAP). The norm of an industry should be ascertained, and then the analyst should be sure to analyze comparable figures.

PART THREE

PORTFOLIO MANAGEMENT

We have gone through the maze of financial analysis that is taught in most business schools. While business schools are more in-depth than our discussion, the basics are the same. We have learned, used, and understood, in a format that is both practical and realistic, the tenets of financial analysis. These tenets are clearly applicable to the task of valuing a financial security. But what about developing a portfolio? Can financial analysis provide today's investor with the all-important fundamentals of portfolio management? An analogy that would probably suffice is something along the lines of the following: financial analysis is the laboratory work of a biotechnology enterprise while portfolio management is the corporate presentation that seeks venture capital backing.

In Chapter 7, we uncover many important issues that plague even the most savvy investor. The importance of a developed Investment Policy Statement and Asset Allocation Model, the emotions involved in the investment management process and the ethical issues encompassing the financial services industry. Where the first two parts provide the framework for the evaluation of a security, this last part discusses how a given security is placed in a portfolio. What is the incremental expected return or risk of this additional security? Are there some diversification benefits to the addition of this security? What is the optimal asset allocation strategy given this investor's Investment Policy?

Although the topics that comprise this section are less focused on the quantitative, empirical constructs of the previous chapters, the tenets of portfolio management are clearly critical to the final success of the investor. The Investment Management Process is the four-step process that each investor should muddle-through in order to attain a better understanding of the basic construction of any given portfolio. It is this four-step process that any pro-active investor is subjected to in order to attempt the fulfillment of any stated investment goal. There are many quantitative formats that also permit a full understanding of the background that comprise this process—correlation's between assets, The Modern Portfolio Theory and the Security Market Line—each of which are discussed in Chapter 7.

Last, several appendices are offered to further the education of the practitioner in the tenets of portfolio management. The ethical issues of the financial services industry are discussed so that an investor may better understand the playing field that regulates today's investment services industry. It is the basics of these ethical issues that make today's investor more empowered than ever before; for the underlying fundamental of ethical behavior in the financial services industry is the creation of a level playing field. With this level playing field today's investor can compete in markets where they could never before—herein lays the mantra of this new era of investing: Become Pro-active and stay Empowered.

Chapter

7

The Investment
Management Process

In this chapter, you will learn:

- ✔ Investment management, a four-step process.
- ✔ The importance of diversification—Modern portfolio (Markowitz) theory.
- ✔ Ethical issues in the investment services industry.

Investment management was first practiced in the 1920s, when it was considered a service of bank trust departments and a few specialty firms. At that time, investment management was the province of the very rich. Not only did the Carnegies, Mellons, and Rockefellers go to banks to have their money managed, they established their own banks.

After World War II, corporations and the public sector began to create pension funds for their employees. These funds soon accumulated millions of dollars of assets, and began to use full-time professionals both to keep the fund safe and provide for a modicum of growth. As the need for professional investment management grew, an industry of advisory firms emerged.

Since the mid-1970s, investment management has grown to address the needs of individual investors as well. The expansion of the managed money business has caused a proliferation of firms specializing in investment management employing well over 22,000 registered investment advisers. Choosing the right investment adviser is a crucial decision.

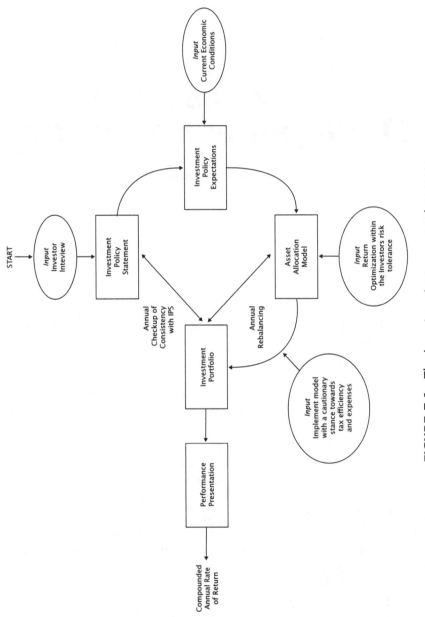

FIGURE 7.1 The investment management process.

This chapter introduces the investment management methodology practiced by many financial advisers. As Figure 7.1 illustrates, four distinct steps make up the investment management process:

1. Ascertainment of the investor's needs and constraints.
2. Understanding of capital markets.
3. Portfolio construction and implementation.
4. Account and manager monitoring.

Although the steps are distinct (with their individual functions and expertise), together they form a process and by definition need to be viewed and operated as such.

STEP 1. INVESTOR DIAGNOSIS—ASCERTAINING ONE'S NEEDS AND CONSTRAINTS

The primary step for the investor is to determine the specific needs and constraints in his investment goals. Questions asked in a medical practice such as "Where does it hurt? How long have you been feeling this way?" and "Are you allergic to any medications?" provide a useful model for the investor's self-assessment of his investment posture. It is easy to see just how critical the interview can be.

In the investment management practice, the client diagnosis, or interview, is also crucial; for only with clearly defined investment objectives and constraints can the professional perform his task effectively. So it is with the individual investor. For example, if Mr. and Mrs. Jones were to open an account with broker Bob Smith without first identifying their requirements, it could lead to disaster: Smith might invest the funds for growth and later learn that the Joneses are retired and require a monthly income to subsidize their living expenses. This exaggerated example highlights the critical need for both professional and client to be proactive in the investment management process. If the professional does not know enough to ascertain his client's needs and constraints, then the client should make them known and then probably seek further counsel.

The *Investment Policy Statement,* as shown in the box "Write Your Investment Policy Statement," enhances the ability of the financial services professional to recognize and better manage a client's expectations. These written guidelines will foster a longer, more productive relationship between financial advisor and client. Although the structure illustrated in

Write Your Investment Policy Statement

Objectives

Return. It is usually advised to align total return objective to some recognizable benchmark. Typically, this benchmark ranges from the total return of the S&P index (Standard & Poor's broad index of 500 actively traded stocks) for those portfolios mostly interested in a growth objective; to Lehman Brothers' Bond Indices for those portfolios whose objective would be more focused on income; or lastly, the CPI (Consumer Price Index) for those portfolios mostly concerned with preserving purchasing power.

Risk. Risk is measured, in investment finance, as the volatility around the mean of not simply one asset in a portfolio but of the entire portfolio's assets working together ("modern portfolio theory"). An investor should expect compensation, by means of a greater return, for any additional risk above the risk-free rate (assumed to be the Treasury bill rate) that he takes on in an investment. An investor needs to be aware of the critical trade-off between return and risk in the investment paradigm. Furthermore, time horizon (discussed next) also takes an important role in defining risk.

To measure accurately an investor's tolerance for risk, the investor must identify his level of comfort with negative market movements. Could the investor withstand negative account performance spanning more than two quarters? More than four quarters? For an extended period of time, given that this is often a trade-off for upside appreciation?

Constraints

Time Horizon. An investor's time horizon can range from one year to as many as several years, even (as in the case of many retirement plans) several decades. For the investor who is focused more on growth, it is recommended that a commitment (to a stated policy program) be made for at least one full market cycle (4–6 years). Investors whose time horizon may be less than that of a full market cycle could cushion any typical market declines by maintaining a high cash position.

Taxes. Taxes and legal issues are certainly categories that warrant professional advice. Each investor needs to examine tax issues carefully, for as the old adage goes, "It is not what you make but what you keep." There are, of course, portfolios such as tax-deferred pension accounts and IRAs, where tax issues are not a major consideration. The investment professional is expected to be aware of tax issues to maximize the after-tax efficiency of the portfolio. For example, in an IRA account the investments would typically be of the high portfolio turnover type that would maximize the tax-deferred growth.

Write Your Investment Policy Statement (Continued)

Legal Issues. Covered in this constraint are all statutes pertaining to the Employee Retirement Income Safety Act of 1974 (ERISA), which applies to pension and retirement accounts. In addition, the standards of prudence in investment management of all portfolios are fundamental to this constraint. Also covered in this constraint are any outstanding legal issues (divorce, estate planning lawsuits, etc.) that may affect the cash flows of the portfolio in question.

Liquidity. The immediate need for cash is always a constraint in the investment management process. Does the investor have other sources of emergency capital at his disposal to withstand any short-term necessities or would the portfolio be subjected to such withdrawals? Liquidity also pertains to the cash-flow generation that may be required by a particular policy statement.

Unique Issues. The catch-all category becomes very important when dealing with circumstances that may be specifically sensitive to the investor (children's educational needs, long-term care insurance concerns, etc.). In addition, certain investment restrictions are also carried in this constraint— such as social-conscious investing (no "sin" stocks, or only environmental sensitive companies), or American-only (non-international) investments.

---

this box is the most common form of the policy statement, it is not the only one. These statements can be written in almost any manner one chooses; however, the information described in the skeleton form provided here (objectives, risk and liquidity constraints, tax and legal issues, time horizon, unique issues) is typically required by the investment management community.

In the following case study, the Investment Policy Statement is demonstrated in a potentially real life circumstance. *Do you have an Investment Policy Statement for your investment account? Why not?* As will be seen later in this chapter, a well-defined IPS will go a long way to optimize a portfolio's return objectives without impeding on its constraints. This case study will teach the fundamentals of developing an Investment Policy Statement from which an investor could formulate an Asset Allocation Model (AAM) that is best suited to his individual needs. The AAM is the crux of the modern portfolio theory and is crucial to the individual investor who seeks the highest risk-adjusted return.

CASE STUDY: INVESTMENT POLICY STATEMENT FOR SUSAN FAIRFAX*

Introduction

Susan Fairfax is president of Reston Industries, a U.S.-based company whose sales are entirely domestic and whose shares are listed on the New York Stock Exchange. The following are additional facts concerning her current situation.

✔ Fairfax is single aged 58. She has no immediate family, no debts, and does not own a residence. She is in excellent health and covered by Reston-paid health insurance that continues after her expected retirement at age 65.

✔ Her base salary of $500,000/year, inflation-protected, is sufficient to support her present lifestyle, but can no longer generate any excess for savings.

✔ She has $2,000,000 of savings from prior years held in the form of short-term instruments.

✔ Reston awards key employees through a generous stock-bonus incentive plan, but provides no pension plan and pays no dividend.

✔ Fairfax's incentive plan participation has resulted in her ownership of Reston stock worth $10 million (current market value). The stock, received tax-free but subject to tax at a 35% rate (on entire proceeds) if sold, is expected to be held at least until her retirement.

✔ Her present level of spending and the current annual inflation of 4% are expected to continue after her retirement.

✔ Fairfax is taxed at 35% on all salary, investment income, and realized capital gains. Assume her composite tax rate will continue at this level indefinitely.

Fairfax's orientation is patient, careful, and conservative in all things. She has stated that an annual after-tax real total return of 3% would be completely acceptable for her if it was achieved in a context where an investment portfolio created from her accumulated savings was not subject to a decline of more than 10% in nominal terms in any given 12-month period.

---

*CFA® Exam questions are reprinted with permission. Copyright (1996), Association for Investment Management and Research, Charlottesville, VA. All rights reserved.

To obtain the benefits of professional assistance, she has approached two investment advisory firms—HH Counselors ("HH") and Coastal Advisors ("Coastal")—for recommendations on allocation of the investment portfolio to be created from her existing savings assets (the "Savings Portfolio") as well as for advice concerning investing in general.

    A. **Create** and **justify** an Investment Policy Statement for Fairfax based *only* on the information provided in the Introduction. Be specific and complete as to objectives and constraints. (An asset allocation is *not* required in answering this question.)

Guideline Answer

    A. An Investment Policy Statement for Fairfax based *only* on the information provided in the Introduction is shown below.

Overview. Fairfax is 58 years old and has seven years to go until a planned retirement. She has a fairly lavish lifestyle but few money worries: Her large salary pays all current expenses, and she has accumulated $2 million in cash equivalents from savings in previous years. Her health is excellent, and her health insurance coverage will continue after retirement and is employer paid. While Fairfax's job is a high-level one, she is not well versed in investment matters and has had the good sense to connect with professional counsel to get started on planning for her investment future, a future that is complicated by ownership of a $10 million block of company stock that, while listed on the NYSE, pays no dividends and has a zero-cost basis for tax purposes. All salary, investment income (except interest on municipal bonds), and realized capital gains are taxed to Fairfax at a 35% rate; this tax rate and a 4% inflation rate are expected to continue into the future. Fairfax would accept a 3% real, after-tax return from the investment portfolio to be formed from her $2 million in savings (the "Savings Portfolio") if that return could be obtained with only modest portfolio volatility (i.e., less than a 10% annual decline). She is described as being conservative in all things.

Objectives

    ✔ *Return requirement.* Fairfax's need for portfolio income begins seven years from now, at the date of retirement when her salary stops. The investment focus for her Savings Portfolio should be on growing the portfolio's value in the interim in a way that provides protection against loss of purchasing power. Her 3% real, after-tax return preference implies a gross total return requirement of at least 10.8%, assuming her investments are fully taxable (as is the case now) and assuming 4% inflation and a 35% tax rate. For Fairfax to maintain her current lifestyle, she would have to generate $500,000 \times (1.04)^7$, or $658,000, in annual income, inflation adjusted, when she retires. If the market value of Reston's stock does not change, and if she has been able to earn a 10.8% return on the Savings Portfolio (or 7% nominal after-tax return = $2,000,000 \times (1.07)^7 = $3,211,500$), she should accumulate $13,211,500 ($10 million in stock plus $3,211,500) by retirement age. To generate $658,000, a return on $13,211,500 of 5.0% would be needed.

✔ *Risk tolerance.* From the information provided, Fairfax is quite risk averse, indicating she does not want to experience a decline of more than 10% in the value of the Savings Portfolio in any given year. This would indicate that the portfolio should have below-average risk exposure to minimize its downside volatility. In terms of overall wealth, she could afford to take more than average risk, but because of her preferences and the nondiversified nature of the total portfolio, a below-average risk objective is appropriate for the Savings Portfolio. It should be noted, however, that truly meaningful statements about the risk of Fairfax's total portfolio are tied to assumptions about the volatility of Reston's stock, if it is retained, and about when and at what price the Reston stock will be sold. Because the Reston holding constitutes 83% of Fairfax's total portfolio, it will largely determine the risk she actually experiences as long as it remains intact.

Constraints

✔ *Time horizon.* Two time horizons are applicable to Fairfax's situation. The first is the medium or intermediate term between now and when she plans to retire, seven years. The second is the long time horizon between now and the expected end of Fairfax's life, perhaps 25 to 30 years from now. The first time horizon represents the period during which Fairfax should set up her financial situation in preparation for the balance of the second time horizon, her retirement period of indefinite length. Of the two horizons, the longer term to the expected end of her life is the dominant horizon because it is over this period that the assets must fulfill their primary function of funding her expenses, in an annuity sense, in retirement.

✔ *Liquidity.* With liquidity defined either as income needs or as cash reserves to meet emergency needs, Fairfax's liquidity requirement is minimal. $500,000 of salary is available annually, health cost concerns are nonexistent, and we know of no planned needs for cash from the portfolio.

✔ *Taxes.* Fairfax's taxable income (salary, taxable investment income, and realized capital gains on securities) is taxed at a 35% rate. Careful tax planning and coordination of tax policy with investment planning is required. Investment strategy should include seeking income that is sheltered from taxes and holding securities for length periods to produce larger after-tax returns. Sale of the Reston stock will have sizable tax consequences because Fairfax's cost basis is zero; special planning will be needed for this. Fairfax may want to consider some form of charitable giving, either during her lifetime or at death. She has no immediate family, and we know of no other potential gift or bequest recipients.

✔ *Laws and regulations.* Fairfax should be aware of and abide by any securities (or other) laws or regulations relating to her "insider" status at Reston and her holding of Reston stock. Although there is no trust instrument in place, if Fairfax's future investing is handled by an investment advisor, the responsibilities associated with Prudent Expert Rule will come into play, including the responsibility for investing in a diversified portfolio. Also, she has a need to seek estate planning legal assistance, even though there are no apparent gift or bequest recipients.

✔ *Unique circumstances and/or preferences.* Clearly, the value of the Reston stock dominates the value of Fairfax's portfolio. A well-defined exit strategy needs to be developed for the stock as soon as is practical and appropriate. If the value of the stock increases, or at least does not decline before it is liquidated, Fairfax's present lifestyle can be sustained after retirement with the combined portfolio. A significant and prolonged setback for Reston Industries, however, could have disastrous consequences. Such circumstances would require a dramatic downscaling of Fairfax's lifestyle or generation of alternate sources of income to maintain her current lifestyle. A worst-case scenario might be characterized by a 50% drop in the market value of Reston's stock and a sale of that stock to diversify the portfolio, where the sale proceeds would be subject to a 35% tax rate. The net proceeds of the Reston part of the portfolio would be $10,000,000 \times 0.5 \times (1 - 0.35) = \$3,250,000$. When added to the Savings Portfolio, total portfolio value would be $5,250,000. For this portfolio to generate $658,000 in income, a 12.5% return would be required.

Synopsis. The policy governing investment in Fairfax's Savings Portfolio shall put emphasis on realizing a 3% real, after-tax return from a mix of high-quality assets aggregating less than average risk. Ongoing attention shall be given to Fairfax's tax planning and legal needs, her progress toward retirement, and the value of her Reston stock. The Reston stock holding is a unique circumstance of decisive significance in this situation: Developments should be monitored closely, and protection against the effects of a worst-case scenario should be implemented as soon as possible.

Now that we have gotten our arms around the IPS, we can turn our attention to some other facets of the first step in the investment management process. Using the IPS as a template, the personality aspects of the investor would be documented under the "unique" constraint in the IPS, because they are important in realizing the investor's needs. While honest self-evaluation may be difficult for someone in this circumstance (What kind of investor are you? Analytical or passive; or both?), it is important to attempt to get a handle on your needs. I recommend seeking the counsel of a financial services provider (FSP) and then take it from there. Or perhaps just talking with someone else will provide you with the necessary information to make a decision.

The Psychographics of the Individual Investor

Psychographics describes psychological characteristics of people and involves the somewhat fuzzy process of classifying people based on their personalities and needs. While much market research is done via demographic approaches, it is also known that any two individual investors can have very different psychological needs in the way their money is invested.

The most popular method of "psychographic labeling" in the financial services industry is the Barnwell two-way model, which studies various occupational groups and develops a superficially simple, yet surprisingly useful model of passive and active investors. A passive investor is defined as that investor who has become wealthy passively (e.g., by inheritance or by risking the capital of others rather than his own).

Passive investors have a greater need for security and less tolerance for risk. Occupational groups that tend to be passive investors include corporate executives, CPAs and attorneys in large firms, medical and dental nonsurgeons, politicians, bankers, and journalists. An active investor is defined as that individual who has earned his own wealth in his lifetime by being actively involved in wealth creation, and by risking his own capital in achieving wealth objectives. Active investors have a high tolerance for risk and a lesser need for security. Related to their high tolerance for risk is the fact that active investors prefer to maintain control of their own investments. By their involvement and control, they feel that they reduce the risk to an acceptable level. Occupationally, active investors are typically small business owners, entrepreneurs, and self-employed consultants.

In addition to this two-way methodology, a quadrant methodology has a growing following among the financial adviser community. The four types of investors in this methodology are:

1. *The In-Control Investor.* These investors are typically entrepreneurs and consequently earn their investment capital by making their own decisions and taking risks. In-control investors usually adopt a tactical asset allocation (versus a strategic asset allocation) strategy—constantly changing their allocation to take advantage of perceived opportunities in the capital markets. This book could be of particular assistance to these proactive investors; in the assembling and organizing of research data, the understanding of the capital markets and the valuing of financial securities.

2. *The Followers.* This group of investors is typically dominated by wealthy, nonbusiness individuals (e.g., medical and dental professionals) who, for fear of "missing the market," choose their investments by seeking the most fashionable, currently "hot" ideas. Typically, however, what is hot on Wall Street today is also quite expensive (read: has high valuation) and tends to correct (decrease in price) in the short run. While this group of investors could be quite profitable for an investment counselor, they usually tend to "burn themselves up" within a short period of time and are destined to the mantra "I am the best reverse indicator on Wall Street—when I buy you should sell short!"

In this case, my advice is simple: Attempt to be a free thinker when it comes to your investment portfolio. Many times, I query my clients to find some of my best investment ideas: What is going on in your industry? Who are the major players? Has demand for the company's goods recently picked up due to an external force that is expected to remain intact for an extended period? When my wife comes home from the store, we go through a similar line of questioning to understand what is happening in the malls and shopping centers (which a fortuitous strain of virus prevents me from ever visiting). This type of investment analysis was popularized by Peter Lynch (former manager of Fidelity's Magellan Fund), who would only buy what he understood and used in his daily life. Once an investor can divorce himself from the emotions involved with the stock itself and boil things down to this rudimentary foundation, investing in equities is simply determining whether you want to buy the "business" at the stated (share) price.

3. *Do-It-Yourselfers.* This investor always brings to mind the commercial featuring a fellow who is attempting to save the $20 on haircut by giving himself a trim (if you haven't seen it, he is forced, by the end of the spot, to wear a hat). The do-it-yourselfers are curious characters who may seek as much information as possible only to make the final decisions themselves. The brokerage community refers to these investors as "professional seminar goers" or "information gatherers." While as an educator as well as a financial services provider, I am in full support of this investor, I believe that investors who fall into this category owe it to themselves to seek professional advice from time to time, in addition to their self-managed portfolio. My advice to these investors: Open more than one account (there is usually no fee or obligation to open an account), one with a professional adviser and one with a discount firm (or for those who are "mouse literate," a computer-linked account) for the self-managed portfolio. Furthermore, a competition (Wall Streeters love a good game) should emerge between the two accounts, the winner being rewarded with a greater commitment in the next period.

4. *The Scared.* These are your certificate of deposit, passbook savings account investors. They may know that the return that they are receiving, on an after-tax, real basis is probably negative, but they cannot make a move. These investors (I use the term loosely) have an unmanageable fear of loss of principal, even though they may have a long-term time horizon. These investors are destined to mediocrity, and unless they have significant wealth (unusual for this group because the wealthy usually get rich by investing), they will be burdened in their retirement with concerns about outliving their assets. It is difficult to suggest a remedy for this type of investor, for there is no panacea to cure the fainthearted. Nor would I ever attempt to convert a scared investor; the ramifications to such an act could be severe. However, I would use every possible means (seminars, face-to-face discussions, books, magazine articles, TV broadcasts), to educate this investor in the hope that he will begin to see the light.

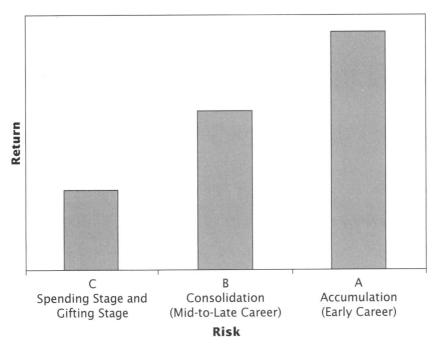

FIGURE 7.2 Risk/return position at various life cycle stages.

In addition to the demographics of wealth and the psychographics of individual investors, there are the demographics of age or, more appropriately, of stages in the life cycle of an investor (see Figure 7.2). These stages are important to understand because of their impact on an individual's risk and return preferences. It is useful to break up this continuous life cycle into four different phases in which individuals exhibit one dominant motif in viewing their wealth: the accumulation (early career), consolidation (mid- to late-career), spending (period of financial independence), and gifting (individual realizes he has more assets than he will ever need for personal security and spending) phases.

Life Cycle of Investors

Phase 1. Accumulation Phase. Typically, these investors have these qualities:

- ✔ They are 25–40 years old.
- ✔ They are spending capital to build home and career.
- ✔ They have a high level of debt and live slightly beyond their means.

In this phase, growth would be the most favored investment objective. The greatest asset that this investor has is the great number of years of compounding ahead. It is the power of this "mechanism" that is truly the investor's greatest resource. One is reminded of the "Rule of 72" (the mathematical construct that permits the determination of the number of years it would take for capital to double by simply dividing the expected rate of growth into 72). See Figure 7.3 as an illustration of what Albert Einstein referred to as "the greatest invention of all time"—compound interest.

To find out how long it will take an amount of money to double, divide 72 by the rate of return.	Rate of Return	Years	Rate of Return	Years
	2.00%	36.0	2.50%	28.8
For example, a $10,000 investment earning a fixed 2.5% will take 28.8 years to double to $20,000 (72 divided by 2.5 is 28.8). If the $10,000 earns 10% a year, it will take only 7.2 years to double your money (72 divided by 10).	3.00	24.0	3.50	20.5
	4.00	18.0	4.5	16.0
	5.00	14.4	5.5	13.0
	6.00	12.0	6.5	11.0
	7.00	10.3	7.5	9.6
You can also determine the rate of return if you divide the number of years it took to double your money into 72. For example, if it took 12 years for you to double your investment, that means you were earning 6%.	8.00	9.0	8.5	8.5
	9.00	8.0	9.5	7.6
	10.00	7.2	10.5	6.9
	11.00	6.5	11.5	6.3
	12.00	6.0	12.5	5.8
	13.00	5.5	13.5	5.3
To determine how long it will take you to double your money or figure out the rate of return you received on your investment, refer to the chart below.	14.00	5.1	14.5	5.0
	15.00	4.8	15.5	4.6
	16.00	4.5	16.5	4.4
	17.00	4.2	17.5	4.1
The chart assumes that the investment earns a fixed rate of return, and is not subject to principal fluctuations. Many investments will fluctuate in value, and this chart is for instructional purposes only and does not depict or predict the return on any specific investment.	18.00	4.0	18.5	3.9
	19.00	3.8	19.5	3.7
	20.00	3.6	20.5	3.5
	21.00	3.4	21.5	3.3
	22.00	3.3	22.5	3.2
	23.00	3.1	23.5	3.0
	24.00	3.0	24.5	2.9
	25.00	2.8	25.5	2.8

FIGURE 7.3 Applying the Rule of 72.

Phase 2. Consolidation. These investors generally have the following characteristics:

✔ They are 40–55 years old.

✔ Career growth is strong; household income tends to rise at a faster rate than in any other phase.

✔ Spending becomes less of a major commitment of total income.

✔ Household debt is reduced as savings (for children's education and retirement) takes a front seat.

Here again, growth of capital is probably best suited; however, there may be a greater liquidity need due to children's education expenses, a cost that is quickly becoming more pervasive than retirement. At least in retirement, there is (or is there?) the prospect of Social Security benefits.

Phase 3. Spending. These investors follow this pattern:

✔ They are 55–70 year old.

✔ Career and income has peaked and is beginning to decline as retirement sets in.

✔ Big ticket spending typically increases as vacation homes and other recreational activities are acquired.

This is the stage where growth is replaced by fixed income as the majority weight in a portfolio. Because much of the investor's assets have been acquired by this time, there is a larger pool of funds from which an income can be generated and subsequently drawn.

Phase 4. Gifting. In this phase, investors fit the following description:

✔ They are 70–85 years old.

✔ They are preoccupied with reduction of estate taxes through the process of gifting away assets.

✔ Potential charity and philanthropic activities may begin to gain importance.

✔ Realization sets in that one's accumulated assets could not be fully spent during the remaining lifetime.

In this stage, the growth/income decision is really based on the final disposition of the assets. Due to estate planning, much of the wealth in the

United States is being passed on to younger generations much earlier than ever before. Because of this phenomenon, the investment horizon is not definitive; is the time horizon the gifter's or the giftee's (possibly the children or even the grandchildren)? Prudent investment counsel is required in this all-important stage.

Vignettes of Investors

These fictional accounts are intended to help investors identify their own investment requirements. I also hope that some entertainment value will be a by-product of this exercise.

Doc. Medical professionals typically go through a life cycle fraught with high debt loads. The average physician has gone through 4 years of undergraduate studies, 4 years of medical school, and then 3 to 4 years of residency and/or specialty program. Unlike other professionals who may also go through an extensive academic apprenticeship, the physician usually can't earn a living outside his chosen profession until this coursework is completed. Few med students would feel comfortable working in their Uncle Joe's insurance office during the summer between their second and third year. Furthermore, the medical professional must witness his contemporaries mature in their respective fields—move up the ladder, start 401(k) plans, take vacations, get married, buy homes while they are still "in school." When the doctor finally begins to make money, he has a lot of catching up to do and spends (read: debt increases) accordingly (see earlier discussion of Followers). Lenders will be knocking on the Doc's door granting the best rates with the most credit without a qualm of default; after all, who could be a better credit risk than a physician? In my experiences, these are unfortunate freedoms, the typical young physician is so mired in debt (especially given school loans) that he is unable to save adequately for his future (not to mention the very real threat of managed care that has altered the profitability of the medical profession).

    Moral. With regard to personal finances, always plan for the unexpected, do not live beyond your means, and always put some (even a tiny amount) to work in investments. For the young and thriving physician, perhaps a disciplined investment program in a tax-deferred retirement account would go a long way to satisfy tax savings as well as investment performance. Here again, due to the age of the investor, growth is the overwhelming investment objective and equities is, consequently, the favored asset class. Fortunately, in my practice, I've come in contact with many medical professionals who understand their predisposition (as illustrated above) and consequently have established investment programs for the long term.

The Timer. Here is the story about Timmy the Timer. Timmy, an avid ice-skater, makes a valiant (and often successful) effort to time the market. Although we are not privy to his methods, rumor has it that much of it is based on the occult and witchcraft. Timmy's contention remains that by pinpointing the perfect time to buy a particular security or sector of the market, he is able to profit in the short run. Unfortunately for Timmy, academically, he has been proven wrong: It has shown that by attempting to time entry (bottoms) and exit (tops) points of the market, an investor would be prone to miss a majority of the entire move. A recent study conducted by various organizations and often bandied about at brokerage firm seminars suggests an investor who missed only 40 trading sessions out of 10 years (about 2200 sessions) would have earned a return of approximately 3% versus 17%; a shortfall that could mean the difference between a retirement sloop and a rowboat.

Moral. While Timmy's ice-skating may be worthy of Olympic play, his timing of the market is bound to slip up. My advice? A disciplined investment program that allows for dollar-cost averaging (the procedure of investing a stated amount into the portfolio periodically) so that the volatility of the capital markets can be put to the investor's advantage. Is dollar-cost averaging a perfect policy that should be adopted by all investors? Probably not, for the jury is still out on the true, quantifiable benefits to such a program (if the markets were to go straight up, the "averager" would be behind the bold and brazened "full amount investor"); however, given the alternative (market timing), dollar-cost averaging, in my estimation, is probably a good practice. Investors should realize that many of us are, and have for some time, employed dollar-cost averaging in our retirement plans—salary deductions to 401(k) plans and the like.

The Gambler. Always looking for the next big "hit." Putting all his investment portfolio on one idea and sticking to it no matter how bad it gets. Meet Donny, the kind of investor who treats brokers as if they are bookies instead of investment professionals. Don makes investment decisions on a whim, without a modicum of research or analysis. When he inquires about the last quote on the stock (as he will every 30 minutes or so), he asks, "What is the score?" as if he were really playing a game. Such clients are more detrimental to an FSP's practice than they are profitable.

Moral. My advice to the Gambler: Risk money at the tables; invest capital seriously and most effectively for your future.

The Do-It Yourselfer. My colleague, Jack Sullivan, tells of an incident that brings this issue of "do-it-yourself" to center stage. It seems a few years ago, Jack and his lovely family were playing host to a family gathering, and Mrs. Sullivan decreed that the driveway repair (including a new-border) was tantamount to the success of the party. So Jack (his real name is John, I just call him Jack) did the perfunctory suburban exercise of seeking estimates for this project. While the estimates ranged from "might-ever-pay-you-that much" to "too cheap to be good quality," the overriding similarity was the additional costs involved for laying a Belgium block border. So Jack decided to go with the median estimate (a fellow of good reputation in such matters), but only for the driveway; Jack was going to "knock out the border over a couple of weekends" and therefore, as he then estimated, save a considerable sum. Jack's calculations, however, failed to include that he was unable to play golf for the next four weeks, was forced to leave work early, and incurred sizable chiropractor bills for his aching back (which to this day is still not right). In the end, Jack had spent more money in doing the job himself than it would have cost him to have it done professionally.

Moral. Leverage the capabilities of those professionals who have a "comparative advantage" in certain areas, and focus your time and attention on those areas where your advantage is known.

STEP 2. THE CAPITAL MARKETS— MANAGING EXPECTATIONS

Understanding the historical interrelationships of the stock and bond markets is necessary to develop an appropriate investment strategy. Figure 7.4 compares the performance of several asset classes and inflation growth (Consumer Price Index) over five time periods (60, 40, 20, 10, and 5 years). In all five time periods, the broad stock market (Standard & Poor's 500 Index) significantly outperformed long-term bonds and Treasury bills and provided the best hedge against inflation.

It is important to recognize that inflation can impact investment returns and erode purchasing power. As mentioned, it is probably best to view inflation as a parasite, eating away the purchasing power of all capital market investments. If an investment makes a return of 5% before inflation (nominal) and if inflation is approximately at 4%, then the inflation-adjusted return is 1% (real return). While this 1% may be keeping your investment portfolio above the inflationary tide, that is, permitting level buying power, are you really meeting your investment needs?

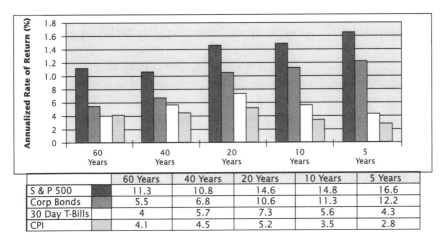

		60 Years	40 Years	20 Years	10 Years	5 Years
S & P 500		11.3	10.8	14.6	14.8	16.6
Corp Bonds		5.5	6.8	10.6	11.3	12.2
30 Day T-Bills		4	5.7	7.3	5.6	4.3
CPI		4.1	4.5	5.2	3.5	2.8

FIGURE 7.4 History of the capital markets (period ending 12/31/95). Used with permission. © 1997 Ibbotson Associates, Inc. All rights reserved. (Certain portions of this work were derived from copyrighted works of Roger G. Ibbotson and Rex Sinquefield.) *Note.* Past performance is no guarantee of future results.

Using the most dramatic example (60 years), as shown in Figure 7.4, you can see that an investment in 90-day T-bills just kept pace with inflation and resulted in no gain in purchasing power while an investment in long-term government bonds yielded returns only slightly greater than inflation's growth. Bear in mind, too, that income taxes paid on the returns from these investments further impair their suitability as inflation hedges. The only asset class to outpace inflation consistently over long time periods is equities.

In all five periods, the annualized returns for the stock market dramatically outpaced inflation. The point, then, is that investors with a long-term view may want to consider equities as a component of their portfolio to enhance returns and, as history illustrates, protect their wealth from dangers of inflation (see Tables 7.1 and 7.2).

The history of the capital markets (as shown in Figure 7.4) relates the returns of each major asset class with respect to a long-term time horizon. As illustrated, again, equities are the best performing of all asset classes, but this outperformance comes with a price—notice the variation of returns in this asset class. While in any 10-year period, the chance of a capital loss in the equity market is quite insignificant, that chance is greatly enhanced in a 1- or 3-year time horizon. As discussed, the issue of

TABLE 7.1   Prepare Yourself for the Ongoing Effect of Inflation

	1970 Price	1990 Price	Percent Increase	Projected Price 2010
One dozen eggs (large)	$ 0.61	$ 1.00	64%	$ 1.64
One pound bacon	0.95	2.28	140	5.47
½ gallon milk	0.66	1.39	111	2.93
One pound coffee	0.91	2.94	223	9.50
Median home price	23,000.00	95,500.00	315	396,533.00
Median income	8,734.00	29,943.00	243	102,654.00

Source. U.S. Department of Commerce except home price data, which were provided by the National Real Estate Board.

time horizon is one of the most critical in the application of an investment policy statement. If an investor came into my office seeking counsel and I learned while interviewing him that his time horizon was "about 1 year because we are looking to buy our first home by then," the advised asset allocation model (AAM) would be quite different from the investor who is investing for his newborn's college education (the AAM, in this case, should consist of at least 80% equities).

Looking at a long-term chart of the asset classes shown in Figure 7.4, has a greater, more personal meaning for me. During the summer of 1929, my grandfather (22 and fresh out of college) was debating his twin brother, Harry, over the state of the stock market at a family dinner in their hometown of Hartford, Connecticut. Uncle Harry, the wide-eyed optimist, had just invested his share of their father's inheritance into the stock market, while Papa kept his share in cash. Furthermore, Papa sold all his previously purchased holdings in the stock market and committed this capital to cash and cash equivalents. As any student of history could already figure out—my grandfather called the Crash of 1929; however, his prowess in the investment field has never earned any recognition since then. When the brothers got back together at Thanksgiving, Papa certainly had the bragging rights over his brother. But Harry, rather than conceding defeat, boldly explained that he had recently begun a program to "save" $20 per month of his newfound job's salary into the market. Well, my grandfather was outraged, he remembers telling Harry that he was crazy and should not be so naive but rather try to become a more "rational" investor. Nevertheless my

		TABLE 7.2 The "Real" Return on Certificates of Deposit		
Year	CD Rate	Less Taxes	Less Inflation	Taxes and Inflation
1978	8.18%	60%	9.0%	−5.73%
1979	11.22	59	13.3	−8.70
1980	13.26	59	12.4	−6.96
1981	16.29	59	8.9	−2.22
1982	13.81	50	3.9	3.01
1983	9.50	48	3.8	1.14
1984	10.92	45	4.0	2.01
1985	8.78	45	3.8	1.03
1986	6.98	45	1.1	2.74
1987	6.80	38	4.4	−0.18
1988	7.83	33	4.4	0.85
1989	9.56	33	4.6	1.81
1990	8.56	31	6.1	−0.19
1991	6.63	31	3.1	1.47
1992	4.15	31	3.1	−0.24
1993	3.39	31	2.8	−0.46
1994	4.57	31	2.7	0.45
1995	6.31	31	2.6	1.75

Taxes reflect Federal tax only at $100,000 income level. Inflation based on Federal Reserve consumer price index.
Source. Salomon Brothers 6-month CD rate (annualized).

brothers and I, when we were young, would always wonder why Harry's grandkids seemed to have the most expensive toys and, as we got older, the Porsches, speedboats, and Yale degrees.

Different asset classes and portfolio management strategies produce varying levels of risk. Generally, as the potential for reward increases, so does the likelihood of increased risk. Equities, therefore, though potentially rich in terms of reward, will almost always be riskier than bonds or T-bills. Think of risk as the degree of certainty with which future returns can be predicted. The less predictable a return, the more risk (uncertainty) it engenders.

While there are different types of risk—the risk of an outcome not occurring, reinvestment risk, credit risk, political risk, purchasing power risk, career risk—the one that is typically used in investment finance is volatility (see Figure 7.5). Financial service providers will typically attempt to measure risk through a series of questionnaires focusing around the fundamental questions: If your portfolio underperforms for 2 to 4 quarters, could you tolerate it? Could you tolerate 6 to 8 quarters of underperformance (versus some stated benchmark) if, as compensation for this risk, you had a chance of a greater upside?

Volatility around the mean (standard deviation of return) is the benchmark that is used in the investment industry. As a review of the discussion of statistics in Chapter 4, examine the following portfolios:

Portfolio A	*Portfolio B*
Return on portfolio (year 1): 0%	Return on portfolio (year 1): 8%
Return on portfolio (year 2): 20%	Return on portfolio (year 2): 12%

While both portfolios have the identical mean (for illustration purposes-arithmetic) return (10%), Portfolio A is quite a bit more volatile than B. In terms of statistics, Portfolio A's standard deviation (or movement around the mean) is greater than that of Portfolio B:

Standard deviation A = Square root of $\{(0 - 10)^2 + (20 - 10)^2\}$
= 14.14

Standard deviation B = Square root of $\{(8 - 10)^2 + (12 - 10)^2\}$
= 2.82

As discussed in Chapter 4, the greater the standard deviation the higher the probability for negative performance. For example, there is a 95% chance that the return of Portfolio A would be between −18% (10% minus 2 standard deviations or 2×14, or 28%) and +38% (10% plus 2 standard deviations or 2×14, or 28%). In Portfolio B, the range is much "tighter": +4.35% (10% minus 2 standard deviations or 2×2.8, or 5.6%) and +15.6% (10% plus 2 standard deviations or 2×2.8, or 5.6%).

To effectively manage this risk or volatility, investment professionals typically prescribe the use of diversification for smoothing out the returns of different asset classes. As explained in the Modern Portfolio Theory discussion in the appendix of this chapter, this "volatility management"

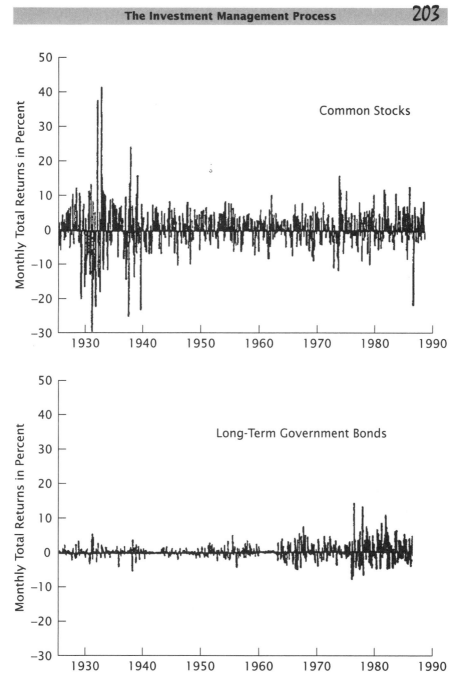

FIGURE 7.5 Volatility of annual returns from the U.S. capital markets (Common stocks versus long-term government bonds). Used with permission. © 1997 Ibbotson Associates, Inc. All rights reserved. (Certain portions of this work were derived from copyrighted works of Roger G. Ibbotson and Rex Sinquefield.)

Investment Styles

Different investment management styles and various investments utilized within these styles produce different results in terms of growth, income, and risk. Your goal in evaluating investment styles is to understand how the approach used for your portfolio will impact overall return without exceeding your risk tolerance. To allow you to differentiate among four common investment management styles, some of their characteristics are presented here.

1. **Value Style.** Appropriate for investors seeking superior long-term total return. Value managers tend to perform better than the market when the market is trending down while providing close (plus or minus) to market returns in a rising equity market. Over a market cycle, the objective is to equal or exceed market returns with less risk. These investment managers are searching through the rubble for the company whose stocks have been irrationally "sold-off" and currently present an outstanding "value." Only patient investors, however, need to apply to this school.

2. **Contrarian Style.** Appropriate for investors seeking superior long-term total return and high current dividend yield. Contrarian managers expect to perform very well in down markets and should participate well in up markets.

3. **Growth Style.** Appropriate for investors seeking superior long-term total return, mostly through capital appreciation. Growth managers must be able to tolerate a higher degree of risk. In this camp, the investment manager is looking for the next "hot" company—one whose earnings are growing at an unsustainably high rate. The growth investor expects to benefit from this earning growth (through increased share price), and will "get off the train" right before the growth ends (so he hopes).

4. **Aggressive Growth Style.** Appropriate for investors with an extremely high tolerance for risk while seeking superior long-term returns through capital appreciation. This style can perform very well in up markets but poorly in down markets.

process is critical to the success of the entire portfolio. It is through the effective use of different investment styles (see box: "Investment Styles"), an investment manager hopes to insulate a portfolio from serious declines. We can think of the asset class decision as a macro one and the style decision as a micro one, both with a common goal of reducing the volatility of a given portfolio.

STEP 3. PORTFOLIO CONSTRUCTION AND IMPLEMENTATION

Step 1 suggests what determines the investment decision—from objective/risk tolerance to mind-set and even lifestyle. Step 2 shows how the capital markets work (the risk and reward paradigm, effects of inflation, different asset classes, etc.) as well as current expectations for capital markets (managing expectations). In this third step, we attempt to use both of the first two steps to formulate an efficient portfolio (in the words of Dr. Markowitz—"optimized") at a given level of risk.

In this step are the expenses involved in the efficient management of a portfolio—a critical red flag. As most investors now realize, almost every investment comes along with certain expenses and fees. With mutual funds, direct money managers and even individual equities have some charges (be it expense ratios, management fees, or bid/offer spreads). The investor should make certain that these fees are not out of line, but are reasonable and competitive. Some investments (in certain sectors) require more fees and expenses (e.g., international and small cap investments) than others (long-term core holdings or passive portfolios).

Fundamental to the efficient construction of an investment portfolio is the Asset Allocation Model which details the commitment of resources to each market sector. It has been proven (Brinson, Beebower, & Hood, *The Determinants of Portfolio's Return,* 1991) that an effective Asset Allocation Model accounts for 91.5% of any account's stated return (see Figure 7.6). All other considerations (market timing, federal reserve intervention, security selection, etc.) have an insignificant effect on the total return of any particular portfolio. What is an Asset Allocation Model? The term is often bandied about in the investment community as being of critical importance to today's investor: "Does your Asset Allocation make sense?" "Which firm's AAM has been the most profitable over the past several months?" Asset allocation is simply the art (or, as some academics would postulate, the science) of positioning

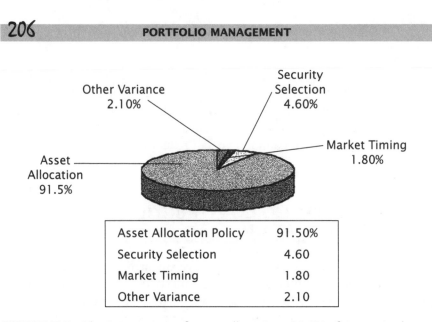

Asset Allocation Policy	91.50%
Security Selection	4.60
Market Timing	1.80
Other Variance	2.10

FIGURE 7.6 The importance of asset allocation: 91.5% of return is due to asset allocation. *Source.* Hood, Brinson B. (1991, May/June). "The Determinants of Portfolio's Return," *Financial Analysts Journal.*

your capital in the asset classes that most reflect your needs without ignoring your constraints. In its most simplistic form, asset allocation is "not investing all of your eggs in one basket." The exercise of deploying one's assets to optimize a return is far from the simplistic, agrarian definition stated here. Asset allocation is of the utmost importance and should not be compromised for the "investment-du jour" nor should it be the sole ingredient in an investment portfolio. Does the Asset Allocation Model assure you success in investing? Perhaps not—there never has been any guarantees in equities—but evidence in the long-term return charts is convincing.

Figure 7.7 depicts a typical Asset Allocation Model for a conservative growth investor (an investor whose objectives require growth of capital and constraints that permit slightly more volatility of returns and a somewhat longer time horizon). As illustrated, there is the importance of style differentiation as well as asset class diversification. Investment history is rich in examples of the importance of style differentiation to the long-term investment performance of a growth-oriented portfolio—perhaps as important as an asset allocation model. Most prominently, the periods of out performance shift between the growth and value style of equity investing.

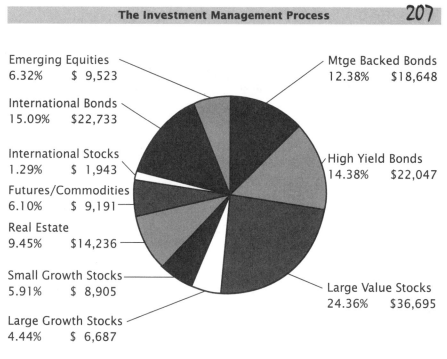

Emerging Equities
6.32% $ 9,523

International Bonds
15.09% $22,733

International Stocks
1.29% $ 1,943

Futures/Commodities
6.10% $ 9,191

Real Estate
9.45% $14,236

Small Growth Stocks
5.91% $ 8,905

Large Growth Stocks
4.44% $ 6,687

Mtge Backed Bonds
12.38% $18,648

High Yield Bonds
14.38% $22,047

Large Value Stocks
24.36% $36,695

FIGURE 7.7 Proposed asset allocation for growth investor.

While one style may prevail for a year or two, typically the other style comes back to out perform.

The following case study focuses on the issue of asset allocation.

CASE STUDY—ASSET ALLOCATION FOR SUSAN FAIRFAX*

Coastal has proposed the asset allocation shown in Table 7.3 for investment of Fairfax's $2 million of savings assets (the "Savings Portfolio"). Assume that only the Current Yield portion of Projected Total Return (comprised of both investment income and realized capital gains) is taxable to Fairfax and that the Municipal Bond income is entirely tax-exempt.

---

*CFA® Exam questions are reprinted with permission. Copyright (1996), Association for Investment Management and Research, Charlottesville, VA. All rights reserved.

	TABLE 7.3 Susan Fairfax—Proposed Asset Allocation—Prepared by Coastal Advisors		
Asset Class	Proposed Allocation (%)	Current Yield (%)	Projected Total Return (%)
Cash equivalents	15.0	4.5	4.5
Corporate bonds	10.0	7.5	7.5
Municipal bonds	10.0	5.5	5.5
Large capital U.S. stocks	0.0	3.5	11.0
Small capital U.S. stocks	0.0	2.5	13.0
International stocks (EAFE)	35.0	2.0	13.5
Real estate investments			
trusts (REITs)	25.0	9.0	12.0
Venture capital	5.0	0.0	20.0
Total	100.0	4.9	10.7
Inflation (CPI)—projected		4.0	

B. Critique the Coastal proposal. Include in your answer *three* weaknesses in the Coastal proposal from the standpoint of the Investment Policy Statement you created for her in Part A (page 187).

Critique. The Coastal proposal produces a real, after-tax return of approximately 5.17%, which is above the 3% level sought by Fairfax. The expected return of the proposal can be calculated by subtracting the tax-exempt yield from the total current yield (4.9% − 0.55% = 4.35%) and converting this to an after-tax yield [4.35% × (1 − 0.35) = 2.82%]. The tax-exempt income is then added back in (2.82% + 0.55% = 3.37%). The appreciation portion of the return (5.8%) is then added to the after-tax yield to get the nominal portfolio return (3.37% + 5.80% = 9.17%). Finally, the 4% inflation factor is subtracted to produce the expected real after-tax return (9.17% − 4.0% = 5.17%). This result also can be obtained by determining these calculations for each of the individual holdings, weighting each result by the portfolio percentage and then adding to a total portfolio result.

From the data available, it is not possible to determine specifically the inherent degree of portfolio volatility. Despite meeting the return criterion, the allocation is neither realistic nor, in its detail, appropriate to Fairfax's situation in the context of an investment policy applicable to her. The primary weaknesses are the following:

✔ *Allocation of equity assets.* Exposure to equity assets will be necessary to achieve the return requirements of Fairfax; however, greater diversification of these assets among other equity classes is needed to produce a more efficient, potentially less volatile portfolio that would meet her risk of tolerance parameters as well as her return requirements. An allocation that focuses the equity investments in U.S. *large-cap* and/or *small-cap* holdings and includes smaller international and Real Estate Investment Trust exposure is more likely to achieve the return and risk tolerance goals. If more information were available concerning the returns and volatility of the Reston stock, an argument could be made that this holding *is* the U.S. equity component of her portfolio. But the lack of this information precludes taking it into account for the Savings Portfolio allocation and creates the need for broader equity diversification.

✔ *Cash allocation.* Within the proposed fixed-income component, the allocation to cash (15%) is excessive given the limited liquidity need and low returns the asset class offers.

✔ *Corporate/municipal bond allocation.* The corporate bond allocation (10%) is inappropriate given Fairfax's tax situation and the superior after-tax yield on municipal bonds relative to corporate (5.5% vs. 4.8%).

✔ *Venture capital allocation.* The allocation to venture capital is questionable given Fairfax's policy statement which reveals that she is quite risk averse and dislikes volatility. Although venture capital may provide diversification benefits, venture capital returns historically have been much more volatile than other risk assets such as large- and small-cap stocks in the United States. Hence, even a small percentage allocation to venture capital may prove vexing.

✔ *Lack of risk/volatility information.* The proposal concentrates on return expectations and ignores risk/volatility implications. Specifically, the proposal should have addressed the expected volatility of the entire portfolio to see if it falls within the risk tolerance parameters of Fairfax.

QUESTION 2

2. HH Counselors has developed five alternative assets allocations (shown in Table 7.4) for client portfolios.

Answer the following questions based on Table 7.4, the Introduction . . . , and the Investment Policy Statement you created for Fairfax in Question 1–Part A.

A. **Determine** which of the asset allocations in Table 7.4 meet or exceed Fairfax's stated return objective. **Show** any calculations.

B. **Determine** the *three* asset allocations in Table 7.4 that meet Fairfax's risk tolerance criterion. Assume a 95% confidence interval is required, with 2 standard deviations serving as an approximation of that requirement. **Show** any calculations.

C. Assume that the risk-free rate is 4.5%.
   i. **Calculate** the Sharpe Ratio for Asset Allocation D. **Show** your calculations. (Your answer should be calculated to 3 decimal places.)
   ii. **Determine** the *two* asset allocations in Table 7.4 having *best* risk adjusted returns, based *only* on the Sharpe Ratio measure.

D. **Recommend** and **justify** the *one* asset allocation in Table 7.4 you believe would be the *best* model for Fairfax's Savings Portfolio. (Your recommendation must be consistent with your answer to Parts A through C above.)

Guideline Answer

A. Fairfax has stated she is seeking a 3% real, after-tax return. Table 7.4 provides nominal, pre-tax figures, which must be adjusted for both taxes and inflation to ascertain which portfolios meet Fairfax's return guideline. A simple solution is for the candidate to subtract the municipal bond return component from the stated return, then subject the resulting figure to a 0.35% tax rate, and add back tax-exempt municipal bond income. This produces a nominal, after-tax return. Then subtract 4% inflation to arrive at the real, after-tax return. For example, Allocation A has a real after-tax return of 3.4%, calculated by

$[0.099 - (0.072) \times (0.4)] \times [1 - 0.35] + [(0.072) \times (0.4)] - [0.04]$
$$= 3.44\% = 3.4\%.$$

Alternatively, it can be calculated by multiplying the taxable returns by their allocations, summing these products, adjusting for the tax rate, adding the result to the product of the nontaxable (municipal bond) return and its allocation, and deducting the inflation rate from this sum. For Allocation A,

$[(0.045) \times (0.10) + (0.13) \times (0.2) + (0.15) \times (0.1) + (0.15) \times (0.1)$
$+ (0.1) \times (0.1)] \times [1 - 0.35] + [(0.072) \times (0.4)] - [0.04] = 3.46\% = 3.5\%.$

TABLE 7.4   HH Counselors—Alternative Asset Allocations

Asset Class	Projected Total Return	Expected Standard Deviation	Asset Allocation A	B	C	D	E
Cash equivalents	4.5%	2.5%	10%	20%	25%	5%	10%
Corporate bonds	6.0	11.0	0	25	0	0	0
Municipal bonds	7.2	10.8	40	0	30	0	30
Large capital U.S. stocks	13.0	17.0	20	15	35	25	5
Small capital U.S. stocks	15.0	21.0	10	10	0	15	5
International stocks (EAFE)	15.0	21.0	10	10	0	15	10
Real estate investment trusts (REITs)	10.0	15.0	10	10	10	25	35
Venture capital	26.0	64.0	0	10	0	15	5
Total			100	100	100	100	100
Summary Data							
Projected total return			9.9%	11.0%	8.8%	14.4%	10.3%
Projected after-tax total return			7.4	7.2	6.5	9.4	7.4
Expected standard deviation			9.4	12.4	8.5	18.1	10.1
Sharpe ratio			0.574	0.524	0.506	?	0.574

Return	Asset Allocation				
Measure	A	B	C	D	E
Nominal return	9.9%	11.0%	8.8%	14.4%	10.3%
Real after-tax return	3.5	3.1	2.5	5.4	3.4

Table 7.4 also provides after-tax returns that could be adjusted for inflation and then used to ascertain the portfolios that meet Fairfax's return guidelines.

Allocations A, B, D, and E meet Fairfax's real, after-tax objectives.

B. Fairfax has stated that a worst case return of −10% in any 12-month period would be acceptable. The expected return less two times the portfolio risk (expected standard deviation) is the relevant risk tolerance measure. In this case, three allocations meet the criterion: A, C, and E.

Parameter	Asset Allocation				
	A	B	C	D	E
Expected return	9.9%	11.0%	8.8%	14.4%	10.3%
Expected standard deviation	9.4	12.4	8.5	18.1	10.1
Worst case return	−8.9	−13.8	−8.2	−21.8	−9.9

C. The Sharpe Ratio for Allocation D, using the Cash Equivalent rate of 4.5% as the risk free rate, is:

$$\text{Sharp Ratio} = \frac{RTN - r_f}{SD}$$

$$\frac{(0.144 - 0.045)}{0.181} = 0.547$$

      i. The two allocations with the best Sharpe Ratios are A and E with ratios of 0.574 each.

  D. The recommended allocation is A. The allocations that meet both the minimal real, after-tax objective and the maximum risk tolerance objective are A and E. These allocations have identical Sharpe Ratios. Both allocations have large exposures to municipal bonds. But Allocation E also has a large position in REIT stocks, whereas Allocation A's counterpart large equity allocation is to a diversified portfolio of large and small cap domestic stocks. Because of the diversification value of the large and small stock representation in A as opposed to the specialized or nondiversified nature of REIT stocks and their limited data history, there can be more confidence that the expectational data for the large- and small-cap stock portfolios will be realized than for the REIT portfolio.

The final piece to this third step is probably the least important but most often concentrated on by individual investors; that is, the actual investments that comprise the Asset Allocation Model. As I am known to say around the office—it is not the product but rather the process. As long as an investor (as well as his professional counsel) abides by a process similar to the one discussed here, where an investor's needs and constraints are identified and upheld, market expectations are realistic and understood, and an Asset Allocation Model is formulated and monitored, the actual choice of specific investments is of less importance. It would take an extensive due diligence process to identify the best investments in a particular asset class. During this due diligence, one would be prudent, once again, to cast a skeptical eye on fees and expenses. This is not an endorsement of "no-load funds," but rather an attempt to raise the flag of caution with regard to unjustifiable fees and expenses. In addition, many investment possibilities other than mutual funds would complete the AAM including individual money managers, diversified equity and bond portfolios, and unit investment trusts.

STEP 4. MONITORING THE PORTFOLIO

The investment management process is not nearly complete until a careful, and extensive review is orchestrated on a continued basis. This review will look to find any changes to the Investment Policy Statement that might have taken place which would deem it crucial to revise this plan and act accordingly. This is an important step in the process and requires prudence and diligence. Typically, investors should deem it appropriate to have quarterly discussions with their advisors to determine whether any personal changes have occurred and to review the account's performance (vs. a benchmark).

PROBLEM SET
INVESTMENT MANAGEMENT*

INTRODUCTION

Ambrose Green, 63, is a retired engineer and a client of Clayton Asset Management Associates ("Associates"). His accumulated savings are invested in Diversified Global Fund ("the Fund"), an in-house investment vehicle with multiple portfolio managers through which Associates manage nearly all client assets on a pooled basis. Dividend and capital gain distributions have produced an annual average return to Green of about 8% on his $900,000 original investment in the Fund, made six years ago. The $1,000,000 current value of his Fund interest represents virtually all of Green's net worth.

Green is a widower whose daughter is a single parent living with her young son. While not an extravagant person, Green's spending has exceeded his after-tax income by a considerable margin since his retirement. As a result, his non-Fund financial resources have steadily diminished and now amount to $10,000. Green does not have retirement income from a private pension plan, but does receive taxable government benefits of about $1,000 per month. His marginal tax rate is 40%. He lives comfortably in a rented apartment, travels extensively, and makes frequent cash gifts to his daughter and grandson, to whom he wants to leave an estate of at least $1,000,000.

Green realizes that he needs more income to maintain his lifestyle. He also believes his assets should provide an after-tax cash flow sufficient to meet his present $80,000 annual spending needs, which he is unwilling to reduce. He is uncertain as to how to proceed and has engaged you, a CFA Charterholder with an independent advisory practice, to counsel him.

Your first task is to review Green's investment policy statement.

AMBROSE GREEN'S INVESTMENT POLICY STATEMENT

Objectives:

- ✔ "I need a maximum return that includes an income element large enough to meet my spending needs, so about a 10% total return is required."
- ✔ "I want low risk, to minimize the possibility of large losses and preserve the value of my assets for eventual use by my daughter and grandson."

Constraints:

- ✔ "With my spending needs averaging about $80,000 per year and only $10,000 of cash remaining, I will probably have to sell something soon."
- ✔ "I am in good health and my non-cancelable health insurance will cover my future medical expenses."

1. **A. Identify** and **briefly discuss** *four* key constraints present in Green's situation not adequately treated in his investment policy statement.

   B. Based on your assessment of his situation and the information presented in the Introduction, **create** and **justify** appropriate *return* and *risk* objectives for Green.

2. Green has asked you to review the existing asset allocation of Diversified Global Fund. He wonders if a 60/30/10 allocation to stocks, bonds, and cash equivalents would be better than the present 40/40/20 allocation. Green also wonders if the Fund is appropriate as his primary investment asset. To address his concern, you decide to do a scenario forecasting exercise using the facts presented in the Introduction and the data in Tables 7.5 and 7.6 provided by Associates.

   Under the "Degearing" scenario, the U.S.-Europe-Far East trading nations experience an extended period of slow economic growth while they reduce prior debt excesses. This scenario is assigned a probability of 0.50, while *each* of the other two scenarios— "Disinflation" and "Inflation"—is assigned a probability of 0.25.

TABLE 7.5 Associates' Diversified Global Fund—Current Asset Allocation

Asset Class	Asset Allocation				
	U.S.	Europe	Far East	Other	Total
Stocks	15%	10%	12%	3%	40%
Bonds	20	12	8	0	40
Cash equivalents	10	5	5	0	20
Totals	45	27	25	3	100

The asset classes shown in Table 7.5 reflect the diversification strategy used by Associates in managing its Diversified Global Fund.

A. **Calculate** the expected total returns associated with the existing 40/40/20 asset allocation *and* with the alternative 60/30/10 mix, given the *three* scenarios shown in Table 7.6. **Show** your work.

TABLE 7.6 Projected Returns by Economic Scenario, 1996–1999 (all data have been weighted to reflect the geographic mix shown in Table 7.5)

		Scenario	
	Degearing	Disinflation	Inflation
Real economic growth	2.5%	1.0%	3.0%
Inflation rate	3.0	1.0	6.0
Nominal total returns:			
Stocks	8.25	−8.00	4.00
Bonds	6.25	7.50	2.00
Cash equivalents	4.50	2.50	6.50
Real total returns:			
Stocks	5.25	−9.00	−2.00
Bonds	3.25	6.50	−4.00
Cash equivalents	1.50	1.50	0.50

B. Justify the 40/40/20 asset allocation shown for the Fund in Table 7.5 versus the alternative 60/30/10 mix and **explain** your conclusion. In formulating your response, use the data in Table 7.5 and Table 7.6, your knowledge of multiple scenario forecasting, and your Part A calculations.

C. Evaluate the appropriateness of the Fund as a primary investment asset for Green, **citing** and **explaining** *four* characteristics that relate directly to his needs and goals.

PROBLEM SET
ANSWERS*

GUIDELINE ANSWERS

Question 1

A. Key constraints are important in developing a satisfactory investment plan in Green's situation, as in all investment situations. In particular, those constraints involving investment horizon, liquidity, taxes, and unique circumstances are especially important to Green. His investment policy statement fails to provide an adequate treatment of the following key constraints:

1. Horizon. At age 63 and enjoying good health, Green still has an intermediate to long investment horizon ahead. When considered in the light of his wish to pass his wealth onto his daughter and grandson, the horizon extends further. Despite his apparent personal orientation toward short-term income considerations, planning should reflect a long-term approach.

2. Liquidity. With spending exceeding income and cash resources down to $10,000, Green is about to experience a liquidity crisis. His desire to maintain the present spending level requires reorganizing his financial situation. This may involve using some capital and reconfiguring his investment assets.

3. Tax considerations. Green's apparent neglect of this factor is a main cause of his cash squeeze and requires prompt attention as part of reorganizing his finances. He should get professional advice and adopt a specific tax strategy. In the United States, such a strategy should include using municipal securities and possibly other forms of tax shelter.

4. **Unique circumstances.** Green's desire to leave a $1,000,000 estate to benefit his daughter and grandson is a challenge whose effects are primary to reorganizing his finances. Again, the need for professional advice is obvious. The form of the legal arrangements, for example, may determine the form the investments take. Green is unlikely to accept any investment advice that does not address this expressed goal.

Other constraints. Three other constraints are present. First, Green does not mention the need to protect himself against inflation's effects. Second, he does not appear to realize the inherent contradictions involved in saying he needs "a maximum return" with "an income element large enough" to meet his considerable spending needs. He also wants "low risk," a minimum "possibility of large losses" and preservation of the $1,000,000 value of his investments. Third, his statements are unclear about whether he intends to leave $1,000,000 or some larger sum that would be the inflation-adjusted future equivalent of today's $1,000,000 value.

B. Appropriate return and risk objectives for Green are as follows:

Return. In managing Green's portfolio, return emphasis should reflect his need for maximizing current income consistent with his desire to leave an estate at least equal to $1,000,000 current value of his invested assets. Given his inability to reduce spending and his constraining tax situation, this may require a total return approach. To meet his spending needs, Green may have to supplement an insufficient yield in certain years with some of his investment gains. He should also consider inflation protection and a specific tax strategy in determining asset allocation. These are important needs in this situation given the intermediate to long investment horizon and his estate-disposition plans.

Risk. Green does not appear to have a high tolerance for risk, as shown by his concern about capital preservation and the avoidance of large losses. Yet, he should have a moderate degree of equity exposure to protect his estate against inflation and to provide growth in income over time. A long time horizon and the size of his assets reflect his ability to accept such risk. He clearly needs counseling in this area because the current risk level is too high given his preferences.

Question 2

Guideline Answer

A. The following shows the calculation of the expected total return associated with the Fund for *each* of the two different asset mixes, given the three scenarios shown in Table 7.6.

Table 7.6 shows projected returns for each of the three economic scenarios. The "Degearing" scenario is for a stable economic environment; economic growth is 2.5% a year and the inflation rate is 3.0%. This scenario provides positive returns for all three asset classes, and stocks outperform both bonds and Treasury bills. The other two scenarios—"Disinflation" and "Inflation"—posit less stable conditions in which stocks do poorly. Bonds also generate losses in the "Inflation" scenario, but provide considerable downside protection under "Disinflation" conditions.

The calculations for the multiple scenario analysis show that of the three asset classes, bonds offer the highest expected real returns, 2.25%, over the forecast horizon. Over the same horizon, stocks are projected to generate a negative real return of −0.125%. Stocks are adversely affected under the "Disinflation" scenario and show losses under the "Inflation" scenario. Given the probabilities assigned to the three scenarios, the stock/bond/cash mix of 40/40/20 provides a superior real return (1.10%) to that from the alternative 60/30/10 mix (0.73%). This analysis reveals that equities do not automatically produce the highest expected returns even when the preponderant economic probability is for a stable environment accompanied by slow growth. If other less favorable outcomes have a reasonable probability of occurring, higher equity exposures may not produce a commensurately higher return. The multiple scenario forecasting methodology provides a valuable tool for effectively exploring the impact of various possibilities via a "what if" approach.

	Real Total Returns			
	Degearing	*Disinflation*	*Inflation*	*Expected Return*
T-bills	$(1.50 \times 0.5) +$	$(1.5 \times 0.25) +$	$(0.5 \times 0.25) =$	1.250%
Bonds	$(3.25 \times 0.5) +$	$(6.5 \times 0.25) +$	$(-4.0 \times 0.25) =$	2.250
Stocks	$(5.25 \times 0.5) +$	$(-9.0 \times 0.25) +$	$(-2.0 \times 0.25) =$	−0.125

	Real Portfolio Returns	
	40/40/20 Mix	*60/30/10 Mix*
T-bills	$1.250 \times 0.2 = 0.25\%$	$1.250 \times 0.1 = 0.125\%$
Bonds	$2.250 \times 0.4 = 0.90$	$2.250 \times 0.3 = 0.675$
Stocks	$-0.125 \times 0.4 = -0.05$	$-0.125 \times 0.6 = -0.725$
Total	1.10%	0.725%

An alternate calculation approach involves finding the portfolio returns under each scenario and then finding the final expected returns using the probabilities:

Real Returns: 40/40/20 Mix

Degearing: $(5.25 \times 0.40) + (3.25 \times 0.40)$
$+ (1.5 \times 0.20) = 3.7\%$

Disinflation: $(-9.00 \times 0.40) + (6.50 \times 0.40)$
$+ (1.5 \times 0.20) = -0.7$

Inflation: $(-2.00 \times 0.40) + (-4.00 \times 0.40)$
$+ (0.5 \times 0.20) = -2.3$

Expected Return $= [(3.7\% \times 0.5)(-0.7\% \times 0.25) + (-2.3\%$
$\times 0.25)] = 1.1\%$

The same alternate procedure applies to the 60/30/10 mix.

B. **Justification.** The answer to Part A provides much of the justification for the Fund's 40/40/20 asset mix. Given the three economic scenarios, each having a reasonable chance of occurring, the expected portfolio real returns are 1.10% for the existing mix versus 0.725% for the 60/30/10 mix. Therefore, the 40/40/20 mix is superior. Although using the scenarios may fail to capture subsequent events, the 40/40/20 mix provides the lowest risk exposure. The return superiority, if any, represents added value. Perversely, the more stocks in the portfolio, the worse the outcomes under circumstances captured by the scenarios.

Explanation. The explanation, also captured in the answer to Part A, lies primarily in the fact that stocks generate losses in both the "Disinflation" and "Inflation" scenarios. Increasing the proportion in stocks increases the portfolio's exposure to their relatively poor performance. Bonds offer the highest expected real returns over the investment horizon, followed by cash equivalents such Treasury bills, whose return is positive under each scenario. Stock's superiority of returns under the "Degearing" scenario is insufficient, even with that scenario given a 0.5% probability of being the dominant set of circumstances, to overcome the "Disinflation" outcome for that asset class.

C. Based on the Introduction and the answer to Question 1, Green's key needs are:

   1. A portfolio offering a long horizon,
   2. tax awareness (if not tax shelter),
   3. control over the timing of gain realization,
   4. an emphasis on production of current income,
   5. a smooth and dependable flow of investment income, and
   6. a below-average risk level, especially as to the possibility of large losses.

Green owns no real estate, receives no private pension income, and has only a small, partly-taxable government benefit payment. He also has no major noninvestment resources and depends entirely on his investment income for his spending. He does not intend to reduce his spending level. Although Green seems ambivalent about inflation, he hopes to leave his present worth to his daughter and grandson for their future financial protection. These factors provide the background for evaluating the appropriateness of the Fund as a primary investment asset.

In the Fund's favor are the following positive characteristics:

   1. **Diversifying agent.** If the Fund were part of a portfolio rather than Green's only investment, it would serve as an excellent diversifying agent.

2. **Adequate return.** Green has owned the Fund shares for six years, over which period (via distributions of both income and gains) he has realized a return on cost averaging 8% a year and has also recorded a $100,000 unrealized gain from Fund value growth beyond the distributions. This is an average but a satisfactory result.

3. **Conservative orientation.** Based on the Question 2.A scenario exercise and the existing 40/40/20 asset allocation, the Fund's management team appears to have a conservative orientation, which meets Green's expressed preference.

Despite the positive aspect of the Fund, most of the evidence suggests that the Fund is *inappropriate* as a primary investment asset for Green for the following reasons:

1. **Risky strategy to achieve Green's goals.** The "all eggs in one basket," single-asset nature of Green's investment is a high-risk strategy, which is clearly inappropriate to Green's circumstances. The 55% out-of-U.S. exposure Green holds via the Fund appears excessive compared with any known needs and goals.

2. **Nonoptimal asset mix of Fund for Green.** Although the Fund's broad global diversification might maximize return and minimize volatility with respect to its own particular asset allocation, its composition is unlikely to meet Green's complex set of specific return needs. The asset mix that is optimal for the Fund is not necessarily optimal for Green.

3. **Excessive volatility.** Much of the distribution flow from the Fund depends on capital gains. Given Green's spending pattern, the volatility of this flow is likely to be excessive in terms of Green's needs for income stability and dependability.

4. **Lack of focus on after-tax returns and control.** The Fund's management focuses on producing total returns, but Green's need is for maximum after-tax returns and for some control over the timing of gain realizations. Under present circumstances, gain realizations are random, uncontrollable events for Green, who must pay taxes on the gain distributions as they occur.

5. **Lack of focus on income needs.** The Fund cannot give the single-minded attention to income type, amount, regularity, and tax nature that this aspect of Green's situation needs.

6. Inflation. The global nature of the Fund's investment means that inflation in the United States, which affects Green directly, probably does not get the concentrated attention that planning for Green must give it.

On balance, the Fund is an inappropriate primary investment for Green, except as a diversifying piece of a much larger, balanced portfolio.

To expand your knowledge of ethics in the financial services industry, the following case study and description of the Disciplinary Process are offered from the *Standards of Practice Casebook.**

AIMR'S DISCIPLINARY PROCESS

The case briefs present short synopses of actual instances of professional misconduct and the related regulatory sanctions that were imposed. Although the individuals in the case briefs were sanctioned only by regulatory bodies, had they been members of AIMR, CFA charterholders, or CFA candidates, their conduct would have subjected them to the disciplinary process of AIMR's Professional Conduct Program (PCP). Similarly, if a member, charterholder, or candidate were to violate the Code or Standards in ways described in the case briefs, AIMR's PCP would have the authority to punish them.

The enforcement effort of the PCP is based on three principles:

1. Fair process to the member, charterholder, or candidate.

2. Confidentiality or proceedings.

3. Peer review.

The AIMR Board of Governors maintains an oversight and responsibility for the PCP, but professional conduct investigations are conducted by AIMR's PCP staff under the supervision of AIMR's Designated Officer and the Professional Standards and Policy Committee. Anyone can write the PCP with a complaint regarding the professional conduct of any member or

---

*Excerpted with permission from *Standards of Practice Handbook.* Copyright 1996, Association for Investment Management and Research, Charlottesville, VA. All rights reserved.

candidate, and the PCP will initiate an inquiry into the member's conduct to determine if a violation of the Code or Standards has occurred. If the Designated Officer determines that disciplinary action is appropriate, the matter is turned over to a review panel drawn from AIMR members involved with the PCP. These panels conduct a hearing on the matter or, if the member has entered into a stipulation with the Designated Officer agreeing to a sanction, review the stipulated agreement.

AIMR members, CFA charterholders, and CFA candidates who violate the Code and Standards will be sanctioned. Authorized sanctions include—in increasing order of severity—private censure, public censure, suspension of membership, revocation of membership, and in the case of CFA charterholders, suspension and revocation of the CFA designation. CFA candidates found to be violating the Code and Standards may be suspended from further participation in the CFA program.

CASE STUDY 1

Pearl Investment Management

Case Facts

Competition for the infrequent job openings at Pearl Investment Management is extensive, both from within the firm and from the outside. After a year in Pearl's back office as one of the account managers, Peter Sherman is told that obtaining a CFA charter would greatly enhance his chances of moving into the firm's research area. Sherman studies at length and passes Level I of the CFA exam.

In the next year, Sherman is helpful in clearing up problems related to the allocation of block trades among certain large client accounts. The most difficult problem is a misallocation related to an Initial Public Offering (IPO) of Gene Alteration Research Corporation. Sherman was assigned this project because of his accounting experience and because none of his client portfolios was involved, although most of his institutional accounts and a few of his larger individual accounts are "total rate of return" portfolios.

Because his review is a rush project, Sherman does not have time to consult the clients' investment policy statement, but he feels certain that the portfolio managers would direct only suitable trades to their client accounts. Furthermore, he believes the Trading Desk would have acted as a second review for client investment guidelines. Sherman reconciles the transactions related to the block trades across all the portfolios in question. As a result, certain securities are shifted among accounts. Sherman believes that with the adjustments and with the transactions reversed and reallocated at the IPO price for the Gene Alteration issue, all clients have been treated fairly, but he wonders how the problems arose in the first place.

Several activities at Pearl are or could be in violation of the Code of Ethics and Standards of Professional Conduct. Identify violations and possible violations, state what actions are required by Sherman and/or the firm to correct the potential violations, and make a short policy statement a firm could use to prevent the violations.

Case Discussion

The pressure of a rush project assigned by one's bosses and faulty assumptions can lead to inappropriate shortcuts even when intentions are good. This case involves violations or potential violations of the CFA candidate's compliance responsibility, fair dealing with clients, fiduciary duty to clients, appropriateness or suitability of investment recommendations or investment action, and correction of trading errors in client accounts.

Responsibility of Candidates to Comply with the Code and Standards. As an employee, Sherman was bound only by Pearl's own personnel policies. As a CFA candidate, he is subject to the Code and the Standards to maintain compliance, with assistance from Pearl's Compliance Department, than to the company explanations of the Code and Standards. As a CFA candidate, Sherman is now subject to disciplinary action by AIMR for violations of the Code and Standards, whether or not Pearl takes action. Because Pearl has incorporated the AIMR Code and Standards into its personnel policies, Sherman is relieved of his duty under Standard III(A), Obligation to Inform Employer of Code and Standards, to give formal notification of his obligations.

Actions Required. Sherman should reacquaint himself with Pearl's personnel policies and read through the AIMR *Standards of Practice Handbook* to increase his familiarity with the Code and Standards and the subtleties of implementing the Standards on a day-to-day basis. The detailed discussion of Standards and examples in the *Handbook* provide explanations and add depth to the meanings of the various Standards. Finally, to be safe, Sherman should document for his supervisor that, as a CFA candidate, he is obligated to comply with

AIMR's Code and Standards and that he is subject to disciplinary sanctions for violations thereof.

Dealing with Clients. The case presents evidence of failure by Pearl Investment Management and its employees to carry out their fiduciary duties and their obligation to treat all clients equitably.

Fiduciary Duty. Standard IV(B.1), Fiduciary Duties, requires members to take investment actions for the sole benefit of the client and in the best interest of the client given the known facts and circumstances. In other words, fiduciaries must manage any pool of assets in their control in accordance with the needs and circumstances of clients. The case notes that Sherman did not consult the clients' investment policy statements, however, when reallocating the IPO trades. He assumed the portfolio managers and/or Trading Desk would have done so. Therefore, Sherman violated his fiduciary duties by not making sure that the reallocations were in the best interests of all clients and suitable to each client.

Fair Dealing. In allocating or reallocating block trades, a member must ensure that Standard IV(B.3), Fair Dealing, is upheld. The case notes that among the problems Sherman was asked to review was allocation of an IPO "among certain large clients." By favoring their large client accounts over others with similar investment objectives, the portfolio managers, the Trading Desk, and the account managers involved violated AIMR's and Pearl's standards on fair dealing.

Members have a duty to treat all clients fairly so that no one client is advantaged or disadvantaged—no matter what the size of the portfolio or other qualifications. Clients' investment guidelines often differ significantly, however, so portfolio managers and the Trading Desk must determine, in advance, which accounts have similar investment objectives and should receive similar allocations when new purchases are made. Even if clients have identical investment objectives, the accounts may have different cash reserves, dissimilar inclinations toward leverage through the use of margin, and distinct minimums for transaction size. All these factors must be taken into account in the decision-making process.

Ultimately, however, Pearl should treat portfolios with similar investment objectives and constraints similarly regardless of the size of the portfolios or the fees that they convey to Pearl. In making new securities purchases, firms should allocate a purchase for all suitable accounts, using a pro rata or similar system of distribution when less than the full order is received.

Actions Required. Sherman must re-investigate the investment objectives for all affected client portfolios to make certain that orders were not entered in violation of client guidelines. He must also ensure that the allocation of block trades is made on an equitable basis for all client portfolios of similar objectives; in carrying out this assignment, he must keep in mind minimum transaction size but include all accounts that have similar investment criteria.

Policy Statements for a Firm. "Employees owe a fiduciary duty to clients, and in all instances, the interest of clients shall come first. Action contrary to this policy is expressly prohibited.

"Allocation of trades shall be on a fair and equitable basis for all portfolios with similar investment objectives and constraints."

Bearing the Financial Risk of Errors in Client Accounts.
When trades are made in error or are misallocated, under no circumstance should client portfolios bear the risk of an inappropriate transaction; nor should the firm shift the burden to another portfolio or client account. The burden of financial risk must be absorbed by the firm, not by the client (either directly or indirectly).

The reversal of trades described in the case and the reallocation of securities at the IPO price comes close to being a complete resolution of the problem Sherman was asked to solve, but Pearl should have credited short-term interest to those accounts from which transactions were removed because the clients' cash accounts were used to cover the trades.

In some instances, investment management firms shift financial risk to a client (or clients) indirectly by using such techniques as letting soft-dollar trades "cover" the financial aspects of a reversal, canceling an order through a "sale" from one account and a coincident "repurchase" in another account, or other transactions to compensate the firm for any loss it incurred by transacting at levels different from the market. Many client portfolios may be involved in order to spread the financial effects over a broad number of portfolios, which complicates the firm's or the manager's efforts to discern this ethical infraction. Any activity of this sort is a violation of AIMR's Code and Standards related to fair dealing and fiduciary duty.

Actions Required. Pearl should see that no client bears a financial loss by the misallocation of block trades by any Pearl employee. As compensation for the use of the clients' funds, Pearl should credit short-term interest to all accounts for which trades were reversed, with Pearl bearing the loss. Short-term interest should not be charged against accounts that received shares.

Policy Statement for a Firm. "The firm will take all steps necessary to ensure the integrity of its client accounts. When errors do occur, the clients' portfolios will be restored with no loss of value to the client. To the extent that such losses occur, Pearl will indemnify its clients and make the appropriate restitution."

CASE STUDY 2

Pearl Investment Management*

Case Facts

After Peter Sherman passed Level II of the CFA exam, Thomas Champa, Pearl Investment Management's director of research, requested that Sherman be transferred to the Research Department with the understanding that his apprenticeship in the department as a junior analyst would last at least until he was awarded the CFA charter. Sherman was thrilled at the prospect of moving into research, and he accepted the transfer.

Champa came to Pearl when he decided to remain in the United States after completing a 5-year U.S. tour of duty for a major international bank with which he had served for 20 years. His background in international banking has made him particularly well suited to be the research director at Pearl. Champa has seven analysts in his department—five senior analysts and two junior analysts. Sherman is one junior analyst, and the other is a Level III CFA candidate.

Champa is anxious to lead the firm's research efforts into international securities and wants to begin with companies in the developing countries whose markets have experienced spectacular performance in recent years. He tells the analysts that Pearl must come up with research recommendations in emerging markets equities quickly or the department will face criticism from senior management and the firm's clients. He also wants to be able to attract prospective clients by demonstrating the firm's expertise in this area.

Although Sherman is new to the department, Champa gives him difficult assignments because he believes Sherman's lack of preconceived notions about emerging market companies makes him an ideal analyst for this area. Sherman is to concentrate on Central and

---

South America, areas where Champa believes he has special insight and can direct Sherman.

Sherman reads several brokerage reports on Latin American markets, spends time with Champa and other members of the Research Department discussing trends in these markets, and browses through the statistical section of Standard & Poor's International Stock Guide. For a briefing by someone with actual experience, Champa refers Sherman to one of his old banking contacts, Gonzalo Alves, who is well connected in Mexico and on the board of directors of a number of important Mexican companies.

Sherman spends several hours speaking with Alves about the Mexican economy and the companies for which Alves serves as a director. Alves tells Sherman about the strategic direction of each company, some potential acquisition targets, and how changes in the Mexican economy will affect each company directly. Sherman now feels comfortable using this information in writing his research reports.

Champa asks Sherman to produce a research report on several Mexican telecommunications and cable companies. Because of the deadline Champa gives Sherman for the report, Sherman cannot develop the research easily on his own, so he plans to incorporate information from his reading of the brokerage firm reports, his conversation with Alves, and other sources. Sherman hastily finishes his two-page report, "Telecommunications Companies in Mexico," which includes excerpts from the brokerage reports, general trends and ratios from the S&P International Stock Guide, and paraphrased opinions from Alves. It concludes with an internal recommendation that stock in the Mexican telecommunications companies be bought for Pearl clients for which such stock is suitable. Sherman does not cite the brokerage reports as sources because they are so widely distributed in the investment community.

Pearl's senior managers applaud Champa and his staff for their quick response to the market demand for emerging market research, and the portfolio managers ask the Research Department for more recommendations. Jill Grant, however, the other junior research analyst, asks Sherman why his report did not include specific details about the Mexican economy or the historical exchange rate fluctuations between the Mexican peso and the U.S. dollar. She questions the comparability of Mexican securities with U.S. securities and notes that the diversification available from investing in global markets is achieved only if the correlation between the specific non-U.S. market and the U.S. market is low. Sherman's response, supported by Champa, is, "Our clients are sophisticated investors; they know these things already."

The case reveals several activities at Pearl that are or could be in violation of the AIMR Code of Ethics and Standards of Professional Conduct. Identify violations, state what actions are required by Sherman or his supervisor to correct the potential violations, and make a short policy statement a firm could use to prevent the violations.

Case Discussion

The pressures to succeed can lead to noncompliance in ordinary, mundane business activities. The violations or potential violations in this case relate to using proper care and independent judgement, use of insider information (particularly under international applications of the Code and Standards and the obligation of members to comply with governing laws and regulations), several aspects of research and research reports, and representation of services.

Proper Care and Independent Judgment. The final requirement stipulated in the AIMR Code of Ethics is to use proper care and exercise independent professional judgement. When Peter Sherman succumbed to the time pressures exerted by Thomas Champa, he was thus violating a basic provision of the Code and Standard IV(A.3), Independence and Objectivity.

Actions Required. Sherman must keep in mind the necessary steps in the research and portfolio decision-making process and resist attempts to rush his analysis.

Policy Statement for a Firm. "Analysts shall use proper care and exercise independent professional judgment in the preparation of research reports to ensure that reports are thorough, are accurate, and include all relevant factors."

Use of Insider Information. Sherman must base any investment recommendations on his research alone, without incorporating material nonpublic information and without engaging in illegal or unethical actions. The situation in which Sherman found himself discussing a number of important corporations with Alves was compromising at best. Based on the local laws and customs with which they were most familiar, Champa and Alves may have found a candid discussion about the corporations where Alves served in a close relationship to be perfectly acceptable. In the course of conversation, however, Alves could have conveyed material nonpublic information to Sherman. If Sherman used such material nonpublic information in his report, which contained recommendations for investment actions, he violated Standard V(A), Prohibition against Use of Material Non-public Information.

One of the more difficult aspects for members is reconciling their obligations under the Code and Standards with the different laws, rules, regulations, and customs of various countries. CFA char-terholders, CFA candidates, and AIMR members are held to the highest standards. Therefore, regardless of local laws, they are oblig-ated by the Code and the Standards to refrain from using confiden-tial information to their advantage or the advantage of their clients.

Being compelled to hold to a higher standard than the local norm can be disadvantageous to CFA charterholders and, some-times, their clients and customers. The higher standard, however, is what sets CFA charterholders apart in terms of the integrity of the investment profession.

Champa's referral of Sherman to Alves can aid Sherman in his research, but Sherman must use the information in an ethical man-ner. A consideration of the mosaic theory can add a useful perspec-tive to judging proper and improper use of information. The mosaic theory states that a compilation of information that is not material or is public is not a violation of the Standards; it is the result of good analytical work. For example, if Sherman is doing a thorough review and analysis of all companies within a specific sector or industry, he may develop a greater sense of the interrelationships among the companies than if he were studying only one or a few of them. In that case, Sherman may be able, based on public information gath-ered from various sources and his unique understanding, to form conclusions about a particular company that may appear to be based on nonpublic information but are not.

Actions Required. Sherman may not use material nonpublic in-formation to take investment action or provide investment advice. If Sherman has come into possession of material nonpublic informa-tion in his contact with Alves, he must disclose this fact to Pearl's Compliance Department or compliance officer.

Policy Statement for a Firm. "Analysts and portfolio managers are prohibited from using material nonpublic information in any form in making investment recommendations or taking investment action. Any employees who have come into possession of material nonpublic information (or who believe they have) shall contact the Compliance Department or compliance officer for guidance. If the information is determined to be material nonpublic information, the employee must refrain acting on it and should take steps to have the information dis-seminated publicly."

Using the Research of Others. Sherman's research reports must acknowledge and give credit to the research of others unless the information is of a statistical nature and widely held to be in the public domain. The case says that Sherman did "not cite the brokerage reports as sources because they are so widely distributed in the investment community." To use the proprietary research of others—brokerage reports, for example—without giving them due credit is a violation of Standard II(C), Prohibition against Plagiarism. Sherman's use of general trends and ratios from the S&P International Stock Guide, however, is a perfectly legitimate use of information widely available in the public domain.

Actions Required. In order to avoid an ethical violation, Sherman must acknowledge the use of someone else's information and must identify its author or publisher. In particular, Sherman must give credit to the author(s) of any brokerage reports he uses extensively in the preparation of internal recommendations.

Policy Statement for a Firm. "Analysts are prohibited from using the work of others without reference and are prohibited from plagiarizing the work of others by not giving due credit to the author, whether or not the author is employed by the firm."

Reasonable Basis for a Research Opinion. Standard IV(A.1), Reasonable Basis and Representations, requires Sherman to "exercise diligence and thoroughness in making investment recommendations," "have a reasonable and adequate basis" for such recommendations, and "avoid any material misrepresentation in any . . . investment recommendation." Sherman's lack of care and independent research in the preparation of his report is a violation of Standard IV(A.1).

Sherman was essentially taking over the recommendations of others, which may or may not have had a reasonable basis. The research he used may have incorporated material misrepresentations that he did not identify or correct. By copying the work and ideas of others, Sherman may have been copying serious deficiencies and attaching his name and approval to them.

Because of the time pressure from Champa, Sherman did not adequately review the entire industry in the context of the overall economy and global markets (as evidenced by Jill Grant's questions). His reliance on a few brokerage firm reports and other sources is not sufficient to be considered, in the words of Standard IV(A.1), "appropriate research and investigation." Furthermore, his report lacks documentation, not only in detail, but also in substance.

Relevant Factors and Fact versus Opinion in Research Reports. Grant was right to question the exclusion of relevant and basic risk factors in Sherman's reports. Sherman has an obligation under Standard IV(A.2), Research Reports, to "use reasonable judgment regarding the inclusion or exclusion of relevant factors in research reports." By excluding important factors, he shirked his responsibility to the firm's clients and violated Standard IV(A.2). Champa's contention that the firm's clients are sophisticated investors who are aware of the characteristics of markets and particular investments does not relieve Sherman of his duty to include relevant factors in his research report.

Actions Required. Sherman's reports should be as thorough as possible. When dealing with markets and economies that are significantly different from domestic markets and economies. Sherman should provide a full explanation. The research reports should provide a reasonable basis for decisions, including all relevant factors that reasonably come into play in an investment recommendation, and avoid material misrepresentation of investment characteristics so that the appropriateness of investments for various clients can be judged. Sherman also must maintain records to support his research reports.

Policy Statement for a Firm. "All relevant factors, including the basic characteristics involved in the investment, are to be included in a research report, with a corresponding discussion of the potential risks involved."

Misrepresentation of Service Performance Presentation. The case raises the issue of potential violations of Standard IV(B.6), Prohibition against Misrepresentation. Whether violations are actual would depend, of course, on how the firm's current and prospective clients are made aware of the qualifications of the firm and the Research Department's experience in emerging markets. If Pearl's research is represented as a reaction to a changing marketplace and the increased globalization of securities markets, no violation has occurred. If Pearl is actively soliciting new and existing clients based on its "expertise" in the research and management of emerging market portfolios, however, then a violation of Standard IV(B.6) has occurred.

The presentation of performance—that is, actual investment returns for its emerging market strategy—will be problematic for Pearl in the beginning. Pearl will not be able to report actual performance until it begins to manage portfolios made up of emerging market securities or portfolios that include some meaningful concentration of securities from emerging markets.

Actions Required. Pearl must not hold itself out as having experience or any "track record" in the management of emerging market portfolios until it actually manages assets in this area. It can suggest to clients, however, that the qualifications of the firm as demonstrated by its current efforts might produce returns that are comparable in a different environment because of the use of a similar methodology.

Policy Statement for a Firm. "Employees shall make only those statements, either verbally or in writing, about the firm and its qualifications that represent the firm properly and with the integrity it has tried to achieve.

"The firm shall not solicit clients, new or existing, for a new investment style without full disclosure of the firm's qualifications and expectations for both risk and potential return.

"Performance results for a new investment style will be in compliance with Standard V(B), Performance Presentation, as discussed in the AIMR *Standards of Practice Handbook*."

APPENDIX 1—CONSIDERATIONS IN PORTFOLIO MANAGEMENT

Modern Portfolio Theory

A caveat is in order before presenting this information: Much of this work is theory and therefore may not be perfectly applicable in the practical sense. We start with a graph of all the risky assets, as depicted in Figure 7.8, with their return and risk coordinates illustrated. The question is then posed: Can we combine these risky assets in some fashion as to optimize the return and minimize the risk of a portfolio? This is where Dr. Harry Markowitz and covariance comes in. Markowitz combined, as illustrated in Figure 7.9, the risky assets in such a way as to produce portfolios that are considered "mean-variance portfolios" or, in other words, the best return with the lowest risk. Markowitz's portfolios combined to make a line known as the "efficient frontier"—those portfolios that have the highest return for a stated level of risk. The efficient frontier provides an investor with the best set (portfolios of assets, otherwise known as asset allocation) of investment combinations, based on historical average returns and standard deviations.

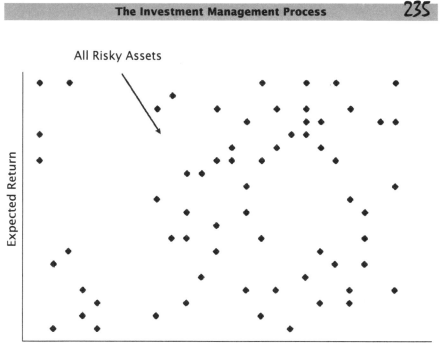

All Risky Assets

Expected Return

Standard Deviation

FIGURE 7.8 The risk/return of all risky assets.

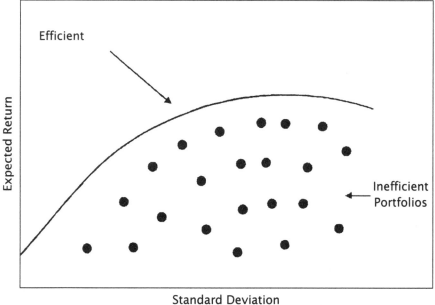

Efficient

Expected Return

Inefficient Portfolios

Standard Deviation

FIGURE 7.9 The efficient frontier.

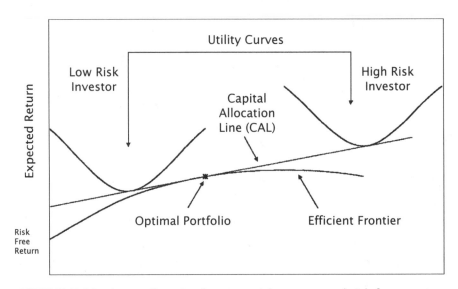

FIGURE 7.10   Asset allocation between risky assets and risk-free assets.

The concept of asset allocation between the risky assets and the risk-free assets is illustrated in Figure 7.10; the capital asset line (CAL) is drawn from the risk-free asset, and the point of tangency with the efficient frontier is the CAL whose slope (also known as the Sharpe Ratio) is maximized. The Sharpe Ratio is the amount of return a portfolio achieves at a given level of risk; in its broadest sense the Sharpe Ratio is a measure of portfolio efficiency. Depending on the individual investor's tolerance for risk, his position along the CAL is demonstrated using utility curves (those closer to the y- or vertical axis are more risk-adverse than those further out on the line).

With the introduction of the market portfolio, The Capital Asset Pricing Model, and the fact that all investors follow Markowitz's tenets would mean that investors would choose the portfolio that is tangent to the efficient frontier, therefore making that portfolio the market portfolio. So with the assumptions imbedded in the Capital Asset Pricing Model, the CAL graph now becomes the Security Market Line (SML) as illustrated in Figure 7.11. Notice the changing risk measure from standard deviation to Beta—the covariance measure between the market and a security.

On Figure 7.11, the distance identified between points F and G is known as alpha—the amount of positive return above the expected return given a stated risk measure. Typically, one would associate this positive alpha with active management; that is, an Asset Allocation Model may

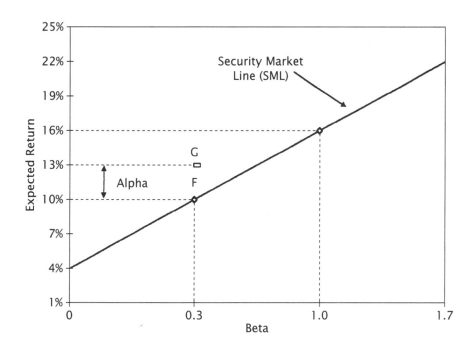

FIGURE 7.11 The security market line.

have an expected return of say 10%, but due to the abilities of the individual managers of these asset portfolios, a return of 13% or a 3% positive alpha may be possible.

Additionally, if we were to take Figure 7.11 one step further and develop four quadrants (separated by the market portfolio's risk and return), a very useful risk-to-reward graph emerges. The managers that are located in the northwest quadrant are, hands down, the very best at their craft—that is, achieving a higher (or equal) return compared to the market with less risk. Where it may be difficult to consistently find managers in this quadrant, an investor may, through portfolio optimization programs, combine managers in such a fashion (asset allocation) that the resulting portfolio resides in the enviable northwest.

Markowitz and the Portfolio Selection Theory

Harry Markowitz, PhD (Baruch College, New York City), is the undisputed father of portfolio theory. He showed quantitatively how diversification works to reduce risk. The key to his seminal work is the covariance relationships between security returns. Markowitz demonstrated how the risk of the portfolio is less than the weighted average of the standard deviations of the individual securities; he developed the concept of efficient portfolios. An efficient portfolio is one with the largest expected return for a given level of risk, or the smallest risk for a given level of return.

Efficient portfolios can be calculated using quantitative techniques. When calculating the risk of a portfolio of securities, it is important to realize that the risk is *not* the simple weighted average of the individual securities' standard deviations; it is critical to take into account the covariance between the securities. Consider the following simple example:

Assume we have data for two companies, ABC and XYZ, with standard deviations (measure of risk) of 37.3% and 23.3%, respectively. The correlation coefficient between their returns is +.15.

> *Note.* As mentioned in statistics chapter that the correlation coefficient is a relative measure of the relationships between security returns. If positive, the security returns move together and the higher the positive correlation, the more the movements are directly related. If negative, security returns are inversely related—they move opposite to each other and therefore, some bad returns can be offset with good returns. A perfectly negative correlation is a theoretical premise only; it does not exist in the real world. If correlation is zero, security returns are independent of each other; that is, they are not related.

Assume the weighting of each security in the portfolio are equal (50% each). With this data, the standard deviation (risk) of the portfolio would be calculated as follows:

$$SD_{port} = [(wt1)^2 (sd1)^2 + (wt2)^2 (sd2)^2 + 2(wt1)(wt2)(sd1)(sd2) \, Corr \, 1,2]^{.5}$$

$$SD_{port} = [(0.5)^2 (0.373)^2 + (0.5)^2 (0.233)^2 + 2(.5)(.5)(.373)(.233) \, Corr \, ABC,XYZ]^{.5}$$

$$= [0.0348 + 0.0136 + 0.0435(0.15)]^{.5}$$

$$= 23.4\%$$

where:

SD port = the total standard deviation of the entire portfolio
wt = the % weight of the security (either 1 or 2, in this
case) in the total portfolio
sd = the standard deviation of the respective security
Corr 1,2 = the correlation measure, as defined above, between
the two securities

It is important to discuss the effect of changes in the correlation between the two securities on the standard deviation of the entire portfolio. Consider the following correlation coefficients for ABC and XYZ:

Corr = +1.0: SD port = $[0.0348 + 0.0136 + .0435(1)]^{.5} = 30.3\%$

Corr = +.5: SD port = $[0.0348 + 0.0136 + .0435(.5)]^{.5} = 26.5\%$

Corr = +.15 SD port = 23.4% (see earlier calculation)

Corr = 0.0: SD port = $[0.0348 + 0.0136 + .0435(0)]^{.5} = 22.0\%$

Corr = −0.5 SD port = $[0.0348 + 0.0136 + .0435(-0.5)]^{.5} = 16.0\%$

Corr = −1.0: SD port = $[0.0348 + 0.0136 + .0435(-0.1)]^{.5} = 7.0\%$

Given the evidence from these calculations, the smaller the correlation between assets (or greater negative correlation) the less the portfolio standard deviation or risk. This indicates that diversification pays. The more diversified a portfolio is, the lower the correlation among assets will be.

Figure 7.12 shows the effect of adding securities to a portfolio. Graphically, this represents what the preceding calculations show quantitatively— the more issues in a portfolio, the more likely the correlation between issues will be less and therefore the portfolio risk is decreased. There are two broad measures of risk, market risk and specific risk. Systematic risk (market risk or nondiversifiable risk) is the amount of risk that cannot be diversified away. Systematic risk is important to investors because they need to be compensated for this risk. It is the result of common sources, such as changing economic conditions, that affect all stocks. Unsystematic risk (firm-specific risk, diversifiable risk) can be decreased as the portfolio begins to diversify. As the number of issues increases, the total risk declines as the diversifiable risk declines. It is possible to diversify away most of the unsystematic risk by adding securities to a portfolio (about 22–30 securities from different industries is optimal for a diversified portfolio). For the individual investor,

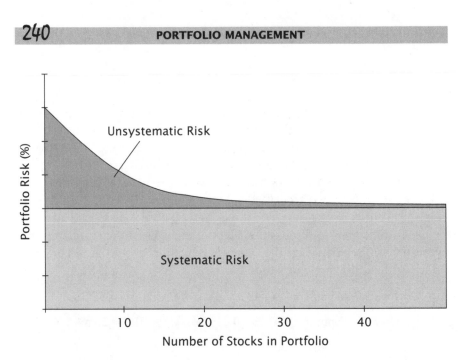

FIGURE 7.12 Reducing risk by adding securities to the portfolio.

however, the growth in the number of mutual funds provides solid footing to achieve this all-important diversification benefit.

The Capital Asset Pricing Model

As discussed in the equity chapter, investors use the Capital Asset Pricing Model (CAPM) equation to ascertain a risk-adjusted capitalization rate that would allow further explanation toward the discounted value of future cash flows. The CAPM is derived on the basis of a set of assumptions such as perfect capital markets (all players have same information; there are no taxes or other fees), homogeneous expectations by all participants, and market players who are all Markowitz (mean-variance) diversifiers.

The CAPM Equation: $E(R_i) = R_f + [E(R_m) - R_f]\beta$

where:

$E(R_i)$ = The expected return for a given security
R_f = The risk-free rate of return
$E(R_m)$ = The expected rate of return for the market portfolio (the index portfolio)
β = Beta, the covariance measure between the return of a security and the market

The CAPM equation states: "The expected return of a security (i) is equal to the risk-free rate (usually a Treasury yield) plus Beta (the covariance of that security's return with the markets') times the difference between the return on the market (usually the S&P 500) and the risk-free rate (this difference is known as the risk premium)."

Consider the following simple example: ABC Company has a beta of .8, the market's rate of return is 12% and the Treasury bond is yielding 5%. The expected rate of return for this security (according to CAPM) is as follows:

$$E(R_{ABC}) = 5\% + [12\% - 5\%]\ (.8)$$
$$= 10.6\%$$

This rate would be useful in determining if the shares were undervalued or overvalued by comparing the expected rates of return with this "calculated" or "theoretical" rate of return. Also, this rate could be used as a discount rate in the valuation process of the particular security.

CAPM is used to estimate the required or expected rate of return for a security or portfolio and is based on systematic risk, which is proxied by beta. Investors should expect to be rewarded for taking risk, but only systematic risk because it cannot be diversified away—the beta in the CAPM equation captures this risk. Although the CAPM model is widely used in finance, it has never been fully supported in empirical tests; furthermore, beta itself has been the subject to criticisms.

Graphical Representation

The Security Market Line (SML) graph (Figure 7.13) is the graphical representation of CAPM. As the SML graph illustrates, there exists an market rate of return associated when beta is equal to 1. In addition, the SML shows an equilibrium rate of return for any measure of beta. This is useful in determining if a security is overvalued or undervalued according to the expected rate of return given its beta.

APPENDIX 2—ETHICS IN THE FINANCIAL SERVICES INDUSTRY

Ethics is difficult to teach because most people adhere to these beliefs intuitively; those who don't grasp the meaning of ethical concepts often

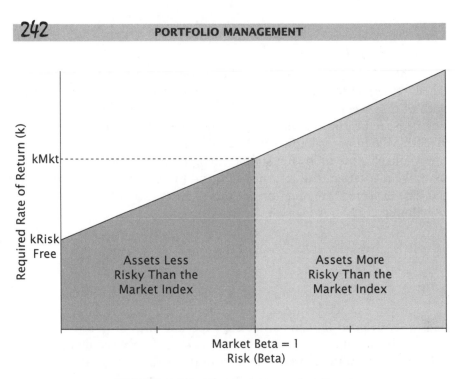

FIGURE 7.13 The security market line.

reveal a character flaw deeply embedded in their subconscious. The financial services industry has gone to great lengths to remove any stigmas of unethical dealings that have damaged their reputation in the past (and to a certain extent still do). The Standards of Professional Conduct of the Association of Investment Management and Research (AIMR) are reproduced in this Appendix. These Standards must be upheld by the thousands of members of the AIMR and are taken seriously by the ethics subcommittee at AIMR. These Standards represent the utmost in ethical requirements in the investment community.

The AIMR's Code of Ethics also is presented here. It is this code that each Chartered Financial Analyst, candidate (currently enrolled in the CFA Program) for the CFA, and member of the AIMR must uphold. Once again it should be clear just how seriously ethics is taken within this organization and consequently by its members. While much of this may seem like fluff, let me assure you that it is anything but; this fact is further evidenced by AIMR's Professional Standards Program. As the language in this extract illustrates, chartered financial analysts are definitely held to a high ethical standard.

Why is any of this information of consequence to the individual investor? Today's investor needs to be aware of the mechanisms that are in place to protect the efficiency and integrity of capital markets. Investors should understand the legal, policy, and ethical constraints that govern the industry they are trusting to preserve and appreciate their hard-earned capital. This is not to say that fraud and deceit are not present in the financial markets, but it is comforting to know that, for the most part, this behavior is in the minority and most likely will be weeded out in the short run. This is the essence of an efficient market—a fair game for each participant if he invests his resources wisely and prudently.

Standards of Professional Conduct*

I. Obligation to Inform Employer of Code and Standards

The financial analyst shall inform his employer, through his direct supervisor, that the analyst is obligated to comply with the Code of Ethics and Standards of Professional Conduct, and is subject to disciplinary sanctions for violations thereof. He shall deliver a copy of the Code and Standards to his employer if the employer does not have a copy.

II. Compliance with Governing Laws and Regulations and the Code of Standards

A. Required Knowledge and Compliance

The financial analyst shall maintain knowledge of and shall comply with all applicable laws, rules, and regulations of any government, governmental agency, and regulatory organization governing his professional, financial, or business activities, as well as with these Standards of Professional Conduct and the accompanying Code of Ethics.

B. Prohibition Against Assisting Legal and Ethical Violations

The financial analyst shall not knowingly participate in, or assist, any acts in violation of any Applicable law, rule, or regulation of any government, governmental agency, or regulatory organization governing his professional, financial, or business activities, nor any act which would violate any provision of these Standards of Professional Conduct or the accompanying Code of Ethics.

C. Prohibition Against Use of Material Nonpublic Information

The financial analyst shall comply with all laws and regulations relating to the use and communication of material nonpublic

(continued)

Source. The Standards of Practice Handbook, copyright 1993 by The Association for Investment Management and Research. Reprinted with permission.

Standards of Professional Conduct (Continued)

information. The financial analyst's duty is generally defined as to not trade while in possession of, nor communicate, material non-public information in breach of duty, or if the information is mis-appropriated.

Duties under the Standard include the following: (1) If the analyst acquires such information as a result of a special or confidential relationship with the issuer or others, he shall not communicate the information (other than within the relationship), or take investment action on the basis of such information, if it violates that relationship. (2) If the analyst is not in a special or confidential relationship with the issuer or others, he shall not communicate or act on material nonpublic information if he knows, or should have known, that such information (a) was disclosed to him, or would result in a breach of a duty, or (b) was misappropriated.

If such a breach of duty exists, the analyst shall make reasonable efforts to achieve public dissemination of such information.

D. Responsibilities of Supervisors

A financial analyst with supervisory responsibility shall exercise reasonable supervision over those subordinate employees subject to his control, to prevent any violation by such persons of applicable statutes, regulations, or provisions of the Code of Ethics or Standards of Professional Conduct. In so doing the analyst is entitled to rely upon reasonable procedures established by his employer.

III. Research Reports, Investment Recommendations, and Actions

A. Reasonable Basis and Representatives

1. The financial analyst shall exercise diligence and thoroughness in making an investment recommendation to others or in taking an investment action for others.

2. The financial analyst shall have a reasonable and adequate basis for such recommendations and actions, supported by appropriate research and investigation.

3. The financial analyst shall make reasonable and diligent efforts to avoid any material misrepresentation in any research report or investment recommendation.

4. The financial analyst shall maintain appropriate records to support the reasonableness of such recommendations and actions.

Standards of Professional Conduct (Continued)

B. Research Reports

1. The financial analyst shall use reasonable judgment as to the inclusion of relevant factors in research reports.
2. The financial analyst shall distinguish between facts and opinions in research reports.
3. The financial analyst shall indicate the basic characteristics of the investment involved when preparing for general public distribution a research report that is not directly related to a specific portfolio or client.

C. Portfolio Investment Recommendations and Actions

The financial analyst shall, when making an investment recommendation or taking an investment action for a specific portfolio or client, consider its appropriateness and suitability for such portfolio or client. In considering such matters, the financial analyst shall take into account (1) the needs and circumstances of the client, (2) the basic characteristics of the investment involved, and (3) the basic characteristics of the total portfolio. The financial analyst shall use reasonable judgment to determine the applicable relevant factors. The financial analyst shall distinguish between facts and opinions in the presentation of investment recommendations.

D. Prohibition Against Plagiarism

The financial analyst shall not, when presenting material to his employer, associates, customers, clients, or the general public, copy or use in substantially the same form material prepared by other persons without acknowledging its use and identifying the name of the author or publisher of such material. The analyst may, however, use without acknowledgment factual information published by recognized financial and statistical reporting services or similar sources.

E. Prohibition Against Misrepresentation of Services

The financial analyst shall not make statements, orally or in writing which misrepresent (1) the services that the analyst or his firm is capable of performing for the client, (2) the qualifications of such analyst or his firm, (3) the investment performance that the analyst or his firm has accomplished or can reasonably be expected to achieve for the client, or (4) the expected performance of any investment.

The financial analyst shall not make, orally or in writing, explicitly or implicitly, any assurances about or guarantees of any

(continued)

Standards of Professional Conduct (Continued)

investment or its return except communication of accurate information as to the terms of the investment instrument and the issuer's obligations under the instrument.

F. Fair Dealing with Customers and Clients

The financial analyst shall act in a manner consistent with his obligation to deal fairly with all customers and clients when (1) disseminating investment recommendations, (2) disseminating material changes in prior investment advice, and (3) taking investment action.

IV. Priority of Transactions

The financial analyst shall conduct himself in such a manner that transactions for his customers, clients, and employer have priority over personal transactions, and so that his personal transactions do not operate adversely to their interests. If an analyst decides to make a recommendation about the purchase or sale of a security or other investment, he shall give his customers, clients and employer adequate opportunity to act on this recommendation before acting on his own behalf.

V. Disclosure of Conflicts

The financial analyst, when making investment recommendations, or taking investment actions, shall disclose to his customers and clients any material conflict of interest relating to him and any material beneficial ownership of the securities or other investments involved that could reasonably be expected to impair his ability to render unbiased and objective advice.

The financial analyst shall disclose to his employer all matters that could reasonably be expected to interfere with his duty to the employer, or with his ability to render unbiased and objective advice.

The financial analyst shall also comply with all requirements as to disclosure of conflicts of interest imposed by law and by rules and regulations of organizations governing his activities and shall comply with any prohibitions on his activities if a conflict of interest exists.

VI. Compensation

A. Disclosure of Additional Compensation Arrangements

The financial analyst shall inform his customers, clients, and employer of compensation or other benefit arrangements in connection with his services to them which are in addition to compensation from them for such services.

Standards of Professional Conduct (Continued)

B. Disclosure of Referral Fees

The financial analyst shall make appropriate disclosure to a prospective client or customer of any consideration paid or other benefit delivered to others for recommending his services to that prospective client or customer.

C. Duty to Employer

The financial analyst shall not undertake independent practice for compensation or other benefit in competition with his employer unless he has received written consent from both his employer and the person for whom he undertakes independent employment.

VII. Relationships with Others

A. Preservation of Confidentiality

A financial analyst shall preserve the confidentiality of information communicated by the client concerning matters within the scope of the confidential relationship, unless the financial analyst received information concerning illegal activities on the part of the client.

B. Maintenance of Independence and Objectivity

The financial analyst, in relationships and contacts with an issuer of securities, whether individually or as a member of a group, shall use particular care and good judgment to achieve and maintain independence and objectivity.

C. Fiduciary Duties

The financial analyst, in relationships with clients, shall use particular care in determining applicable fiduciary duty and shall comply with such duty as to those persons and interests to whom it is owed.

VIII. Use of Professional Designation

The qualified financial analyst may use, as applicable, the professional designation "Member of the Association for Investment Management and Research," "Member of the Financial Analysts Federation," and "Member of the Institute of Chartered Financial Analysts," and is encouraged to do so, but only in a dignified and judicious manner. The use of the designations may be accompanied by an accurate explanation (1) of the requirements that have been met to obtain the designation, and (2) of the Association for Investment Management and

(continued)

Standards of Professional Conduct (Continued)

Research, the Financial Analysts Federation, and the Institute of Chartered Financial Analysts, as applicable.

The Chartered Financial Analyst may use the professional designation "Chartered Financial Analyst," or the abbreviation "CFA," and is encouraged to do so, but only in a dignified and judicious manner. The use of the designation may be accompanied by an accurate explanation (1) of the requirements that have been met to obtain the designation, and (2) of the Association for Investment Management and Research, and the Institute of Chartered Financial Analysts.

IX. Professional Misconduct

The financial analyst shall not (1) commit a criminal act that upon conviction materially reflects adversely on his honesty, trustworthiness or fitness as a financial analyst in other respects, or (2) engage in conduct involving dishonesty, fraud, deceit or misrepresentation.

Code of Ethics

Members of the Association for Investment Management and Research shall:

- ✔ Act with integrity, competence, dignity, and in an ethical manner when dealing with the public, clients, prospects, employers, employees, and fellow members.

- ✔ Practice and encourage others to participate in a professional and ethical manner that will reflect credit on members and their profession.

- ✔ Strive to maintain and improve their competence and the competence of others in the profession.

- ✔ Use reasonable care and exercise independent professional judgment.

Source. The Standards of Practice Handbook, copyright 1993 by The Association for Investment Management and Research. Reprinted with permission.

AIMR Professional Standards Programs

All members of AIMR, whether regular members or affiliates, including whose who are retired but maintain an active presence within the profession, are included, as are all those who are awarded the CFA professional designation, whether or not they are members of AIMR, and all candidates for the CFA designation.

The definition of financial analyst and financial analysis in the AIMR bylaws is broad. It provides that a financial analyst "is an individual who spends a substantial portion of time collecting, evaluating, or applying financial, economic, and statistical data, as appropriate, in the investment decision making process. This process is referred to as financial analysis."

Because the definition of a financial analyst is broad, the *Handbook* often employs the term "investment professional" to indicate the variety and complexity of the functions of members, CFAs, and CFA candidates in a changing and increasingly diverse investment environment.

Extensive diversity exists in the occupations of regular members and affiliates of AIMR, both of whom are referred to as members in the *Handbook* and elsewhere. Regular members either have three years' experience and have passed CFA I or have six years' experience and have passed a self-administered examination based on the Code and Standards. Affiliates lack the minimum experience requirement or do not meet the strict definition of financial analyst but are engaged in related activities, such as corporate pension fund sponsorship or consulting, options and futures analysis and management, corporate financial and investor relations activities, bank and loan decisions, and real estate analysis and management.

Violations of the Code and Standards

The bylaws of AIMR, FAF, and ICFA provide, in addition to the required compliance by members, that violations of the Code and Standards are grounds for disciplinary sanctions by AIMR, as are other grounds set forth in the respective bylaws.

AIMR has established in its bylaws the basic structure for enforcing the Code and Standards, implemented through Rules of Procedure (Rules) adopted by AIMR. Authorized sanctions, in increasing order of severity, include an administrative sanction, private reprimand, private censure, public censure, suspension, revocation of membership, and in the case of CFAs, suspension or revocation of the CFA charter. With the exception of summary suspension as outlined in Rule VII, the latter four sanctions can only be imposed by the AIMR Board of Governors. Appropriate notice of disciplinary sanction is also authorized.

(continued)

AIMR Professional Standards Programs (Continued)

Enforcement Procedures

The AIMR Code and Standards are enforced through the procedures based on due process that involve staff investigation and peer review on a confidential basis. (The Rules of Procedure for Proceedings Related to Professional Conduct are printed in AIMR's membership directory.) The AIMR designated officer is responsible for administration of the rules. The AIMR Professional Conduct Committee (PCC) consists of a chairman, one or more vice chairmen, and other members who chair ten regional committees. The more than 80 members of these regional committees provide an additional peer review mechanism.

Each member, CFA, and CFA candidate must submit a member's agreement, and an initial Professional Conduct Statement and subsequent annual statements, which require disclosure pertinent to the Code and Standards. Information received by AIMR relating to an individual's professional conduct, including disclosure in his or her statement or from other sources of legal or regulatory proceedings against him or her or complaints by members or nonmembers, may lead to an inquiry. Complaints regarding professional conduct must be in written form.

Inquiries are conducted by staff operating under the supervision of the designated officer and in consultation with legal counsel. When an inquiry is undertaken, the individual against whom a complaint has been filed is requested to submit a written explanation supported by documents when appropriate.

The designated officer, upon reviewing the explanation, may take one of the following steps: (1) dismiss the complaint, with the concurrence of the regional chairman in the case of a nonmember's complaint; (2) impose a private reprimand; (3) enter into a stipulation agreement with the individual, subject to the approval of the AIMR Board of Governors; or (4) submit the matter to a regional committee for further investigation.

The regional committee may submit a statement of charges resulting in the appointment by the PCC chairman of a panel to hear the charges and any defense offered. The hearing panel reports its findings and recommendations to the AIMR member, CFA, or CFA candidate, and to the AIMR Board of Governors if a sanction is recommended. Any proposed sanction must be approved by the board. Notices of sanctions are published in the AIMR newsletter or other publication of the organization.

Source. The Standards of Practice Handbook, copyright 1993 by The Association for Investment Management and Research. Reprinted with permission.

Insider Trading

The ethics of inside information is an important topic in the financial services industry. As purveyors of research, the financial analyst community often comes in contact with information that they, because of their position, are trusted with. In most cases, the analyst who comes in contact with nonpublic information will not be explicitly warned about the confidential nature of such information. It is incumbent upon the analyst to be aware of what material nonpublic information is and to make every effort to seek its public disclosure.

Firms may, for strategic reasons, decide to keep this information nonpublic until such time that it is required to be public. The analyst should "divorce" himself or herself from any dealings with the security and cease from any trading in this security. Furthermore, the analyst also has a duty to inform his firm of any lax policies with regard to the disclosure of nonpublic information. There should be firm policies with regard to material nonpublic information. There should also be educational programs to inform employees of these policies. Watch lists and restricted lists should be used. Different departments in the firm should be separated, to some degree, by an information barrier (called a Chinese or fire wall).

The legal issues surrounding trading in material nonpublic information has evolved over the last 50 years or so. Has a breach of fiduciary duty been consummated? Under the classical theory, this breach of fiduciary duty is defined as being between the company and their investment bankers, accountants, and lawyers. If XYZ Company tells their accountant of a lucrative new contract and the accountant then buys shares in anticipation of such an announcement, the accountant is clearly breaching the fiduciary duty between himself and the company. The same thing applies for the company's attorneys and investment bankers—a breach of fiduciary duty results in violations of inside information.

Now consider the employee of XYZ's financial printer who, through his work, comes into contact with material nonpublic information. He trades on this information. Is this an insider trading violation? As illustrated in the *Chiarella vs. United States* case, the employees of the printer do not have a fiduciary relationship (as required by the Classical Theory) with XYZ and therefore cannot breach such a relationship. Enter the Misappropriation Theory; it was this theory that sanctioned the illegality of the use of material, nonpublic information for any breach not just those of a fiduciary nature. According to the Misappropriation Theory, if a person misappropriates material nonpublic information and uses or conveys this information to someone else, then that person has breached a duty that then imposes an illegal act.

Definitions

Material Information.   Information that would (with a high degree of certainty) upon its dissemination cause a significant effect on the price of the securities involved. In addition, materiality can be illustrated if a knowledgeable investor would expect this information to affect his or her trading in this security.

Nonpublic Information.   Information that is not in the public domain; that is, it has not yet been disseminated and made available to all investors who seek it.

Fiduciary.   One who has a special relationship of trust with someone (person or institution) else. This fiduciary has a duty to this counterparty to serve in a manner which is fair, honest, and to keep counterparty's best interests as the sole beneficiary of the fiduciary's actions. Simply put, a fiduciary must put the interests of the beneficiaries before that of his own or his firm.

Misappropriation Theory.   Pertains to violations of 10-b(5) that occur when material, nonpublic information is misappropriated in a breach of duty or similar relationship of trust and confidence. The breach need not be one of fiduciary nature (as in the Classical Theory) but only a breach of duty (as in the case of an employee to an employer). Further, this information is then used in transactions or is communicated to others for their use. This theory is the basis of insider trading laws.

The Chinese Wall (or the Fire Wall).   While all confidential information must be handled in accordance with the policies and procedures set forth by the firm's compliance handbook, the securities laws require more specific procedures to separate the disparate business activities of the firm. These procedures, known collectively as the Chinese Wall, are reasonably designed to restrict the flow of inside information and to prevent those employees engaged in research, sales, trading, portfolio management, and administrative activities (marketing) from gaining access to inside information that the firm may have acquired or developed in connection with investment or merchant banking activities of other employees of the firm (banking side), except pursuant to specific wall-crossing procedures.

In general, banking employees must obtain prior authorization (usually written) on a project-by-project and person-by-person basis from a senior banking employee before contacting the marketing employee to bring him across the Wall.

Mosaic Theory.   Pertains to the act of researching through the use of public information and nonpublic, nonmaterial information a company's history and business dealings. This research may allow the analyst to "piece together" (hence, the term mosaic) facts that lead to conclusions that are the basis of material, nonpublic information. The analyst, for his own protection, is expected to keep detailed records of his research that allowed him to build the mosaic and the consequent conclusions.

Watch List.   A confidential list of securities about which the firm may have received or may expect to receive inside information. These lists are ordinarily used to monitor sales, trading (especially that of employees), and research activities in these securities and to monitor compliance with the Chinese Wall.

Legal Restricted List.   A confidential list of securities that are subject to restrictions in handling customer orders, trading for proprietary accounts, trading for discretionary accounts, trading for employee and related accounts, and other activities. The Restricted List refers to those securities that the firm may have or expect to have a fiduciary relationship with in the near future.

Employee Education.   A firm has a duty to educate its employees about the internal compliance procedures, especially those dealing with inside information. There are several methods that Wall Street firms use to increase the awareness of ethical and legal violations including courses on ethics, firmwide retreats, policy manuals, and even pop-quizzes.

Insider Trading Laws

Insider Trading & Securities Fraud Enforcement Act (ITS-FEA)–1988.   Increased criminal penalties for securities law violations (maximum jail term increased from 5 to 10 years, maximum individual fine increased from $100,000 to $1,000,000, maximum fine for business entities increased from $500,000 to $2,500,000); allows SEC to pay bounties to informants of up to 10% of penalty imposed; authorizes SEC to exchange information with foreign governments; and establishes joint liability for "contemporaneous traders" (total damages may be assessed against any and all users of insider information).

Securities Enforcement Remedies & Penny Stock Reform Act (SERPSRA)–1990.   Provides SEC additional remedies including civil penalties in administrative proceedings; penalties can be assessed by the SEC in its own hearings or by the courts in civil cases; SEC can issue permanent or temporary cease-and-desist orders after finding that a person or entity is or will violate securities laws. Allows SEC to bar brokers, investment advisors and dealers (firms) from participating in the industry for any period of time, including lifetime.

Epilogue

Okay, the journey you embarked on in Chapter 1 has come to an end; or has it? I hope you have become a more proactive investor, fully aware of the implications embedded in periodic economic releases, the valuation techniques of financial assets, and the process by which professional investment managers formulate portfolios.

When asked what type of investment (a strategy requiring a relatively minor research commitment; typically suggested for retirement and custodial accounts) I would recommend to an investor, my response is the same for the novice or the seasoned investor—the Dow dividend theory. This theory is a time tested strategy that illustrates the performance of a portfolio of 10 stocks chosen through the calculation of the highest dividend yield from the 30-stock Dow Jones Industrial Average. This portfolio is then held for 12 months and, on maturity, is restructured to the next 10 highest yielding stocks in the Dow Average. This strategy is one of the best investment strategies for a conservative investor seeking long-term capital appreciation. While a limited venue of stock choices (only the 30 Dow stocks are included in this strategy) is available in this strategy, the investor is comforted by knowing that these companies are among the most conservative and largest companies in the United States. As I often describe it, with this strategy the investor is "shopping" in the best neighborhood and therefore the best values abound. Furthermore, the calculation of the highest yields is straightforward and removes any of the emotion that often roils the most seasoned investor. Also by focusing on the dividend rather then the earnings, the investor gets to the true measure of the company's ability to generate cash flow. A company's stated dividend is typically treated with care and respect. The dividend is seen, by both the investor and the company, as an unwritten covenant that is not subjected to the vagaries and whims of management and their policies. Therefore, a greater level of stability is present with dividends than with most other factors.

Dow Dividend Theory Performance Numbers—1972–1997

Year	DJIA Total Return (%)	Top Ten
1972	18.21	23.26
1973	−13.21	−1.02
1974	−23.14	−0.31
1975	44.40	57.02
1976	22.72	34.81
1977	−12.71	−0.83
1978	2.69	0.16
1979	10.52	12.35
1980	21.41	26.37
1981	−3.40	7.47
1982	25.79	25.46
1983	25.68	38.46
1984	1.06	7.34
1985	32.78	28.63
1986	26.91	34.57
1987	6.02	6.97
1988	15.95	21.50
1989	31.71	27.30
1990	−0.57	−7.94
1991	23.93	33.37
1992	7.34	8.32
1993	16.72	26.92
1994	4.95	3.89
1995	36.48	36.48
1996	28.57	27.94
1997	24.78	19.62

Average Annual Rate of Return

3 year	29.85	26.24
5 year	21.81	20.69
10 year	18.41	17.31
25 year	13.01	16.09

Notes. DJIA = Dow Jones Industrial Average; Top Ten = The strategy described by the Dow dividend theory.

The above performance numbers are based on a calendar year basis and do not reflect any sales charges, expenses, or taxes. The total returns are based on price appreciation plus any dividends.

The performance numbers above were calculated by taking the year-end prices, subtracting them from the beginning-year prices, and adding dividends received for the period. The author does not represent these to be exact figures, but rather as a close estimate.

These numbers represent historical performance and in no way does this performance guarantee any future performance.

APPENDIXES

Appendix A

Internet Directory

INVESTMENT RESEARCH USING THE INTERNET

The development of the Internet has had a fundamental and profound effect on business, education, and entertainment. Fortunately, the individual investor has not been denied the benefits of cyberspace. The Internet offers unparalleled research opportunities for investors through quick access to documents and free exchange of ideas. With a few keystrokes, an investor anywhere in the world can instantly obtain information that was once only available from a broker or investment firm. This empowerment of today's investor provides a good part of the fuel of the current bull market.

One of the most useful Internet resources is the World Wide Web (popularly called the "Web"), a seemingly endless array of documents and files. Think of the Web as a huge, all-encompassing database that, if queried properly, can return a wealth of investor information. Web pages often incorporate pictures, sounds, and other interactive utilities that make accessing material easy, informative, and fun. Newsgroups are another useful feature of the Internet. These are the equivalent of electronic bulletin boards that allow people to read and respond to postings submitted by the many "Net-izens" who inhabit cyberspace. Newsgroups are organized by subject matter and may contain Internet links to related files (e.g., pictures, sounds, documents, spreadsheets) or copies of the files themselves embedded in the body of a message. Another common resource of the Internet is E-mail. This basic tool allows users to send electronic letters around the corner or around the world. The most popular means of accessing E-mail is through an Internet Service Provider (ISP) such as America Online, CompuServe, or Prodigy. These providers usually offer supplementary services to subscribers (e.g., electronic games, chat rooms, and shopping). Browsing through the many areas of America Online is not quite the same as "surfing the 'Net." The Web and newsgroups represent an entire world beyond the cozy realm of America Online and similar services. The simplicity and user-friendly format of these services, however, provide an easy way for even the novice computer user to explore some of the Internet's benefits.

So, how does the average investor take full advantage of all that the Internet has to offer? Often, the best way to perform investment research via the Internet isn't by directly searching the Web or newsgroups, but by using one of the many quality Web sites available from financial firms, consumer groups, and government agencies. These Internet sites go through the trouble of collecting and verifying information for you, and allow you to find quickly and easily what you need, be it the latest quarterly EPS release for Intel, or the number of new housing starts for the month of November. The following list describes some of the best investment research sites. Happily, these sites are all free, although some require a free registration to obtain a user name and password. (*Note.* As with anything on the Internet, these sites are subject to rapid change or closure without notice. Usually, when a site changes address, the old address will remain active with a link to the site's new home.)

Individual Company Research

http://www.dailystocks.com
Perhaps the finest site for company research available on the Web, DailyStocks has it all. You can start out by screening for stocks that match your own customized set of requirements (like growth rates, P/E ratios, and debt factors), then perform detailed fundamental and technical analysis. The site acts as a bridge between the investor and other sites offering information. From here, you can find links to company news from sources like Dow Jones; articles from magazines like *Fortune* and *Business Week;* discussion groups from the Motley Fools; company fundamentals via Morningstar, Hoovers, Zack's, and others; technical charts and graphs; earnings estimates and research reports from investment firms; SEC filings;

stock quotes; and much, much more. You can also research recent IPOs, discover EPS surprises, learn how professional investors and insiders are trading your stock, research mutual funds, and collect data on the U.S. economy.

(Although this site is free and requires no registration, some links may require registration, and a small few are pay sites.)

http://www.wsrn.com

Another excellent site similar to DailyStocks, this page contains over 250,000 links to company information, mutual fund research, and economic data.

http://www.peerscape.com

This site, administered by the accounting firm Deloitte & Touche, contains a wealth of historical data for most companies, including detailed balance sheets and income statements. Additionally, the site provides comprehensive company analysis reports that include key operating measures for a company (like profit margins, return on equity, and credit ratios), as well as useful graphs and charts comparing a selected company to 10 of its closest industry peers.

(Free registration required.)

http://www.prars.com

This is the largest annual report ordering service firm in the country. Through the Public Registers Annual Report Service, you can have free copies of annual reports from any of 3200 companies sent to you. Another useful feature of this site is its database of the 50 top financial Web sites, according to its continuously updated survey of Internet investors.

http://edgar.stern.nyu.edu/EDGAR/toolSearch.html

Retrieve the Securities and Exchange Commission filings of any publicly listed company. You can access 10-Ks, 10-Qs, 8-Ks, 13F-Es, and most other filings for up to a year in the past, within 24 hours of the time of filing. You can search by ticker, company, form type, industry, or sector code. This is a much faster alternative to the SEC's own database of filings (http://www.sec.gov) and to other EDGAR sites, which can become quite slow during business hours.

Quotes

http://www.quote.com

Free stock quotes, as well as popular market and industry index quotes.

http://quote.pathfinder.com/money/quote/qc

http://www.secapl.com/cgi-bin/qs

http://fast.quote.com/fq/zacks/ticker
Stock quotes, plain and simple. Just enter a ticker—or search for one if you don't know it—and retrieve 10–20-minute delayed quotes. (Many sites on-line offer up-to-the-minute quotes, live streaming stock charts, and other high-tech novelties, but only for a price.)

http://www.secapl.com/secapl/quoteserver/mw.html
Delayed quotes of popular indices such as the S&P 500, the NYSE, and NASDAQ.

U.S. Economy

http://www.bog.frb.fed.us/fomc/bb/current
Who better to turn to for information about the U.S. economy than the Federal Reserve Board? This is an on-line version of what is commonly called the "Beige Book," a summary of current economic conditions from each district of the Federal Reserve Bank.

http://www.census.gov/econ/www
Now that you've learned about the various economic indicators compiled regularly by the Census Bureau, put your knowledge to use by browsing through the latest retail, manufacturing, poverty, labor, and other indicators. Not sure when that indicator you're interested in is released? Well, the site also includes an economic indicator calendar for every day of the current year, so you'll never have to miss out.

http://www.webcom.com/~yardeni
An extremely comprehensive and helpful site covering macroeconomic analysis of the U.S. and other markets. Maintained by the chief economist of Deutsche Morgan Grenfell, this site also includes some of his own opinions and analysis of the economy.

General Information/Educational

http://www.morningstar.net
Articles, discussions, interviews, topic forums, market news, and interactive investment tools all designed with the individual investor in mind.

http://www.aaii.org
This is an educational and informative Web site for individual investors maintained by the American Association of Individual

Investors. Here you'll find a host of interesting investment articles covering topics from stocks, to fixed income securities, to mutual funds, as well as stocks screened by the AAII.

Fixed Income Securities

http://www.bonds-online.com
People who want information about bonds go here to do their research. Some parts of this site require a paid subscription, but most are free. You can research T-bills; corporate, municipal, and savings bonds; read up on news in the bond market; and learn about investing in bonds.

http://www.ratings.standardpoor.com
Retrieve bond ratings and research reports from one of the most popular and authoritative sources available.

International and Emerging Markets

http://www.ifc.org
This is the International Finance Corp.—the private-sector arm of the World Bank—providing current information about companies in international and emerging markets.

http://www.emgmkts.com
For the "big picture" view of an emerging market, including information on an emerging market's government, economic indicators, and related business news, try this site.

E-mail, Newsgroups, and Other Resources

http://www.infobeat.com
Receive a daily e-mail message containing closing prices and news for a personalized portfolio of market indices, mutual funds, and securities from the three major U.S. exchanges. Go to this site to register for free. (Resources like this—known as "push technology"—try to bring information to you, rather than forcing you to go out and find it yourself. See also "http://www.pointcast.com.")

http://www.liszt.com
Here you can search for mailing lists that might interest you. Once you subscribe, simply send an E-mail to the list, and everyone else on the list will receive it. And, when anyone else sends an E-mail, it

will automatically be distributed to you. List services are a great forum for discussing investment ideas and picking up investment tips. At this site, you can also search for relevant newsgroups.

http://www.reference.com
Another source for searching mailing lists and newsgroups.

misc.invest.stocks

misc.invest.funds

misc.invest.technical
A few popular newsgroups. Be warned that all newsgroups are unverified sources of information that may contain leading or entirely inaccurate information. Many times, these newsgroups are simply sounding boards for people to hype stocks they own, or advertise the latest get-rich-quick scheme. However, through patient detective work, the wary investor can usually glean some valuable information.

(*Note.* These are not World Wide Web addresses. You can access a newsgroup through a browser like Netscape by choosing "Add Newsgroup" within the Newsgroup function.)

http://www.dejanews.com
If you're researching a particular stock but don't feel like reading through thousands of newsgroup postings, try a newsgroup search here.

http://www.pointcast.com
Another example of push technology, this program acts as a screen saver for your computer. When the screen saver is activated, it broadcasts the latest news of your choosing over your desktop. And, while you're working, a scrolling ticker at the bottom of the screen relays the latest information. If a headline intrigues you, you're just a double-click away from the full story. News sources include the Wall Street Journal Interactive Edition, CNN, CNNfn, company and index quotes from S&P Comstock, and general information about companies or industries you wish to track. (Also track other news items, like weather, sports, and entertainment.)

If you've used all the listed resources and still haven't found what you're looking for, you can try directly searching the Internet. But before doing so, you should be aware of the biggest pitfall inherent in searching any database as vast as the Web. To put it simply, the problem is information overload, for the sheer volume of data available can become quite overwhelming. This issue of "information retrieval" has been the subject of much academic research and debate, most of it showing that retrieving information from huge databases is almost impossible to do effectively using any standard query tools. One study found that a group of lawyers searching their own relatively small database of case files couldn't even do so with much accuracy. They didn't retrieve many articles relevant to their case, but did retrieve much that was entirely useless.

The problems associated with information retrieval make for a daunting challenge for the average investor looking for information, but a few simple steps can help you find what you need. A useful starting point in your search is one of the many Internet search engines available. Some of the more popular search engines include:

- ✔ AltaVista—http://www.altavista.com
- ✔ Yahoo!—http://www.yahoo.com
- ✔ Infoseek—http://www.infoseek.com
- ✔ WebCrawler—http://www.webcrawler.com
- ✔ Hotbot—http://www.hotbot.com
- ✔ Lycos—http://www.lycos.com

Although these sites may have small differences, the basic formats are similar. You will usually have many options to help define your search, such as what part of the Internet to search (the Web or newsgroups) and what to display as matching search results (full descriptions of a page, brief descriptions, or simply an address telling you where to go). It is often best to search only the Web, and to include at least a brief description of the page.

The most difficult part of an Internet search is specifying what you're looking for and retrieving documents that are relevant to what you need. Say you're searching for information about Warren Buffett, the billionaire investor and Chairman of Berkshire Hathaway. Simply searching under the key phrase "Buffett" will inundate you with hundreds, if not thousands of documents, including everything from the music of Jimmy Buffett, to the poor fellow who has misspelled his advertisement for his "All-You-Can-Eat Lunch Buffet." (Though this may sound funny, it happens often. In the study mentioned earlier, one problem that the lawyers encountered while searching their database was that the names of the people involved in the case were often spelled wrong. Therefore, important articles were not retrieved because the search would not recognize a misspelled name as a "match" for the search words.) The trick here is to narrow down your search to include only what you really want.

There are certain criteria by which you can narrow your search using several words. For example, typing "Warren Buffett" will search for documents with "Warren" or "Buffett" in them. Doing this can help, but you'll still find yourself learning more than you ever needed to know about "Margaritaville." What's more, you'll now be wading through the description of every Web page maintained by, or about someone named Warren. A better method of linking words is the AND concatonator. Typing "Warren AND Buffett" or "+Warren +Buffett" will search for documents with Warren AND Buffett in them (by default, after listing all pages with Warren AND Buffett in them, most search engines then list search results for Warren OR Buffett). This increases the effectiveness of your search by weeding out irrelevant documents. However, this can lead to trouble as well. For example, typing "Warren Buffett AND Washington Post" is great if you want to learn about Buffett's spectacular investment in this company, but isn't very good if you're interested in any of his other investments. Too much detail might exclude documents that are in fact quite valuable. The paradoxical advice here: Be specific, but not *too* specific. (Are you starting to understand why those lawyers had so much trouble searching their own database?)

It is also a good idea to try several different search engines, as each has subtle nuances. More importantly, due to the system of "registering" pages employed by most search engines, often the same search on two different engines will yield entirely different results. This is because the person who maintains a Web page must add his page to a search engine database before a search on that engine can consider it. A great page about Warren Buffett may have been registered on AltaVista, but not on Infoseek. Therefore, if you search only using Infoseek, you'll miss out on the information.

Keeping the preceding in mind, let's say that you've found some good information about Warren Buffett. We now encounter a second major problem of the Web: the accuracy and quality of the information. Because anyone can say almost whatever they want on the Web, many people usually do. Just because you've found an article saying that Warren Buffett has purchased a major stake in Nike doesn't mean that this information is necessarily true. (Actually, this rumor wasn't true—it just seemed that way when Berkshire Hathaway purchased Geico. Yet, there were indeed many less reputable sources on the Web heralding the marriage between the "Oracle of Omaha" and "Air Jordan.")

Pay particular attention to the source of any information that you find on the Web.

Appendix

B

Selected Tables

TABLE B.1 ABC Products—Balance Sheet 12/31/94

Current Assets		Current Liabilities	
Cash	$ 256,663	Accrued expense	$ 188,539
Accounts payable	388,834	Income tax payable	13,394
Accounts receivable	578,745	Short-term notes payable	425,000
Inventory	978,094	**Total current liabilities**	**$1,015,767**
Prepaid expenses	117,176	**Long-term notes payable**	**$ 550,000**
Total current assets	**$1,930,687**		
Property, plant & equipment	$0		
Land, building, machines	0		
Equipment & furniture	1,986,450	**Stockholder's equity**	
Accumulated depreciation	(452,140)	Capital Stock	$1,534,310
		Retained earnings	725,000
			1,174,230
Other assets	0		**$1,889,230**
Total assets	**$3,464,997**	**Total liabilities & stockholders' equity**	**$3,464,997**

TABLE B.2 ABC Products—Income Statement 12/31/94

Sales revenue		$6,019,040
Cost of goods sold expense		3,912,376
Gross profit		$2,106,664
Operating expenses:		
S,G & A	$323,288	
Utilities	200,000	
Salaries	700,000	
Marketing/Advertising	300,000	
Total Operating Expenses	$1,523,288	
Operating earnings before depreciation		$ 583,376
Depreciation expense		112,792
Operating earnings		470,584
Interest expense		76,650
Earnings before income tax		393,934
Income tax expense		133,938
Net income		$ 259,996

**TABLE B.3   Parrot Computers Inc.
Balance Sheet, 1994 (in thousands)**

Assets		Liabilities and Equity	
Cash	$ 300	Accounts payable	$ 400
Accounts receivable	200	Long-term debt	250
Inventory	700	Common stock	1,000
Fixed assets	1,200	Retained earnings	750
Total assets	$2,400	Total liabilities and equity	$2,400

*Parrot Computer has A/R terms of net 45 days.
*Long-term debt principal repayment due in 1995 is $100.

**TABLE B.4   Parrot Computers Inc.
Income Statement, 1994 (in thousands)**

Sales (credit only)	$6,000
COGS	(4,000)
Depreciation	(300)
EBIT	$1,700
Interest expense	(100)
Pretax income	1,600
Taxes (40%)	(640)
Net income	$ 960

TABLE B.5 Selected Financial Ratios

Fiscal Year	EBIT + Assets		Total Assets + Common Equity		Net Earnings + Pretax Earnings		Net Sales + Total Assets	
	KO	PEP	KO	PEP	KO	PEP	KO	PEP
1983 (est.)	21.1%	14.7%	1.78x	2.56x	56.0%	58.0%	1.33x	1.82
1982	23.7	16.9	1.68	2.57	55.0	57.2	1.47	1.82
1981	24.3	17.7	1.60	2.53	55.4	58.5	1.69	1.89
1980	24.3	18.3	1.59	2.39	55.1	56.5	1.77	1.90
1979	26.2	18.5	1.51	2.20	55.4	59.8	1.70	1.92
1978	27.8	19.8	1.46	2.13	54.4	56.1	1.69	1.89
1977	27.9	20.1	1.41	2.31	54.0	55.4	1.59	1.83
1976	28.3	16.9	1.39	2.55	53.4	54.4	1.57	1.77
Averages								
1980–83	23.3	16.9	1.66x	2.51x	55.4	57.5	1.57x	1.84x
1976–79	27.6	18.8	1.44	2.30	54.3	56.4	1.64	1.85
1976–83	25.4	17.9	1.55	2.41	54.8	57.0	1.60	1.86

Average of beginning and end of year assets and equity used where applicable in computing ratios.

TABLE B.6 Selected Financial Ratios

Fiscal Year	Pretax Earnings + Net Sales		Net Earnings + Total Assets		Net Earnings + Common Equity		Dividends + Net Earnings	
	KO	PEP	KO	PEP	KO	PEP	KO	PEP
1983 (est.)	14.8%	6.4%	11.0%	6.5%	19.6%	16.6%	64.6%	53.1%
1982	14.9	7.1	12.1	7.4	20.3	18.9	62.8	48.9
1981	13.7	7.2	12.8	8.0	20.6	20.3	59.5	44.1
1980	13.1	7.7	12.8	8.3	20.3	19.8	63.2	44.1
1979	15.2	8.2	14.3	9.4	21.6	20.8	57.6	40.9
1978	16.2	9.2	14.9	9.8	21.8	20.9	57.4	40.6
1977	17.5	9.7	15.1	9.9	21.3	22.8	57.5	38.6
1976	18.0	9.6	15.1	9.2	21.1	23.4	55.7	35.4
Averages								
1980–83	14.1	7.1	12.2	7.6	20.2	18.9	62.5	47.6
1976–79	16.7	9.2	14.9	9.6	21.4	22.0	57.1	38.9
1976–83	15.4	8.1	13.5	8.6	20.8	20.4	59.8	43.2

Average of beginning and end-of-year assets and equity used where applicable in computing ratios.

TABLE B.7 Selected Financial Statistics, The Coca-Cola Company (in millions)

Fiscal Year

	1983 (Est.)	1982	1981	1980	1979	1978	1977	1976
Operations								
Sales	6,820.0	6,249.0	5,889.0	5,621.0	4,689.0	4,095.0	3,394.0	2,989.0
Depreciation	180.0	148.9	136.9	131.0	110.0	91.0	80.0	70.0
Interest	73.0	74.6	38.3	35.1	10.7	7.8	NA	NA
Income taxes	444.0	419.8	360.2	330.4	318.0	303.0	273.0	251.0
Net earnings	565.0	512.2	447.0	406.0	395.0	361.0	321.0	288.0
Financial Position								
Cash	616.4	311.0	393.0	289.0	209.0	369.0	418.0	403.0
Receivables	831.3	751.8	483.5	523.1	435.1	338.3	279.9	237.3
Current assets	2,444.2	2,076.6	1,636.2	1,622.3	1,305.6	1,236.6	1,103.5	1,027.3
Total assets	5,331.0	4,923.3	3,564.8	3,406.0	2,938.0	2,582.8	2,254.5	2,007.0
Current liabilities	1,702.7	1,326.8	1,006.3	1,061.6	884.2	744.0	596.3	506.4
Long-term debt	475.0	462.3	137.3	133.2	31.0	15.2	15.3	11.0
Common equity	2,990.0	2,778.7	2,270.8	2,074.7	1,918.7	1,739.6	1,578.0	1,434.0

TABLE B.8 Selected Financial Statistics, PepsiCo, Inc.* ($ Millions)

				Fiscal Year				
	1983 (Est.)	1982	1981	1980	1979	1978	1977	1976
Operations								
Sales	7,700.0	7,499.0	7,027.0	5,975.0	5,089.0	4,300.0	3,649.0	3,109.0
Depreciation	260.0	230.4	205.5	172.9	142.1	117.0	93.7	79.1
Interest	156.0	166.2	149.7	114.7	73.1	52.0	46.0	45.0
Income taxes	206.0	226.8	210.8	200.8	168.2	174.3	158.3	135.3
Net earnings	285.0	303.7**	297.5	260.7	250.4	223.0	196.7	161.7
Financial Position								
Cash and equivalents	397.3	280.3	239.0	232.0	205.0	167.0	256.0	231.0
Receivables	785.7	746.1	741.4	596.7	557.2	433.6	374.4	324.5
Current assets	1,739.4	1,590.6	1,762.5	1,326.5	1,201.4	1,010.5	997.0	903.7
Total assets	4,588.9	4,197.5	4,040.0	3,399.9	2,888.9	2,416.8	2,130.3	1853.6
Current liabilities	1,440.0	1,345.6	1,430.7	1,005.3	843.6	650.7	574.5	478.9
Long-term debt	786.7	864.2	816.1	781.7	619.0	479.1	427.9	278.6
Common equity	1,786.3	1,650.5	1,556.3	1,381.0	1,247.0	1,165.0	971.9	753.0

*Amounts for 1978–1981 restated to reflect overstatement of net income aggregating $92.1 million.
**Before unusual charge of $79.4 million.

Table B.9 Present Value of $1

$$PVIF = 1/(1+k)^t$$

Period	1%	2%	3%	4%	5%	6%	7%	8%	9%	10%	12%	14%	15%	16%	18%	20%	24%	28%	32%	36%
1	.9901	.9804	.9709	.9615	.9524	.9434	.9346	.9259	.9174	.9091	.8929	.8772	.8696	.8621	.8475	.8333	.8065	.7813	.7576	.7353
2	.9803	.9612	.9426	.9246	.9070	.8900	.8734	.8573	.8417	.8264	.7972	.7695	.7561	.7432	.7182	.6944	.6504	.6104	.5739	.5407
3	.9706	.9423	.9151	.8890	.8638	.8396	.8163	.7938	.7722	.7513	.7118	.6750	.6575	.6407	.6086	.5787	.5245	.4768	.4348	.3975
4	.9610	.9238	.8885	.8548	.8227	.7921	.7629	.7350	.7084	.6830	.6355	.5921	.5718	.5523	.5158	.4823	.4230	.3725	.3294	.2923
5	.9515	.9057	.8626	.8219	.7835	.7473	.7130	.6806	.6499	.6209	.5674	.5194	.4972	.4761	.4371	.4019	.3411	.2910	.2495	.2149
6	.9420	.8880	.8375	.7903	.7462	.7050	.6663	.6302	.5963	.5645	.5066	.4556	.4323	.4104	.3704	.3349	.2751	.2274	.1890	.1580
7	.9327	.8706	.8131	.7599	.7107	.6651	.6227	.5835	.5470	.5132	.4523	.3996	.3759	.3538	.3139	.2791	.2218	.1776	.1432	.1162
8	.9235	.8535	.7894	.7307	.6768	.6274	.5820	.5403	.5019	.4665	.4039	.3506	.3269	.3050	.2660	.2326	.1789	.1388	.1085	.0854
9	.9143	.8368	.7664	.7026	.6446	.5919	.5439	.5002	.4604	.4241	.3606	.3075	.2843	.2630	.2255	.1938	.1443	.1084	.0822	.0628
10	.9053	.8203	.7441	.6756	.6139	.5584	.5083	.4632	.4224	.3855	.3220	.2697	.2472	.2267	.1911	.1615	.1164	.0847	.0623	.0462
11	.8963	.8043	.7224	.6496	.5847	.5268	.4751	.4289	.3875	.3505	.2875	.2366	.2149	.1954	.1619	.1346	.0938	.0662	.0472	.0340
12	.8874	.7885	.7014	.6246	.5568	.4970	.4440	.3971	.3555	.3186	.2567	.2076	.1869	.1685	.1372	.1122	.0757	.0517	.0357	.0250
13	.8787	.7730	.6810	.6006	.5303	.4688	.4150	.3677	.3262	.2897	.2292	.1821	.1625	.1452	.1163	.0935	.0610	.0404	.0271	.0184
14	.8700	.7579	.6611	.5775	.5051	.4423	.3878	.3405	.2992	.2633	.2046	.1597	.1413	.1252	.0985	.0779	.0492	.0316	.0205	.0135
15	.8613	.7430	.6419	.5553	.4810	.4173	.3624	.3152	.2745	.2394	.1827	.1401	.1229	.1079	.0835	.0649	.0397	.0247	.0155	.0099
16	.8528	.7284	.6232	.5339	.4581	.3936	.3387	.2919	.2519	.2176	.1631	.1229	.1069	.0930	.0708	.0541	.0320	.0193	.0118	.0073
17	.8444	.7142	.6050	.5134	.4363	.3714	.3166	.2703	.2311	.1978	.1456	.1078	.0929	.0802	.0600	.0451	.0258	.0150	.0089	.0054
18	.8360	.7002	.5874	.4936	.4155	.3503	.2959	.2502	.2120	.1799	.1300	.0946	.0808	.0691	.0508	.0376	.0208	.0118	.0068	.0039
19	.8277	.6864	.5703	.4746	.3957	.3305	.2765	.2317	.1945	.1635	.1161	.0829	.0703	.0596	.0431	.0313	.0168	.0092	.0051	.0029
20	.8195	.6730	.5537	.4564	.3769	.3118	.2584	.2145	.1784	.1486	.1037	.0728	.0611	.0514	.0365	.0261	.0135	.0072	.0039	.0021
25	.7798	.6095	.4776	.3751	.2953	.2330	.1842	.1460	.1160	.0923	.0588	.0378	.0304	.0245	.0160	.0105	.0046	.0021	.0010	.0005
30	.7419	.5521	.4120	.3083	.2314	.1741	.1314	.0994	.0754	.0573	.0334	.0196	.0151	.0116	.0070	.0042	.0016	.0006	.0002	.0001
40	.6717	.4529	.3066	.2083	.1420	.0972	.0668	.0460	.0318	.0221	.0107	.0053	.0037	.0026	.0013	.0007	.0002	.0001	•	•
50	.6080	.3715	.2281	.1407	.0872	.0543	.0339	.0213	.0134	.0085	.0035	.0014	.0009	.0006	.0003	.0001	•	•	•	•
60	.5504	.3048	.1697	.0951	.0535	.0303	.0173	.0099	.0057	.0033	.0011	.0004	.0002	.0001	•	•	•	•	•	•

* The factor is zero to four decimal places.

Table B.10 Present Value of an Annuity of $1 Per Period for *n* Periods

$$PVIFA = \sum_{t=1}^{n} \frac{1}{(1+k)^t} = \frac{1 - \dfrac{1}{(1+k)^n}}{k}$$

Number of Payments	1%	2%	3%	4%	5%	6%	7%	8%	9%	10%	12%	14%	15%	16%	18%	20%	24%	28%	32%
1	0.9901	0.9804	0.9709	0.9615	0.9524	0.9434	0.9346	0.9259	0.9174	0.9091	0.8929	0.8772	0.8696	0.8621	0.8475	0.8333	0.8065	0.7813	0.7576
2	1.9704	1.9416	1.9135	1.8861	1.8594	1.8334	1.8080	1.7833	1.7591	1.7355	1.6901	1.6467	1.6257	1.6052	1.5656	1.5278	1.4568	1.3916	1.3315
3	2.9410	2.8839	2.8286	2.7751	2.7232	2.6730	2.6243	2.5771	2.5313	2.4869	2.4018	2.3216	2.2832	2.2459	2.1743	2.1065	1.9813	1.8684	1.7663
4	3.9020	3.8077	3.7171	3.6299	3.5460	3.4651	3.3872	3.3121	3.2397	3.1699	3.0373	2.9137	2.8550	2.7982	2.6901	2.5887	2.4043	2.2410	2.0957
5	4.8534	4.7135	4.5797	4.4518	4.3295	4.2124	4.1002	3.9927	3.8897	3.7908	3.6048	3.4331	3.3522	3.2743	3.1272	2.9906	2.7454	2.5320	2.3452
6	5.7955	5.6014	5.4172	5.2421	5.0757	4.9173	4.7665	4.6229	4.4859	4.3553	4.1114	3.8887	3.7845	3.6847	3.4976	3.3255	3.0205	2.7594	2.5342
7	6.7282	6.4720	6.2303	6.0021	5.7864	5.5824	5.3893	5.2064	5.0330	4.8684	4.5638	4.2883	4.1604	4.0386	3.8115	3.6046	3.2423	2.9370	2.6775
8	7.6517	7.3255	7.0197	6.7327	6.4632	6.2098	5.9713	5.7466	5.5348	5.3349	4.9676	4.6389	4.4873	4.3436	4.0776	3.8372	3.4212	3.0758	2.7860
9	8.5660	8.1622	7.7861	7.4353	7.1078	6.8017	6.5152	6.2469	5.9952	5.7590	5.3282	4.9464	4.7716	4.6065	4.3030	4.0310	3.5655	3.1842	2.8681
10	9.4713	8.9826	8.5302	8.1109	7.7217	7.3601	7.0236	6.7101	6.4177	6.1446	5.6502	5.2161	5.0188	4.8332	4.4941	4.1925	3.6819	3.2689	2.9304
11	10.3676	9.7868	9.2526	8.7605	8.3064	7.8869	7.4987	7.1390	6.8052	6.4951	5.9377	5.4527	5.2337	5.0286	4.6560	4.3271	3.7757	3.3351	2.9776
12	11.2551	10.5753	9.9540	9.3851	8.8633	8.3838	7.9427	7.5361	7.1607	6.8137	6.1944	5.6603	5.4206	5.1971	4.7932	4.4392	3.8514	3.3868	3.0133
13	12.1337	11.3484	10.6350	9.9856	9.3936	8.8527	8.3577	7.9038	7.4869	7.1034	6.4235	5.8424	5.5831	5.3423	4.9095	4.5327	3.9124	3.4272	3.0404
14	13.0037	12.1062	11.2961	10.5631	9.8986	9.2950	8.7455	8.2442	7.7862	7.3667	6.6282	6.0021	5.7245	5.4675	5.0081	4.6106	3.9616	3.4587	3.0609
15	13.8651	12.8493	11.9379	11.1184	10.3797	9.7122	9.1079	8.5595	8.0607	7.6061	6.8109	6.1422	5.8474	5.5755	5.0916	4.6755	4.0013	3.4834	3.0764
16	14.7179	13.5777	12.5611	11.6523	10.8378	10.1059	9.4466	8.8514	8.3126	7.8237	6.9740	6.2651	5.9542	5.6685	5.1624	4.7296	4.0333	3.5026	3.0882
17	15.5623	14.2919	13.1661	12.1657	11.2741	10.4773	9.7632	9.1216	8.5436	8.0216	7.1196	6.3729	6.0472	5.7487	5.2223	4.7746	4.0591	3.5177	3.0971
18	16.3983	14.9920	13.7535	12.6593	11.6896	10.8276	10.0591	9.3719	8.7556	8.2014	7.2497	6.4674	6.1280	5.8178	5.2732	4.8122	4.0799	3.5294	3.1039
19	17.2260	15.6785	14.3238	13.1339	12.0853	11.1581	10.3356	9.6036	8.9501	8.3649	7.3658	6.5504	6.1982	5.8775	5.3162	4.8435	4.0967	3.5386	3.1090
20	18.0456	16.3514	14.8775	13.5903	12.4622	11.4699	10.5940	9.8181	9.1285	8.5136	7.4694	6.6231	6.2593	5.9288	5.3527	4.8696	4.1103	3.5458	3.1129
25	22.0232	19.5235	17.4131	15.6221	14.0939	12.7834	11.6536	10.6748	9.8226	9.0770	7.8431	6.8729	6.4641	6.0971	5.4669	4.9476	4.1474	3.5640	3.1220
30	25.8077	22.3965	19.6004	17.2920	15.3725	13.7648	12.4090	11.2578	10.2737	9.4269	8.0552	7.0027	6.5660	6.1772	5.5168	4.9789	4.1601	3.5693	3.1242
40	32.8347	27.3555	23.1148	19.7928	17.1591	15.0463	13.3317	11.9246	10.7574	9.7791	8.2438	7.1050	6.6418	6.2335	5.5482	4.9966	4.1659	3.5712	3.1250
50	39.1961	31.4236	25.7298	21.4822	18.2559	15.7619	13.8007	12.2335	10.9617	9.9148	8.3045	7.1327	6.6605	6.2463	5.5541	4.9995	4.1666	3.5714	3.1250
60	44.9550	34.7609	27.6756	22.6235	18.9293	16.1614	14.0392	12.3766	11.0480	9.9672	8.3240	7.1401	6.6651	6.2402	5.5553	4.9999	4.1667	3.5714	3.1250

$$FVIF_{k,n} = (1+k)^n$$

Period	1%	2%	3%	4%	5%	6%	7%	8%	9%	10%	12%	14%	15%	16%	18%	20%	24%	28%	32%	36%
1	1.0100	1.0200	1.0300	1.0400	1.0500	1.0600	1.0700	1.0800	1.0900	1.1000	1.1200	1.1400	1.1500	1.1600	1.1800	1.2000	1.2400	1.2800	1.3200	1.3600
2	1.0201	1.0404	1.0609	1.0816	1.1025	1.1236	1.1449	1.1664	1.1881	1.2100	1.2544	1.2996	1.3225	1.3456	1.3924	1.4400	1.5376	1.6384	1.7424	1.8496
3	1.0303	1.0612	1.0927	1.1249	1.1576	1.1910	1.2250	1.2597	1.2950	1.3310	1.4049	1.4815	1.5209	1.5609	1.6430	1.7280	1.9066	2.0972	2.3000	2.5155
4	1.0406	1.0824	1.1255	1.1699	1.2155	1.2625	1.3108	1.3605	1.4116	1.4641	1.5735	1.6890	1.7490	1.8106	1.9388	2.0736	2.3642	2.6844	3.0360	3.4210
5	1.0510	1.1041	1.1593	1.2167	1.2763	1.3382	1.4026	1.4693	1.5386	1.6105	1.7623	1.9254	2.0114	2.1003	2.2878	2.4883	2.9316	3.4360	4.0075	4.6526
6	1.0615	1.1262	1.1941	1.2653	1.3401	1.4185	1.5007	1.5869	1.6771	1.7716	1.9738	2.1950	2.3131	2.4364	2.6996	2.9860	3.6352	4.3980	5.2899	6.3275
7	1.0721	1.1487	1.2299	1.3159	1.4071	1.5036	1.6058	1.7138	1.8280	1.9487	2.2107	2.5023	2.6600	2.8262	3.1855	3.5832	4.5077	5.6295	6.9826	8.6054
8	1.0829	1.1717	1.2668	1.3686	1.4775	1.5938	1.7182	1.8509	1.9926	2.1436	2.4760	2.8526	3.0590	3.2784	3.7589	4.2998	5.5895	7.2058	9.2170	11.703
9	1.0937	1.1951	1.3048	1.4233	1.5513	1.6895	1.8385	1.9990	2.1719	2.3579	2.7731	3.2519	3.5179	3.8030	4.4355	5.1598	6.9310	9.2234	12.166	15.916
10	1.1046	1.2190	1.3439	1.4802	1.6289	1.7908	1.9672	2.1589	2.3674	2.5937	3.1058	3.7072	4.0456	4.4114	5.2338	6.1917	8.5944	11.805	16.059	21.646
11	1.1157	1.2434	1.3842	1.5395	1.7103	1.8983	2.1049	2.3316	2.5804	2.8531	3.4785	4.2262	4.6524	5.1173	6.1759	7.4301	10.657	15.111	21.198	29.439
12	1.1268	1.2682	1.4258	1.6010	1.7959	2.0122	2.2522	2.5182	2.8127	3.1384	3.8960	4.8179	5.3502	5.9360	7.2876	8.9161	13.214	19.342	27.982	40.037
13	1.1381	1.2936	1.4685	1.6651	1.8856	2.1329	2.4098	2.7196	3.0658	3.4523	4.3635	5.4924	6.1528	6.8858	8.5994	10.699	16.386	24.758	36.937	54.451
14	1.1495	1.3195	1.5126	1.7317	1.9799	2.2609	2.5785	2.9372	3.3417	3.7975	4.8871	6.2613	7.0757	7.9875	10.147	12.839	20.319	31.691	48.756	74.053
15	1.1610	1.3459	1.5580	1.8009	2.0789	2.3966	2.7590	3.1722	3.6425	4.1772	5.4736	7.1379	8.1371	9.2655	11.973	15.407	25.195	40.564	64.358	100.71
16	1.1726	1.3728	1.6047	1.8730	2.1829	2.5404	2.9522	3.4259	3.9703	4.5950	6.1304	8.1372	9.3576	10.748	14.129	18.488	31.242	51.923	84.953	136.96
17	1.1843	1.4002	1.6528	1.9479	2.2920	2.6928	3.1588	3.7000	4.3276	5.0545	6.8660	9.2765	10.761	12.467	16.672	22.186	38.740	66.461	112.13	186.27
18	1.1961	1.4282	1.7024	2.0258	2.4066	2.8543	3.3799	3.9960	4.7171	5.5599	7.6900	10.575	12.375	14.462	19.673	26.623	48.038	85.070	148.02	253.33
19	1.2081	1.4568	1.7535	2.1068	2.5270	3.0256	3.6165	4.3157	5.1417	6.1159	8.6128	12.055	14.231	16.776	23.214	31.948	59.567	108.89	195.39	344.53
20	1.2202	1.4859	1.8061	2.1911	2.6533	3.2071	3.8697	4.6610	5.6044	6.7275	9.6463	13.743	16.366	19.460	27.393	38.337	73.864	139.37	257.91	468.57
21	1.2324	1.5157	1.8603	2.2788	2.7860	3.3996	4.1406	5.0338	6.1088	7.4002	10.803	15.667	18.821	22.574	32.323	46.005	91.591	178.40	340.44	637.26
22	1.2447	1.5460	1.9161	2.3699	2.9253	3.6035	4.4304	5.4365	6.6586	8.1403	12.100	17.861	21.644	26.186	38.142	55.206	113.57	228.35	449.39	866.67
23	1.2572	1.5769	1.9736	2.4647	3.0715	3.8197	4.7405	5.8715	7.2579	8.9543	13.552	20.361	24.891	30.376	45.007	66.247	140.83	292.30	593.19	1178.6
24	1.2697	1.6084	2.0328	2.5633	3.2251	4.0489	5.0724	6.3412	7.9111	9.8497	15.178	23.212	28.625	35.236	53.108	79.496	174.63	374.14	783.02	1602.9
25	1.2824	1.6406	2.0938	2.6658	3.3864	4.2919	5.4274	6.8485	8.6231	10.834	17.000	26.461	32.918	40.874	62.668	95.396	216.54	478.90	1033.5	2180.0
26	1.2953	1.6734	2.1566	2.7725	3.5557	4.5494	5.8074	7.3964	9.3992	11.918	19.040	30.166	37.856	47.414	73.948	114.47	268.51	612.99	1364.3	2964.9
27	1.3082	1.7069	2.2213	2.8834	3.7335	4.8223	6.2139	7.9881	10.245	13.110	21.324	34.389	43.535	55.000	87.259	137.37	332.95	784.63	1800.9	4032.2
28	1.3213	1.7410	2.2879	2.9987	3.9201	5.1117	6.6488	8.6271	11.167	14.421	23.883	39.204	50.065	63.800	102.96	164.84	412.86	1004.3	2377.2	5483.8
29	1.3345	1.7758	2.3566	3.1187	4.1161	5.4184	7.1143	9.3173	12.172	15.863	26.749	44.693	57.575	74.008	121.50	197.81	511.95	1285.5	3137.9	7458.0
30	1.3478	1.8114	2.4273	3.2434	4.3219	5.7435	7.6123	10.062	13.267	17.449	29.959	50.950	66.211	85.849	143.37	237.37	634.81	1645.5	4142.0	10143.
40	1.4889	2.2080	3.2620	4.8010	7.0400	10.285	14.974	21.724	31.409	45.259	93.050	188.88	267.86	378.72	750.37	1469.7	5455.9	19426.	66520.	●
50	1.6446	2.6916	4.3839	7.1067	11.467	18.420	29.457	46.901	74.357	117.39	289.00	700.23	1083.6	1670.7	3927.3	9100.4	46890.	●	●	●
60	1.8167	3.2810	5.8916	10.519	18.679	32.987	57.946	101.25	176.03	304.48	897.59	2595.9	4383.9	7370.1	20555.	56347.	●	●	●	●

FVIFA > 99.999

Table B.12 Future Value of an Annuity of $1 Per n Periods

$$FVIFA_{k,n} = \sum_{t=1}^{n}(1+k)^{t-1} = \frac{(1+k)^{n}-1}{k}$$

Number of Periods	1%	2%	3%	4%	5%	6%	7%	8%	9%	10%	12%	14%	15%	16%	18%	20%	24%	28%	32%	36%
1	1.0000	1.0000	1.0000	1.0000	1.0000	1.0000	1.0000	1.0000	1.0000	1.0000	1.0000	1.0000	1.0000	1.0000	1.0000	1.0000	1.0000	1.0000	1.0000	1.0000
2	2.0100	2.0200	2.0300	2.0400	2.0500	2.0600	2.0700	2.0800	2.0900	2.1000	2.1200	2.1400	2.1500	2.1600	2.1800	2.2000	2.2400	2.2800	2.3200	2.3600
3	3.0301	3.0604	3.0909	3.1216	3.1525	3.1836	3.2149	3.2464	3.2781	3.3100	3.3744	3.4396	3.4725	3.5056	3.5724	3.6400	3.7776	3.9184	4.0624	4.2096
4	4.0604	4.1216	4.1836	4.2465	4.3101	4.3746	4.4399	4.5061	4.5731	4.6410	4.7793	4.9211	4.9934	5.0665	5.2154	5.3680	5.6842	6.0156	6.3624	6.7251
5	5.1010	5.2040	5.3091	5.4163	5.5256	5.6371	5.7507	5.8666	5.9847	6.1051	6.3528	6.6101	6.7424	6.8771	7.1542	7.4416	8.0484	8.6999	9.3983	10.146
6	6.1520	6.3081	6.4684	6.6330	6.8019	6.9753	7.1533	7.3359	7.5233	7.7156	8.1152	8.5355	8.7537	8.9775	9.4420	9.9299	10.980	12.135	13.405	14.798
7	7.2135	7.4343	7.6625	7.8983	8.1420	8.3938	8.6540	8.9228	9.2004	9.4872	10.089	10.730	11.066	11.413	12.141	12.915	14.615	16.533	18.695	21.126
8	8.2857	8.5830	8.8923	9.2142	9.5491	9.8975	10.259	10.636	11.028	11.435	12.299	13.232	13.726	14.240	15.327	16.499	19.122	22.163	25.678	29.731
9	9.3685	9.7546	10.159	10.582	11.026	11.491	11.978	12.487	13.021	13.579	14.775	16.085	16.785	17.518	19.085	20.798	24.712	29.369	34.895	41.435
10	10.462	10.949	11.463	12.006	12.577	13.180	13.816	14.486	15.192	15.937	17.548	19.337	20.303	21.321	23.521	25.958	31.643	38.592	47.061	57.351
11	11.566	12.168	12.807	13.486	14.206	14.971	15.783	16.645	17.560	18.531	20.654	23.044	24.349	25.732	28.755	32.150	40.237	50.398	63.121	78.998
12	12.682	13.412	14.192	15.025	15.917	16.869	17.888	18.977	20.140	21.384	24.133	27.270	29.001	30.850	34.931	39.580	50.894	65.510	84.320	108.43
13	13.809	14.680	15.617	16.626	17.713	18.882	20.140	21.495	22.953	24.522	28.029	32.088	34.351	36.786	42.218	48.496	64.109	84.852	112.30	148.47
14	14.947	15.973	17.086	18.291	19.598	21.015	22.550	24.214	26.019	27.975	32.392	37.581	40.504	43.672	50.818	59.195	80.496	109.61	149.23	202.92
15	16.096	17.293	18.598	20.023	21.578	23.276	25.129	27.152	29.360	31.772	37.279	43.842	47.580	51.659	60.965	72.035	100.81	141.30	197.99	276.97
16	17.257	18.639	20.156	21.824	23.657	25.672	27.888	30.324	33.003	35.949	42.753	50.980	55.717	60.925	72.939	87.442	126.01	181.86	262.35	377.69
17	18.430	20.012	21.761	23.697	25.840	28.212	30.840	33.750	36.973	40.544	48.883	59.117	65.075	71.673	87.068	105.93	157.25	233.79	347.30	514.66
18	19.614	21.412	23.414	25.645	28.132	30.905	33.999	37.450	41.301	45.599	55.749	68.394	75.836	84.140	103.74	128.11	195.99	300.25	459.44	700.93
19	20.810	22.840	25.116	27.671	30.539	33.760	37.379	41.446	46.018	51.159	63.439	78.969	88.211	98.603	123.41	154.74	244.03	385.32	607.47	954.27
20	22.019	24.297	26.870	29.778	33.066	36.785	40.995	45.762	51.160	57.275	72.052	91.024	102.44	115.37	146.62	186.68	303.60	494.21	802.86	1298.8
21	23.239	25.783	28.676	31.969	35.719	39.992	44.865	50.422	56.764	64.002	81.698	104.76	118.81	134.84	174.02	225.02	377.46	633.59	1060.7	1767.3
22	24.471	27.299	30.536	34.248	38.505	43.392	49.005	55.456	62.873	71.402	92.502	120.43	137.63	157.41	206.34	271.03	469.05	811.99	1401.2	2404.6
23	25.716	28.845	32.452	36.617	41.430	46.995	53.436	60.893	69.531	79.543	104.60	138.29	159.27	183.60	244.48	326.23	582.62	1040.3	1850.6	3271.3
24	26.973	30.421	34.426	39.082	44.502	50.815	58.176	66.764	76.789	88.497	118.15	158.65	184.16	213.97	289.49	392.48	723.46	1332.6	2443.8	4449.9
25	28.243	32.030	36.459	41.645	47.727	54.864	63.249	73.105	84.700	98.347	133.33	181.87	212.79	249.21	342.60	471.98	898.09	1706.8	3226.8	6052.9
26	29.525	33.670	38.553	44.311	51.113	59.156	68.676	79.954	93.323	109.18	150.33	206.33	245.71	290.08	405.27	567.37	1114.6	2185.7	4260.4	8233.0
27	30.820	35.344	40.709	47.084	54.669	63.705	74.483	87.350	102.72	121.09	169.37	238.49	283.56	337.50	479.22	681.85	1383.1	2798.7	5624.7	11197.9
28	32.129	37.051	42.930	49.967	58.402	68.528	80.697	95.338	112.96	134.20	190.69	272.88	327.10	392.50	566.48	819.22	1716.0	3583.3	7425.6	15230.2
29	33.450	38.792	45.218	52.966	62.322	73.639	87.346	103.96	124.13	148.63	214.58	312.09	377.16	456.30	669.44	984.06	2128.9	4587.6	9802.9	20714.1
30	34.784	40.568	47.575	56.084	66.438	79.058	94.460	113.28	136.30	164.49	241.33	356.78	434.74	530.31	790.94	1181.8	2640.9	5873.2	12940	28172.2
40	48.886	60.402	75.401	95.025	120.80	154.76	199.63	259.05	337.88	442.59	767.09	1342.0	1779.0	2360.7	4163.2	7343.8	22728	69377.	•	•
50	64.463	84.579	112.79	152.66	209.34	290.33	406.52	573.76	815.08	1163.9	2400.0	4994.5	7217.7	10435.	21813.	45497.			•	•
60	81.669	114.05	163.05	237.99	353.58	533.12	813.52	1253.2	1944.7	3034.8	7471.6	18535.							•	•

FVIF > 99.999

Bibliography

Association for Investment Management and Research (1993). *Standards of Practice Handbook*. Charlottesville, VA: AIMR.

Association for Investment Management and Research (1996). *Standards of Practice Casebook*. Charlottesville, VA: AIMR.

Billingsley, R. S. (1993). "Equity Securities Analysis Case Study: Merck & Company." In *Equity Securities Analysis and Evaluation*. Charlottesville, VA: AIMR.

Bodie, Z., Kane, A., & Marcus, A. J. (1993). *Investments* (2nd ed.). Burr Ridge, IL: Irwin.

Caccese, M. S. (1994). "Compliance Guidelines: Introduction." In *Good Ethics: The Essential Element of a Firm's Success.*Charlottesville, VA: AIMR.

Casey, J. L. (1988). *Ethics in the Financial Marketplace*. New York: Scudder, Sterns, & Clark.

Clayman, M. (1987, May/June). "In Search of Excellence: The Investor's Viewpoint," *Financial Analyst's Journal.*

Cohen, J. B., Zinbarg, E. D., & Zeikel, A. (1987). *Investment Analysis and Portfolio Management* (5th ed.). Homewood, IL: Irwin.

Der Hovanessian, A. (1992, Nov.). "Guide to Evaluating Sovereign Credits," *Fixed Income Credit Research,* Morgan Stanley & Co.

Fabozzi, F. J. (1993). *Bond Markets, Analysis and Strategies* (2nd ed.). Englewood Cliffs, NJ: Prentice Hall.

Fabozzi, F. J., Fabozzi, T. D., & Pollack, I. M. (Eds.). (1991). *The Handbook of Fixed Income Securities* (3rd ed.). Homewood, IL: Irwin.

Frumkin, N. (1987). *Tracking America's Economy*. Armonk, NY: ME Sharpe.

Gillis, J. G., & Ciotti, G. J. (1992, Nov./Dec.). "Insider Trading Update," *Financial Analyst's Journal.*

Hakkio, C. S. (1992). "Is Purchasing Power Parity a Useful Guide to the Dollar?" *Economic Review,* Federal Reserve Bank of Kansas City (Third Quarter).

Higgins, R. C. (1993). *Analysis for Financial Management* (2nd ed.). Burr Ridge, IL: Business One Irwin.

Kritzman, M. (1995). "The Portable Financial Analyst," *Financial Analyst's Journal.* Charlottesville, VA: AIMR, pp. 3–5.

Lewis-Beck, M. S. (1980). *Applied Regression, An Introduction.* Thousand Oaks, CA: Sage Publications.

Longstreth, B. (1987). "The Prudent Man Rule Today—Variations on a Single Theme." In *Modern Investment Management and the Prudent Man Rule.* New York: Oxford University Press.

Magnin, J. L., & Tuttle, D. L. (1990). *Managing Investment Portfolios: A Dynamic Process* (2nd ed.). New York: Warren, Gorman & Lamont.

McNees, S. K. (1991). "The Accuracy of Macroeconomic Forecasts." In *Improving the Investment Decision Process—Better Use of Economic Inputs in Securities Analysis.* Charlottesville, VA: AIMR.

Nelson, C. (1987). *The Investor's Guide to Economic Indicators.* New York: John Wiley & Sons.

Peters, Thomas J. & Waterman, Robert H. (1982). *In Search of Excellence: Lessons from Ameria's Best Run Corporations.* New York: Random House.

Porter, M. E. (1985). "Competitive Strategy: The Core Concepts." In *Competitive Advantage: Creating and Sustaining Superior Performance.* New York: The Free Press/Macmillan.

Reilly, F. K. (1994). *Investment Analysis and Portfolio Management* (4th ed.). Fort Worth, TX: The Dryden Press.

Shapiro, A. C. (1992). *Multinational Financial Management* (4th ed.). Needham Heights, MA: Allyn & Bacon.

Siegel, J. J. (1991, Fall). "Does It Pay Stock Investors to Forecast the Business Cycle?" *Journal of Portfolio Management.*

Solnik, B. (1991). *International Investments* (2nd ed.). Reading, MA: Addison-Wesley.

"S&P's Corporate Finance Criteria." (1994). *Standard & Poor's Debt Ratings.* New York: Standard & Poor's Corporation.

Tracy, J. A. (1994). *How to Read a Financial Report* (4th ed.). New York: John Wiley & Sons.

White, G. I., Sondhi, A. C., & Fried, D. (1994). *The Analysis and Use of Financial Statements.* New York: John Wiley & Sons.

Index

Accelerated depreciation method
    (ACRS), 22, 27, 159
Accounting:
    balance sheet, 17–19
    credit analysis and, 160
    financial analysis and, 11
    income statement, 19–27
    industry analysis and, 178
    merger methods, 27–34
    overview, 15–16
    policies, generally, 4
    positive, 155
Accounts payable, 18
Accounts receivable:
    collection period, 154
    function of, generally, 18
    turnover, 152
Accumulation phase, investor life cycle,
    193–194
Acid test, 153
Acquisitions, see Merger and
    acquisitions
    credit analysis and, 175–176
    impact on operations, 9
Active investor, 191
Agency relationship, 148
Aggressive growth managers, 204
AIMR, see Association of Investment
    Management and Research (AIMR)
Amortization, 21, 114
Annuity:
    net present value, 72
    sample values, 276, 278

Arbitrage:
    economic health and, 35–36
    interest rate, 72–73, 76–77
Arbitrage Pricing Theory (APT),
    138–139
Arithmetic mean, 90–91
Asset:
    allocation, see Asset allocation; Asset
        Allocation Model (AAM)
    current, 17
    defined, 114
    equity investments and, 7
    equity performance, 199
    fixed (noncurrent), 17–18, 151
    in pooling accounting method, 34
    in purchase accounting method, 33
    risky, return on, 235
    turnover (ATO), 117
    understatement of, 34
Asset allocation:
    case study, Susan Fairfax, 207–213
    defined, 205, 234
    importance of, 206
    model, see Asset Allocation Model
        (AAM)
Asset Allocation Model (AAM):
    investor life cycle and, 200
    modern portfolio theory, 185
    portfolio construction and
        implementation, 205
    typical, 206–207
Asset market approach, exchange rate
    forecasts, 61

Asset turnover ratio, 151
Asset utilization/efficiency ratios, 152–153
Association of Investment Management and Research (AIMR), 3
  Board of Governors, 223
  Code of Ethics, 242
  Professional Conduct Program (PCP), case study, 223–234
  Professional Standards Programs, 249–250
  Standards of Professional Conduct, 243–248
Average inventory, 152

Bad debt, 159
Balance of payments method, exchange rate forecasts, 61
Balance sheet:
  assets, 17–18
  defined, 114
  importance of, 4, 7
  liabilities, 18, 156
  samples, 268, 270
Barnwell two-way model, 190
Benchmarks, 202
Beta, 113, 128, 237
Bid/offer spreads, 205
Board of directors, function of, 115, 133
Bonds, *see specific types of bonds*
  characteristics of, 165
  definitions, 164–165
  investments in, generally, 76
  risk management, 201
  types of, 165–167
Bonus plan hypothesis, 155
Book value ratio, 135
Boom-and-bust cycle, 158
British pound, 40–41, 71–72, 74–76
Brittany Company, managerial accounting sample, 23–24
Buffett, Warren, 265–266
Bureau of Economic Analysis, 61
Business cycle:
  impact of, 35
  investments and, 56–57

LCL (leading, coincident, lagging) turning points, 55–56
  stock performance and, 182
Buyers, power of, 127

Capital:
  expenses and, 9–10
  growth evaluation and, 133
Capital asset line (CAL), 236
Capital Asset Pricing Model (CAPM):
  equity valuation and, 135
  formula for, 128–129
  function of, generally, 113
  graphical representation, 241
  in modern portfolio theory, 234, 236–237
  overview, 240–241
  sample problems, 129
Capitalization rate, 128
Capital markets, managing expectations, 198–205
Capital reserve requirements, 46
Cash flow:
  annuities and, 80–81
  coupon bonds and, 164
  discounted method, 16
  EBITDA (earnings operating before interest, taxes, depreciation and amortization), 21
  free, 136
  future, discounted value, 119
  growth evaluation and, 133
  inflation and, 35
  liquidity and, 185
  net present value (NPV) and, 78–80
  operating, 157
Cash flow statement, 4
Cash ratio, 153
Cellular communications, 21
CFA chartholders, professional conduct code, 224–234, 243–248
Champa, Thomas, 228–233
Charitable contributions, 195
Chiarella vs. United States, 251
Chinese Wall, 252–253
Classical theory, accounting methods, 16

Coca-Cola, 9, 124, 273
Coincident index, 55–56
Common-size financial statements, 116
Company, generally:
  entrants, 10
  life cycle, 122–123
  position of, 3–4
Competition:
  credit analysis and, 177
  forces of, see Competitive forces
  industry, 121
Competitive forces:
  buyers, power of, 127
  company life cycle, 122–123
  credit analysis and, 158
  impact of, 112
  listing of, 121
  new entrants, threat of, 127
  rivalry among existing firms, 128
  substitutes, threat of, 127
  suppliers, power of, 127
Compounded annual growth rate (CAGR), 92
Compounding, 12, 72, 74
Compound interest, 194
Concessions, selling, 131
Conference Board, 51, 54–55
Confidence limits, 96–97
Consolidation, growth trends, 176
Consolidation phase, investor life cycle, 195
Constant growth model, 135–136
Consumer basket, purchasing power parity (PPP) and, 44
Consumer confidence, as economic indicator, 54
Consumer Price Index (CPI), 42, 43, 44, 58–59, 184, 198
Contracts:
  with credit rating agency, 161
  as economic indicator, 52–53
Contrarian managers, 204
Conversion ratio, 167
Convertible bonds, 166–167
Corporate bond investors, 163

Correlation, regression analysis, 103–104
Cost, purchasing power parity (PPP) and, 71. See also specific types of costs
Cost-effective management, equity investments and, 9–10
Cost of goods sold (COGS):
  income statement, 19–20
  inventory, LIFO vs. FIFO, 22
Coupon bond, 164
Covariance, regression analysis, 102–103
Covered interest arbitrage, 73
Credit analysis:
  bonds, basics of, 164–167
  function of, 33, 109, 147–148
  problem set, 171–178
  qualitative analysis, 157–160
  rating agencies, 160
  rating process, overview, 161–163
  tools of, 149–157
Credit rating:
  changes in, 163–164
  downgrade in, 162–163
  financial ratios, relationship with, 171
  purpose of, 162
Creditworthiness, 160
Culture, purchasing power parity (PPP) and, 70
Currency market:
  business cycles and, 57–58
  international parity conditions, 39–42, 70
  purchasing power parity, 70–71
Current assets, 17
Current income, 132
Current liabilities, 18
Current ratio, 153
Current yield, 164

Days' sales in cash, 153
Debt:
  credit ratings and, 167–169
  financing, 114
  long-term, 18–19
  trade-related, 18

Debt-to-equity ratio, 156
Default risk, 165–166
Dent, Harry, 106
Department of Labor, 51, 58
Dependent variable, regression analysis, 100, 102
Depreciation, 20–22, 114, 159. _See also specific types of depreciation_
Disclosures, 159
Discount rate, 46, 128
Diversification:
  bond market and, 165
  growth industries and, 133, 176
Dividend Discount Model, 5, 8, 135
Dividends:
  decrease in, 131
  discount methods, 109
  focus on, 255–256
  growth evaluation and, 131–133
  increase in, 132
  model, _see_ Dividend Discount Model
  record and policy, 4
Dog and pony shows, 131
Do-it-yourselfer investors, 192, 198
Double taxation, 132
Due diligence, 5, 213
Duff & Phelps, Inc., 160
DuPont Method, Return of Equity Equation, 5
Durable goods, 57, 70

Earnings:
  operating, generally, 21
  operating before interest, taxes, depreciation and amortization (EBITDA), 21
  projected, 19
  quality of, 159
  ratios, 135
  retained, 19
Earnings before interest and taxes (EBIT), 114
Earnings per share (EPS), 176, 261
EBITDA (earnings operating before interest, taxes, depreciation and amortization), 21

Economic releases:
  automobile sales, 57, 70
  calendar of, 70
  consumer price index (CPI), 42, 43, 58–59, 70
  employment situation, 50–51, 70
  gross national product (GNP), 59–60, 70
  impact of, generally, 42, 44, 46
  inventories and, 70
  leading economic indicators, index of, 51–52
  listing of, generally, 48–49
  manufacturer's shipments, inventories, and new orders for consumer goods, 49–50
  National Association of Purchasing Managers (NAPM), report on business, 50, 70
  personal income and expenditures, 57, 70
  producer price index (PPI), 59–60, 70
Economics, generally:
  determining health of the economy, 36–39
  financial analysis and, 11
  government releases and indicators, 42–45, 47–61
  interest rate parity, 72–77
  international parity conditions, 39–42, 69–70
  purchasing power parity, 69, 70–72
Economist, 39
EDGAR, 261
Efficient frontier, 236
Efficient portfolios, 237–238
Einstein, Albert, 194
Employee:
  benefit plans, 159
  Education, defined, 253
  morale, significance of, 6
Employee Retirement Income Security Act (ERISA), 185
Employment:
  cost indicator, 47
  economic trends and, 50–51
  situation indicator, 51

Employment Cost Index, 51
Equity:
    defined, 114
    investments, 76
    securities, see Equity securities,
        valuation of
    valuation, see Equity valuation
Equity analysis, see Equity valuation
    equity securities, valuation of,
        128–135
    financial analysis and, 112–113
    industry analysis, 121–128
    investment, defined, 111
    qualitative analysis, 119–121
    return on equity (ROE), 113–119
Equity securities, valuation of:
    CAPM, 129
    growth evaluation, 129
    risk evaluation, 128–129
Equity valuation:
    analysis methods, 135–137
    case study, Merck & Company,
        138–145
    sample problems, 137
Escrow, bond market and, 165
Estate planning, 195
Ethics:
    AIMR's disciplinary process case study,
        223–234
    definitions, 252–253
    in financial services industry, 241–250
    insider trading, 251–252
Excellent company, attributes of,
    120–121
Exchange rate:
    currency market, 40–42
    interest rate arbitrage, 74–75
    purchasing power parity (PPP), 71
Expenditures, personal, 57, 70
Expense ratios, 205
Expenses:
    deductibility of, 21
    operating, 20–21
    prepaid, 18
Explanatory variable, regression
    analysis, 100

Facilities, defined, 4
Fairfax, Susan, 186–190, 207–213
Fair market value, 28
FASB 115, 156
Fast-growth companies/industry, 158, 176
Federal funds rate, 46
Federal Reserve, 42–47
Federal Reserve Bank of New York, 55
Fees:
    advisory, 131
    credit rating agency, 161–162
    management, 205
Fiduciary, generally:
    breach of duty, 251–252
    defined, 252
FIFO (first in-first out), 12, 22
Financial analysis, 11, 112
Financial ratios:
    defined, 112
    samples, 271–273
Financial services provider (FSP), 38,
    202
Financial statements, see Balance sheet;
    Cash flow statement; Income
    statement
    analysis of, 12
    common-size, 116
    merger and acquisition accounting, 28
Fire Wall, 252–253
Fitch Investors Service, 160
Fixed assets, 17–18, 151
    turnover, 152–153
Fixed cost, 20, 23–24
Fixed income, 163–164, 195
    investment research, on Internet, 265
Flexibility, financial, 150, 153
Follower investors, 191–192
Forecasts:
    economic health and, 36
    economic indicators and, 52
    exchange rates, 61
    interest rates, 163
Forms 10-K, 10-Q, 8-K, 13F-E, 261
Forward rate, 61
Free-profit, 35
Fundamental analysis, 21, 109

Future value (FV):
of annuities, 81–82
defined, 73–74
of $1.00, 277
sample problems, 75–76, 83–85
FVFA (future value factor of an
annuity), 81–82

GAAP (Generally Accepted Accounting
Principles), 154, 160, 178
Geometric mean (average), 91–92
Gifting, investor life cycle, 195
Global economy, 8
Goodwill, 28–31, 33, 159
Government releases and indicators,
42–45, 47–61
Grant, Jill, 229, 232
Great Boom Ahead, The (Dent), 106
Green, Ambrose, 214–217
Greenspan, Alan, 54
Gross domestic product (GDP), 50, 57
Gross national product (GNP), 59–61
Gross profit margin, 20
Growth evaluation:
components of, 129–133
in credit analysis, 158, 176–177
sample problems, 134–135
Growth managers, 204
Growth matrix, 139–140, 143

Handbook of Fixed Income Securities
(Howe), 176
Hedges, 103
Hewlett Packard (HP) 12C financial
calculator, 73, 74, 84
High yield bonds, 165–166
Historical cost, 156
H Model, 130, 135–136
Howe, Jane, 176–178

Imports/exports, currency market and,
40–41
Income, dividends as, 132
Income statement:
components of, 19–22
defined, 4

managerial accounting samples,
23–26
merger and acquisition accounting,
sample, 31–32
samples, 269–270
Income tax, 18, 21, 199
In-control investor, 191
Indenture, 165
Independent variable, regression
analysis, 100, 102
Index of Industrial Production, 50
Indicators, economic, 12, 37–38
Industrial Lifecycle Model, 113, 130
Industry, generally:
analysis of, see Industry analysis
average return on equity, 118
economic health of, 44, 45
fragmentation, 10
growth trends in, 176
life cycle, see Industrial Lifecycle Model
significance of, 3
Industry analysis:
competitive forces, 121–128
credit analysis and, 158
equity securities
function of, 121–123
problem set, 123–127
Inflation:
defined, 43–44
economic indicators and, 54
impact of, generally, 16
purchasing power parity, 72
rate, defined, 61
In Search of Excellence: Lessons from
America's Best Run Corporations
(Peters/Waterman), 120
Insider trading:
definitions, 252–254
laws, 253–254
overview, 251–252
Insider Trading & Securities Fraud
Enforcement Act (ITS-FEA),
253–254
Institutional Investor, All-Star List, 163
Insurance claims, unemployment, 53
Intangible assets, 21, 28, 159

Interest:
  burden, 117
  defined, 71
  expense, 21
  rate, *see* Interest rate
Interest rate, *see* Interest rate parity
  calculation of, 77
  defined, 61
  fluctuation of, 176
  forecasts, 163
  foreign, 35
Interest rate parity (IRP):
  defined, 72–73
  interest rate arbitrage, 73–74, 76–77
  mathematical notation, 73
  quick math method, 73–74
  sample problems, 75–77
Internal rate of return (IRR):
  bond market, 165
  defined, 78
  examples of, 79–80
Internal Revenue Service (IRS),
    18, 28
International Fisher Parity Condition,
    43, 76
International investing, 40
International parity conditions, 39–42,
    69–70
International strategy, equity
    investments and, 8
Internet directory:
  information retrieval, 264–266
  investment research, 259–266
  search engines, 265
Internet Service Provider (ISP), 260
Inventories/inventory:
  accounting methods and, 16
  accumulation rate, 53
  composition of, 18
  control, 7
  LIFO *vs.* FIFO, 22
  ratio, 151
  turnover (ITO), 151–152
Investment, generally:
  analysis of, *see* Investment analysis
  defined, 111

mathematics, *see* Investment
    mathematics
  styles, 204
Investment analysis, geometric mean,
    91–92
Investment Management Process:
  capital markets, managing
    expectations, 198–205
  case study, AIMR's disciplinary
    process, 223–234
  function of, 179–180
  historical perspective, 181
  investor diagnosis, overview,
    183–197
  monitoring the portfolio, 213–214
  portfolio construction and
    implementation, 205–213
  problem set, 214–223
Investment mathematics:
  annuities, 80–83, 85–86
  financial analysis and, generally,
    11–12, 71–73
  future value of money, 73–74,
    83–85
  internal rate of return, 76–80,
    86–87
  net present value, 76–80, 86–87
  present value of money, 75–76,
    83–85
  sample problems, 83–87
Investment Policy Statement:
  case study, Susan Fairfax, 186–190
  changes to, 213–214
  purpose of, 183, 185
  writing guidelines, 184–185
Investment research, Internet:
  e-mail, newsgroups, and other
    resources, 263–264
  fixed income securities, 263
  general information/educational,
    262–263
  individual company, 260–261
  international and emerging markets,
    263
  quotes, 261–262
  U.S. economy, 262

Investor(s):
  guidelines, report checklist, 3–4
  life cycle of, 193–196
  vignettes of, 196–198
IRAs, 184

Japanese yen, 41

Keynesian economists, 70

Labor, significance of, 178
Lagging index, 55–56
Land, valuation of, 18
Large-cap holdings, 209
Lawsuits:
  pension and retirement accounts, 185
  reserves for, 159
Leading Economic Indicators (LEI):
  components of, 52–54
  defined, 51–52
  principles of, 52–53
Leading index, 54–55
Legal issues, investment policy
    statement, 185
Legal Restricted List, 253
Lehman Brothers' Bond Indices, 184
Lenders, role in credit analysis, 148
Leverage:
  equity analysis, 117–119
  growth and, 131
  ratios, 156–157
Levers, 112
Liabilities, 18, 156
Life cycle stages, risk/return position,
LIFO (last in-first out), 12, 16, 22, 159
Linear regression, 101
Line workers, 6
Liquidity:
  investment policy statement, 185
  ratios/financial flexibility, 153
Lone Hill Company, managerial
    accounting sample, 26
Lower-of-cost-or-market (LCM) method,
    32
Lump sum payments, 80
Lynch, Peter, 192

McCarthy, Crisanti & Maffei, Inc., 160
McDonald's, 9
McNees, Stephen, 36
Macroeconomics, 3, 36
Management, generally:
  accounting methods and, 16
  investment process, see Investment
      Management Process
  investment styles, 204
Managerial accounting, 22–24
Market-based research, accounting
    methods, 13
Market risk, 239
Market share, 122
Markowitz, Harry, PhD., 205, 234, 237,
    240
Material information, defined, 252
Material nonpublic information, 251
Maturity date, bonds, 166
Median, 92–93
Membership of the Business Survey
    Committee, 50
Merck & Company, equity valuation
    case study:
  business profile, 139–140
  company profile, 139
  financial data, 140–141
  intrinsic value, calculation of,
      141–145
  overview, 138–139
Merger and acquisitions, accounting
    methods:
  pooling-of-interest method, 28–29
  purchase method, 28
  samples, 29–34
Middle management, 6
Minor ratios, 153–154
Misappropriation Theory, 252
Misery Index, 59
Mitchell, Wesley, 55
Mode, 93
Modern Portfolio Theory, 16, 180, 202
Money, generally:
  future value of, 73–74, 83–85
  present value of, 75–76, 83–85
  time value of, 72

Money supply (M2), as economic indicator, 53, 77
Moody's Investor Service, 160
Morale, significance of, 6
Mosaic Theory, 253
MS EAFE (Morgan Stanley Europe Asia Far East) index, 39
Multinational corporation (MNC):
  international parity conditions, 41
  purchasing power parity (PPP), 71
Multistage (2-Stage) Model:
  application of, generally, 130
  defined, 135, 137
  equity valuation case study, 141–145
Municipal bonds, 166, 174–175
Mutual funds, 213, 240

National Association of Purchasing Managers (NAPM), 44, 45
National Association of Realtors, 70
Net income, 21, 33, 114
Net present value (NPV):
  defined, 19, 72, 76–80
  examples of, 77–78
  growth evaluation and, 133
  positive, 119
New Age, of investment management, 39
New entrants, threat of, 127
New equity, 131
New orders, as economic indicator, 53
New products, 10
Newsgroups, as information resource, 263–264
No-load funds, 214
Noncurrent assets, 17–18
Nondurable goods, 57
Nonfinancially interested individuals (NFIIs), 35, 39, 82
Nonpublic information, 252
Normal distributions, 96

Offering memorandum, 162
Oligopoly, 177
Operating expenses, 20–21
Operating margin, 117

Operations, equity investments and, 8–9
Outliers, 93
Ownership, equity investments and, 6

Parity:
  interest rate, 72–77
  international conditions, 39–42, 69–70
  purchasing power, 69, 70–72
Passive investor, 190–191
PATIROC, 5, 10
Payout ratio, 131
Pearl Investment Management, AIMR Professional Conduct case studies, 224–234
People, equity investments and, 5–6
PepsiCo, Inc., 9, 124, 274
Performance management, 111–112
Performance ratios, 154–155
Permits, as economic indicator, 52–53
Peters, Tom, 120
PFVA (present value factor of an annuity), 82–83
Philanthropy, 195
Pooling method, merger and acquisition accounting:
  defined, 28–29
  sample, 30–31
Porter, Michael E., 112, 121, 158
Portfolio, generally:
  efficient, 239
  construction and implementation of, 205–207
  management, see Portfolio management
  modern theory, see Modern Portfolio Theory
  monitoring, 213–214
Portfolio management:
  Capital Asset Pricing Model (CAPM), 240–241
  decision-making, 162
  ethics, in financial services industry, 241–250
  investment management process, see Investment Management Process

Portfolio management (*Continued*)
  Modern Portfolio Theory, 234–241
  Portfolio Selection Theory, 237–240
  Security Market Line (SML), 241
Positive accounting, 13, 155
Premium, bonds, 166
Present/Future Value and Annuity
    Tables, 73
  of annuity, 83
  defined, 75–76
  net, *see* Net present value (NPV)
  sample problems, 75–76, 83–85
  samples, 275–277
Present value factor (PVF), 77, 79
Price:
  bond market, 164
  increase in, 131
  to sales, 135
  stocks, 167
Proactive investors, 5, 119, 138
Proactive treasurer, 8
Producer price index (PPI), 58–59
Profitable pruning, 131
Property, plant, and equipment, 18
Psychographics, individual investors,
    190–191
Purchase method, merger and
    acquisition accounting, 28, 33
Purchasing power parity (PPP):
  defined, 69, 70–72
  equation, 12
  mathematical notation, 72
  quick math notation, 72
PV (present value), *see* Present value
    (PV)

Qualitative analysis:
  in credit analysis:, 157–160
  equity analysis, 119–121
Quantitative analysis:
  basic statistics, overview, 90–98
  importance of, 11, 13
  problem sets, 98–99
  roots of, 89
Quick ratio, 153
Quotes, on Internet sources, 261–262

Range, 93
Rate of return:
  CAPM equation, 240
  internal, *see* Internal rate of return
    (IRR)
  risk evaluation, 128
Rating agencies, 160. *See also* Standard
    & Poor's (S&P) Corporation,
    Corporate and Municipal Rating
    Definitions
Ratio analysis, 149–151
Ratios, *see specific types of ratios*
Real estate investments, 76
Red flags, in credit analysis, 158
Regression, example of, 121
Regression analysis:
  application of, 37
  correlation, 103–104
  covariance, 102–103
  financial analysis and, 11
  linear regression, 101
  problem set, 107–108
  regression, defined, 100
  sample, 101–102
  simple, example of, 104–106
Regulatory environment, 159, 178
Releases, economic, *see* Economic
    releases
Research:
  economic, 36
  investment, *see* Investment research,
    Internet
Research and development, 7, 176–177
Reserves, 159
Restrictive covenants, 162
Retention ratio, 129
Retirement planning, 195–197
Return, equity investments and, 8
Return on assets (ROA):
  credit analysis and, 154
  defined, 119, 154–155
Return on equity (ROE):
  components of, 116–119
  credit analysis, 151, 154–155
  credit rating and, 173
  definitions, 114–116

Du Pont Derivation Equation, 113
equity valuation, 135
function of, 112
growth evaluation, 129–130
industry average, 118
net, 119
Revenue, income statement, 19
Revenue recognition methods, 159
Risk:
active investors and, 191
in bond market, 165–166
CAPM equation and, 242
equities *vs.* bonds, 201
equity valuation, 128–129
international investments, 41
investment policy statement, 184
investor life cycle and, 201
portfolio selection theory, 237–240
Rivalry, among existing firms, 128
Roach, Stephen, 59
Rule of 72, 194

Sayles, Tom, 107
Scared investors, 192–193
Seasonality, 151
Securities Enforcement Remedies &
Penny Stock Reform Act
(SERPSRA), 254
Securities and Exchange Commission
(SEC), 254, 261
Security, characteristics of, 4
Security Market Line, 180, 236
Self-assessment, investors', 183
Self-managed portfolios, 192, 198
Senior management, 5–6, 10
Sensitive materials, 54
Shapiro, Alan, 43
Shareholders, 115
Sharpe Ratio, 236
Sherman, Peter, 224–234
Short-term money market instruments, 7
Simple regression, 104–106
Slow-growth companies/industry, 158,
176
Small-cap holdings, 209
Social Security, 195

Solnik, Bruno, 70
Sounds-too-good-to-be-true
investments, 82
Specific risk, 239
Spending phase, investor life cycle, 195
Spot rate, 61
Standard & Poor's (S&P) Corporation,
160
Corporate & Government Bond Yield
Index, 170
Corporate and Municipal Rating
Definitions, 167–169
International Stock Guide, 229, 232
Standard & Poor's 500 Index, 39, 198
Standard deviation, 95–97
Standard industrial classification (SIC),
50
Standards of Practice Handbook (AIMR),
3–4, 223, 225
Start-up costs, 159
Statement of Financial Accounting
Concepts (SFAC) 5, "Recognition
and Measurement in Financial
Statements of Business Enterprises,"
114
Statistics, *see* Quantitative analysis
central tendency measures, 90–93
confidence limits, 96–97
dispersion measures, 93–95
financial analysis and, 11
sample problems, 98–99
Stock(s):
options, 16
performance, business cycle and,
57
prices, 54, 78, 167
repurchase, 29
Stockholders' equity, 18–19
Straight-line depreciation, 22, 26, 32
Substitutes, threat of, 127
Sullivan, Jack, 198
Sum-of-the-years digits (SOYD), 27
Suppliers, power of, 127
Supply sources, 177–178
Symmetrical distributions, 96
Systematic risk, 239

Tangible assets, 21
Taxation:
    dividends and, 132
    double, 132
    estate, 195
    income, 199
    investment policy statement, 184
Tax burden, 117
Tax law, corporate, 21
Technological advances:
    equity investments and, 7–8
    impact of, 127
Telecommunications industry, 21
Third party endorsement, 162
Time horizon, investment policy
    statement, 184, 200
Times interest earned, 157–157
Top management, 119. See also Senior
    management
Trade-related debt, 18
Treasury bills, 184, 201
Trend analysis, 34, 57–58

Uncertainty, 201. See also Risk
Understates theory, 59
Underwriter, 161–162
Unemployment rate, 50–51
Unique issues, investment policy
    statement, 185
U.S. Department of Commerce, 50–51,
    61
U.S. dollar, 35, 40–41, 71, 74–76
U.S. international trade in goods and
    services, 57–58
Unsystematic risk, 239

UTA Company, managerial accounting
    sample, 24–26

Valuation, generally:
    analysis, 33
    equity, see Equity valuation
    financial analysis and, 112
    significance of, 15–16
Value investors, 5
Value managers, 204
Variable cost, 20, 24
Variance, 94–95
Variation, 93–94
Vendors, multiple, 127
Vertical integration, 158–159
Very financially interested individuals
    (VFIIs), 35–39, 71, 82
Volatility:
    in capital markets, 203
    credit ratings and, 173
    growth evaluation and, 130
    management, 202

Wall Street Journal, The, 39
Watch List, 253
Waterman, Robert H., 120
Wells Fargo Bank, 9
Working capital, 153
Workweek, average, 53
World Wide Web, 259, 264. See also
    Internet directory

Yellow flag, in credit analysis, 154
Yield, in bond market, 164–165
Yield to maturity (YTM), 164–165